IBSEN

Four Major Plays

RICK DAVIS is Artistic Director of Theater of the First Amendment, a professional company in residence at George Mason University in Fairfax, Virginia. He worked at Baltimore's Center Stage as Resident Dramaturg and Associate Artistic Director, and was cofounder and Associate Artistic director of the American Ibsen Theater in Pittsburgh. He is a regular contributor to *American Theatre* magazine, and is the librettist for Kim D. Sherman's opera *Love's Comedy*, based on an early Ibsen play. He taught at Washington College in Maryland before joining T.F.A. and George Mason University, where he also serves as Director of the Division of Theater within GMU's Institute of the Arts, teaching directing, dramatic literature, and criticism. He was educated at Lawrence University in Appleton, Wisconsin, and the Yale School of Drama.

BRIAN JOHNSTON has taught at universities in Britain, Norway, the Middle East, and the United States, and is currently Associate Professor of Dramatic Literature at Carnegie Mellon University, Pittsburgh. He is the author of three highly acclaimed studies of Ibsen's drama: *To The Third Empire: Ibsen's Early Drama* (University of Minnesota Press, 1980), *Text and Supertext in Ibsen's Drama* (1989) and *The Ibsen Cycle* (Revised Edition) (1992), both published by the Pennsylvania State University Press.

Smith and Kraus *Books For Actors*

THE MONOLOGUE SERIES
> The Best Men's / Women's Stage Monologues of 1994
> The Best Men's / Women's Stage Monologues of 1993
> The Best Men's / Women's Stage Monologues of 1992
> The Best Men's / Women's Stage Monologues of 1991
> The Best Men's / Women's Stage Monologues of 1990
> One Hundred Men's / Women's Stage Monologues from the 1980's
> 2 Minutes and Under: Original Character Monologues for Actors
> Street Talk: Original Character Monologues for Actors
> Uptown: Original Character Monologues for Actors
> Ice Babies in Oz: Original Character Monologues for Actors
> Monologues from Contemporary Literature: Volume I
> Monologues from Classic Plays
> 100 Great Monologues from the Renaissance Theatre
> 100 Great Monologues from the Neo-Classical Theatre
> 100 Great Monologues from the 19th C. Romantic and Realistic Theatres

YOUNG ACTORS SERIES
> Great Scenes and Monologues for Children
> New Plays from A.C.T.'s Young Conservatory
> Great Scenes for Young Actors from the Stage
> Great Monologues for Young Actors
> Multicultural Monologues for Young Actors
> Multicultural Scenes for Young Actors

SCENE STUDY SERIES
> Scenes From Classic Plays 468 B.C. to 1960 A.D.
> The Best Stage Scenes of 1994
> The Best Stage Scenes of 1993
> The Best Stage Scenes of 1992
> The Best Stage Scenes for Men / Women from the 1980's

CONTEMPORARY PLAYWRIGHTS SERIES
> Romulus Linney: 17 Short Plays
> Eric Overmyer: Collected Plays
> Lanford Wilson: 21 Short Plays
> William Mastrosimone: Collected Plays
> Horton Foote: 4 New Plays
> Israel Horovitz: 16 Short Plays
> Terrence McNally: 15 Short Plays
> Humana Festival '93: The Complete Plays
> Humana Festival '94: The Complete Plays
> Women Playwrights: The Best Plays of 1992
> Women Playwrights: The Best Plays of 1993
> EST Marathon '94: One-Act Plays

GREAT TRANSLATION FOR ACTORS SERIES
> The Wood Demon by Anton Chekhov, tr. by N. Saunders & F. Dwyer
> The Sea Gull by Anton Chekhov, tr. by N. Saunders & F. Dwyer
> Three Sisters by Anton Chekhov, tr. by Lanford Wilson
> Mercadet by Honoré de Balzac, tr. by Robert Cornthwaite
> Villeggiatura: The Trilogy by Carlo Goldoni, tr. by Robert Cornthwaite

CAREER DEVELOPMENT SERIES
> The Job Book: 100 Acting Jobs for Actors
> The Smith and Kraus Monologue Index
> What to Give Your Agent for Christmas and 100 Other Tips for the Working Actor
> The Camera Smart Actor
> The Sanford Meisner Approach
> Anne Bogart: Viewpoints
> The Actor's Chekhov
> Kiss and Tell: Restoration Scenes, Monologues, & History
> Cold Readings: Some Do's and Don'ts for Actors at Auditions

If you require pre-publication information about upcoming Smith and Kraus books, you may receive our semi-annual catalogue, free of charge, by sending your name and address to *Smith and Kraus Catalogue, P.O. Box 127, One Main Street, Lyme, NH 03768. Or call us at (800) 895-4331, fax (603) 795-4427.*

IBSEN

FOUR MAJOR PLAYS

translated by Rick Davis
and Brian Johnston

Great Translations for Actors

SK

A Smith and Kraus Book

A Smith and Kraus Book
One Main Street, PO Box 127, Lyme, NH 03768
603.795.4331

Cover illustration (detail), Edouard Manet, *Gare Saint-Lazare* Gift of Horace Havemeyer in memory of his mother, Louisine W. Havemeyer, ©1995 Board of Trustees, National Gallery of Art, Washington.

First Edition: April 1995
10 9 8 7 6 5 4 3 2 1

Library of Congress Cataloging-in-Publication Data
Ibsen, Henrik, 1828-1906.
    [Plays. English. Selections.]
    Ibsen: four major plays / translated by Rick Davis and Brian Johnston. --1st ed.

    p. cm. --(Great translations for actors)
    Contents: A doll house -- Ghosts -- An enemy of the people -- Hedda Gabbler.

    ISBN 1-880399-67-9 (alk. paper)
    I. Davis, Rick. II. Johnston, Brian, 1932- . III. Title. IV. Series.

PT8854.D38   1995
839.8'226--dc20   95-13632
                                        CIP

CONTENTS

A TRANSLATOR'S NOTE

I. BEGINNINGS (AND SOME NOTES ON THE TEXTS)

The original impetus for these collaborative translations was a directorial one. I was working at Center Stage in Baltimore as resident dramaturg, helping Stan Wojewodski, Jr. and a team of dramaturgs (Walter Bilderback and Anthony Fichera, to be exact) prepare for Stan's upcoming production of *An Enemy of the People.* The dramaturgs and I dug out every English version that we thought had the potential to hold the stage and presented them to Stan; after comparing them, he declared his dissatisfaction with the existing texts and suggested that Brian Johnston and I prepare a new translation. This possibility had not occurred to any of us before, but in retrospect seems like an inevitable conclusion. All of us involved in the project held too great a respect for the translator's art—and, I like to think, too stringent ethical standards—to do a "compilation" version, modifying a single translation by an unwillingly anonymous writer (who also, thereby, is spared from receiving his or her due royalties!) or taking the best lines from a variety of versions and whirling them together in what might be called "Cuisinart translation." So the drive to create a new text was on.

Brian, fresh from the triumphant publication of *Text and Supertext In Ibsen's Drama,* and steeped in the Norwegian originals, began sending pieces of the new English text interlarded with the most stimulating and theatrically inspiring notes—so much so that the notes often occupied as much space on the page as the dialogue. I then worked through the options Brian presented—bearing in mind, to the extent my insight and the necessities of a speakable stage text permitted, the range of supertextual resonances that dance around every line—and slowly a playable version was shaped. We held a workshop of this text at Center Stage with Stan and the dramaturgs, and from that the eventual performance version emerged.

A word about the profanity in *An Enemy of the People*; the Norwegian text is sprinkled with many oaths and imprecations, including the irresistibly evocative word *skitt*, which, when pronounced with good Norwegian sound, is homonymic with the English oath we have come to know and love. We decided that, in Brian's words, "Stockmann is the most impious (as well as impish) of Ibsen's heroes, and his oaths, in the 19th century, are at least as vehement as our choices in the 20th." In performance these little verbal punctuation marks lend an agreeable sense of urgency to the linguistic world of the small-town-in-crisis that Ibsen creates.

A Doll House was also commissioned by Center Stage, and our text became the basis for a fairly aggressive adaptation by the director, Jackson Phippin, who had stylistic goals for his production that required a number of cuts and modifications in the direction of a terser language. I was fortunate to be involved in the shaping of that performance "variation" (to steal a word from Eric Bentley) and the resulting quite successful production, which was fascinating in the gains and losses achieved by the emendations; the text published here represents a return to a style more harmonious with our other texts and more representative of the fullness of Ibsen's expression, including the purposeful repetition of images and words (such as Nora's ever-more-complex use of the term "wonderful," which grows from a description of material comfort in the first act to a fundamentally new understanding of the structure of marriage by the play's end).

Ghosts was commissioned by Atlanta's Alliance Theatre, where Walter Bilderback was serving as dramaturg, and Brian and I conducted a lengthy long-distance workshop on the text by fax and phone with Walter, since we could not be present at the early rehearsals. The production was a lovely illustration of the power that Ibsen has when liberated from an overly naturalistic stage environment—about which there is more to be said below. In *Ghosts*, Brian and I experimented with a diction for Pastor Manders that captures his orotund, biblical tone in those moments of high rhetorical passion—for example, his attempt to lead Mrs. Alving back to the path of righteousness. On opening night, we were gratified to see that this strategy works in the playing, though we became aware of several excesses that we have since modified.

Hedda Gabler was created for a production I directed at George Mason University, which provided the opportunity to workshop this text rather fully with Brian in residence for several days. This translation is informed by Brian's understanding of the insistent dialectic between the pagan and Christian worlds that forms the very *agon* of the play, and my own belief that the spirit of *Hedda Gabler* is very often a comedic one, partaking of character typologies and patterns of excessive behavior that would not be out of place in Congreve or Wycherley.

There is, additionally, a strong theatrical metaphor running through the play, revealed in Hedda's self-consciously histrionic behavior—she seems often to be playing, or playing *at*, a role, varying her style to suit the context—and in some of Ibsen's stage directions. Notice how the moments leading up to Hedda's last exit (from the stage and then from the world) are set up in theatrical terms. Hedda mimics and parodies the language of Tesman and Judge Brack, then withdraws behind an archway strongly suggestive of the proscenium stage to perform (an overture or a postlude?) on her piano. She makes her last appearance by poking her head through the curtains she has previously drawn, creating a sly and comic visual reference to an old-fashioned curtain call. Brian and I have made several choices in the language to point up the theatrical metaphor, none more significant than in Judge Brack's famous last line (which is itself an echo of Hedda's language earlier in the play). The canonical version has Brack saying something like "People don't do such things," but we have rendered the line—just as faithfully, by the way—as "People don't act that way," offering one great final summation of Hedda's ultimately fatal attempt to find a role to play in a drama with no place for her.

II. IBSEN IN THE THEATER

Producing Ibsen used to be a somewhat archeological matter, concerned with matching stage wallpaper patterns, fjordscapes, and somber tones of cloth to their Norwegian originals. But no longer. The experience of the last decade or so has shown us that Ibsen can profit from a theatrical life freed from the burdens of realism. The decade of the 1980s provided several salutary examples of stylistic departures including such landmark productions as Lloyd Richards's Munch-inspired, red-drenched Yale Rep staging of *Hedda Gabler* in 1981; Travis Preston's three expressionistic, revolutionary productions (*A Doll House,* 1983; *Little Eyolf,* 1984; and *Ghosts,* 1985) for the

American Ibsen Theater in Pittsburgh; Lucian Pintilie's passionate, operatic *The Wild Duck* for Arena Stage in 1986; and Stan Wojewodski, Jr.'s lyrical yet architectonic *The Lady From the Sea* at Center Stage in 1988 or his spirited and image-rich *An Enemy of the People* in 1990.

These productions—all distinguished by design values and performances that leapt beyond the literal—and others that have followed, prove that Ibsen's dramaturgy is cast from the classical mold; that his plays, like those of Shakespeare or the Greeks, can be liberated from their local and temporal origins and survive the transplantation even prosper thereby. At the root of this realization, of course, is a suspicion about what theater's proper business is.

It is now a commonplace to say that the stage cannot compete with film or television in the arena of realism and should not try. But that piece of folk wisdom is more honored in the breach than the observance; we still tend to drag out the box sets (or fragments of them—that doesn't count any longer as a nonrealistic approach) and, more importantly, the overly psychologized, behavioristically cluttered acting styles of our supposed realistic traditions. Almost invariably, the result is reductive when applied to the scale of artistic endeavor represented by great playwriting, whether classical or contemporary. With Ibsen, specifically, the archival approach tends toward productions that can too easily be written off as "quaint," "nostalgic," giving the bemused audience a glimpse of a time long gone that we have now, happily, transcended in the blinding progress of our civilization toward a higher state of humanity.

Released from the shackles of naturalism, Ibsen will speak to us as powerfully and as rudely as Shakespeare or Euripides. *An Enemy of the People* remains a bitterly comic struggle between brothers for the soul of a community, of course, and a cautionary, satiric parable about the tyranny of the majority; but it becomes something larger as well, a battleground in which the antagonists are truth and deception, ideals and realities, and the stakes are life and death. *A Doll House* will always be the story of a woman who begins to understand the concept of an independent self, but it can also become a shattering tragedy of the dissolution of marriage as the founding institution of our civilization. *Ghosts* can acquire mythic overtones that enlarge our sense of the awesome struggle our species faces to wriggle forward to the next step in the evolution of our consciousness in the face of dead ideas and actions that work to hold us back. *Hedda Gabler* is liberated to be a wickedly comic *agon* between Apollo and Dionysos, or perhaps Christ and Pan, instead of a domestic tragedy that more liberal employment practices would ameliorate.

III. Acting Ibsen: A Few Stray Thoughts

The actor in an Ibsen play has a fascinating challenge. Ibsen's characters are within the range of recognizable humanity—I'm stopping short of saying that they're conceived "realistically," because I'm not exactly sure that I can locate a precise meaning for that idea. But the Ibsen character is also an *instrumental* component of the larger dramatic whole, and the actor does well to consider performance issues that go well beyond motives (though these are always present) and psychological tics (these are usually invented)—issues that include the emblematic content of a given moment, its relation to the "super-text" or range of references outside the immediate world of the play, and the ways in which the actor as interpretive artist can give a human shape to this large reservoir of meaning that shadows the overt level of the play's action. Image-based (as opposed to archival) design helps enormously in this task; so does bold, unfettered use of the voice and body; and of course a great deal depends on the ability of the imagination of the director and all of the collaborative artists to take the all-important next step beyond the basic understanding of action and situation (vital building blocks though they are) to the creation of imagery that communicates something of the scale and audacity of these works to a contemporary audience.

—Rick Davis

THE PLAYS AND THE CYCLE

A Doll House, Ghosts, and *An Enemy of the People* belong to the first group of four plays in Ibsen's realist cycle that opened with *Pillars of Society.* These plays take as their subject our humanity seen predominantly in terms of social politics and the family. *Pillars of Society* and *An Enemy of the People,* as their opposing titles proclaim, are notably 'civic' with public confrontations and crowd scenes and the leading male figures, Karsten Bernick, Thomas Stockmann. The two inner plays, *A Doll House* and *Ghosts,* whose leading characters are the women, Nora Helmer, Helene Alving, focus on the impact of this social realm and its conflicts within the setting of the home. As the group advances, so does its dramatic argument. The characters of these plays, and the audience in the theater, are to be shaken into a perception that they do not know the world they think they know (either civic or domestic), do not know what a perversion of truth and freedom they (and we) have made of it. And this will be Ibsen's dialectical procedure throughout the cycle.

Pillars of Society had revealed a community of self-deceivers and cheats whose proclaimed moral principles bore no relation to its capitalist practices; so in this play the most violent confrontation took place between the "spirit of truth and freedom" and the characters onstage. The heroine of that play was Lona Hessel whose first name "is short for Abelone from Greek Apollonia, i.e. the divine, the one who belongs to the god Apollo."[1] An apparition from the past, she brings to the guilty community and its leading citizen, Karsten Bernick, the disquieting Apolline values of truth and self-knowledge. Jan Kott, for one, has noted: "Into the houses of Ibsen's imagination descend the ghosts of Oedipus, Electra, Orestes, and Iphigenia... the summoning of Greek shadows reveals... parallels between Ibsen and Freud."[2] These Greek shadows particularly haunt the first four plays. For it was Greek drama, in such works as Sophocles' *Antigone,* that most deeply explored the collision between the family and the state.[3]

A Doll House evolves out of the subethical situation dramatized in *Pillars of Society.* Both Torvald and Nora Helmer need to be shaken into an awareness of the unreality of the world their doll home embodies. But Torvald, unlike Bernick, is no criminal, he is living up to his principles, however fragile these prove to be. Nora, through whose *agon* the values of the doll home will be shattered, figuratively re-enacts the action of Alcestis in Euripides' play: of the wife 'dying' for her husband and returning from the dead as a stranger. The imagery of Act Two is of her death by drowning and of the tarantella, the dance of death of the victim of the tarantula's poison. In Act Three, as Jan Kott observes, Ibsen reverses Euripides' recognition scene and in the now famous confrontation of Nora with Torvald "the wife discovers the Stranger in her own husband."4

In *Ghosts* ethical principles shaped the whole life of Helene Alving, and these now return as tragic nemeses. Under the disastrous tutelage and dogmatic moral principles of Pastor Manders and of her community, Helene had constructed a world of lies, whose emblem is the Alving Memorial Home, raised to obliterate the memory of Alving. The play opens with her in triumphant possession of this world of lies and will end in her (and its) total devastation as the past utterly destroys the fraudulent present. In Act One she eloquently justifies her life to Manders from *her* point of view, and her speeches are filled with the rancorous iteration against Alving, "I had to... I had to..." In Act Three, she sees her young husband's "joy of life" resurrected in her son and sees, also, life from *his* point of view, her speeches repeating "He had to... He had to..." She has come to love her husband just when she will be called upon to kill him in his filial reincarnation. Beginning in confident verbal and rhetorical control of her world, she will end virtually speechless, able only to gasp the monosyllables, "No, no, no!—Yes!—No, no!"

This level of tragic consciousness in both Helene and Osvald emerges and detaches itself from the comic-melodramatic consciousness of Manders, Engstrand, and Regine, who, warily evading tragic insight, never will attain to tragic self-knowledge. By the end of Act One, Manders is a spent force, even a comic figure, while the voice of Osvald's tragic identity, displacing Manders, now moves to center stage.

Under Osvald's merciless prompting, tragic self-knowledge and heroic resolution will be the path taken by Helene Alving, her desolating victory over the forces that disastrously shaped her life. Fully to understand what this implies, we must remember that Osvald has come home to search out someone capable of killing him! The Greek ghosts of this play are notable: of the Orestes story, of Oedipus and of *The Bacchae*.[5] In Helene and Osvald Alving the tragic spirit, the privilege of the spiritual aristocrat, is born in the Cycle. From *Pillars of Society* through *A Doll House*, Ibsen had been training his audience to rise to this level of tragedy. They could not, and *Ghosts* became the most vilified drama in the history of the theater, banned from public performance and, along with its author, hysterically attacked by the bourgeois press of Europe.

This Greek tetralogy of modern plays ends, like its classical Athenian counterpart (three tragedies and a satyr play), with a comedy, *An Enemy of the People*, where the central figure of the drama has evolved from the hypocritical 'pillar' Bernick, to the Socratic rebel Thomas Stockmann. The Hellenic "joy of life" that haunted and eluded the tragic protagonists of *Ghosts* now emerges in the ebullient Stockmann, in a play in which, within the terms of the nineteenth century theatre, something of Aristophanic political comedy, and even some of its incidents, are recovered.[6]

In Ibsen's theatre the symbolic is always the real seen from another perspective—often a perspective a play's characters try to evade. In *An Enemy of the People*, the baths are a practical, functioning institution, but increasingly they take on symbolic identity. Their polluted waters parallel the community's polluted spirit; they are not built high enough into the world of Nature and so become infected by the intervention of greedy industrial interests. Finally, they are the center of an intense struggle for political power. The community, in other words, creates the symbol by which it can be judged. The patriotic doctor, Thomas, who heals sick *bodies* and delights in the spectacle of *physical* appetites in the young at the beginning of the play, gradually becomes the outlawed prophet determined to heal sick *souls* and will set about nourishing the *minds* of starving street urchins (he decides upon *twelve* such disciples). Beginning in a *dining room*, the play ends in Stockmann's *study* as he outlines his program for the re-education of his society.[7] Such symbolism, like the fraudulent Memorial in *Ghosts*, permeates Ibsen's dramatic method because, to the 'awakened' imagination, it permeates reality.

The fourth play in this volume, *Hedda Gabler*, concludes the second group of four plays which included, in order, *The Wild Duck*, *Rosmersholm*, and *The Lady from the Sea*.[8] These plays dramatize the evolution of a distinctly 'subjective' world, where conflicts are more internalized than in the first group. In *Hedda Gabler* we find not an 'objective' conflict between competing rights and duties as in the three other plays in this volume, but rather conflicts within the "state of mind" of the heroine profoundly alienated from a world that, as Ibsen noted, "threatens her very being."

Hedda Gabler is richly haunted by other texts. Its scene of almost claustrophobic confinement re-enacts the Pagan-Christian collision of Ibsen's *Emperor and Galilean*, and figures and themes from that immense drama (and from Western cultural history) invade the stage. The characters in the cast divide into mutually antagonistic groups. The 'Christian' world of Tesman and his aunts and Thea shades into the ambiguous Judge Brack, one of Ibsen's playful 'satanic' figures to whom Hedda observes, "it is a treat to see you by daylight..." (Brack's satanic predecessors in this volume are Krogstad, Engstrand, and Morten Kiil). The 'pagan' world of Hedda, her father, and Løvborg shades into the disreputable world of Diana who, as her name implies, rules the 'night world' of bohemian orgy as Hedda rules the 'day world' of social proprieties. Thea's description of the strange woman in Løvborg's past, and Hedda's agreement that it is Diana, link the two together. Løvborg accuses Diana of committing the crime ('killing the child') which Hedda commits. He is shot in Diana's apartment with Hedda's pistol, and Judge Brack threatens Hedda with the possibility of her appearing with Diana in court. Hedda, with her 'military' discipline and restraint is the Apolline counterpart of the wildly Dionysian Løvborg whom she envisages reborn with "vine leaves in his hair." Such patterning throughout the play does not take away from its human urgency and appeal; but we get only a fraction of Ibsen's intention if we read his plays as photographic naturalism. With all Ibsen's drama, it is best to set aside those accounts that conveniently fit him into anthologies as the "father of modern realism" and confine his audacious dramas to concern with "social problems" or with psychological case-histories. Such received ideas predispose us to see him small scale. We should let ourselves be open to his strange, huge and multilayered artistry, receptive to the ghosts that haunt his texts.

For the plausibly modern stage of Ibsen's realist method is also occult ground, providing a more adequate space than strict realism for

Ibsen's poetic imagination and a more adequate portrait of our human identity. Merely to imitate our fallen and imprisoned world, the psychopathology of everyday life created by our bungling and unhappy intellect, would be imitating a bad work of art. For just as we have debased and polluted our natural world, so have we debased and polluted our spiritual inheritance. To restore what has been lost or disfigured, the artist must create, in Michel Foucault's phrase, a 'counter-discourse' to the world's false discourse. Art, wrote Ibsen's son, Sigurd, "gives liberty of action to forces and possibilities to which life does not grant the chance of coming into their rights."[9] The characters on Ibsen's realist stage are animated by forces and powers thousands of years old. Their actions raise the reproachful ghosts that have shaped our modern identities.

—*Brian Johnston*

NOTES

1. This information was supplied to me by Dr. Einar Haugen.

2. Kott, Jan. *The Theater of Essence.* (Evanston: Northwestern University Press, 1984) 58, 59

3. Cf. Johnston, Brian, *The Ibsen Cycle: Revised Edition.* (University Park, Pa.: The Pennsylvania State University Press, 1992) 101–122.

4. *Theater of Essence* 32.

5. Critics who have seen the Greek aspect of *Ghosts* include P.O. Schott (Ibsen's Norwegian contemporary), G. Wilson Knight, Francis Fergusson, Jan Kott. Cf. *The Ibsen Cycle: 'Archetypal Repetition in Ghosts.'*

6. Johnston, Brian. *Text and Supertext in Ibsen's Drama* (University Park, Pa.: The Pennsylvania State University Press, 1989) 165–191.

7. This sequence first was pointed out by Kenneth Burke in *A Grammar of Motives* (Berkeley: University of California Press, 1945) 3–4.

8. Cf. *The Ibsen Cycle.* 123–153.

9. Ibsen, Sigurd. *Human Quintessence.* (New York: B. W. Huebach, 1972) 93. Most recently, Harold Bloom, in *The Western Canon.* (New York: Harcourt, Brace & Co, 1994) 350–367. *passim.* has made the same observation about Ibsen's realism: that it is occult rather than photographic, containing demonic forces.

IBSEN'S PROSE CYCLE

Pillars of Society	1877
A Doll House	1879
Ghosts	1881
An Enemy of the People	1882
The Wild Duck	1884
Rosmersholm	1886
The Lady from the Sea	1888
Hedda Gabler	1890
The Master Builder	1892
Little Eyolf	1894
John Gabriel Borkman	1896
When We Dead Awaken	1899

A Doll House

A DOLL HOUSE was originally produced May 26-28, 1994 at Lawrence University, Appleton, Wisconsin under the direction of Mark Dintenfass. The cast was as follows in order of appearance:

Nora . . . . Melinda Hein
Torvald . . . . Tim McKellips
Dr. Rank . . . . Bill Parker
Kristine . . . . Jessica Roegler
Krogstad . . . . Eric Westphal
Anne-Marie . . . . Kristine Wendland
Maid . . . . Katra Byram
Ivar . . . . Joey Biese
Emmy . . . . Brittany Pahnke

A Doll House

ACT ONE

A comfortable, tasteful but not expensively furnished room. A door to the right in the back wall leads out to the hall; another door to the left leads in to Helmer's study. Between these doors is a piano. In the middle of the left wall, a door, and farther back, a window. Near the window a round table with armchairs and a small sofa. In the right wall, upstage, a door and, on this same side nearer the foreground, a porcelain stove with a pair of armchairs and a rocking chair. Between the stove and the door, a little table. Engravings on the walls. An etagère with porcelain figures and other small art objects; a small bookcase with books in rich bindings. Carpet on the floor; the fire burns in the stove. A winter's day.

(A bell rings in the hallway; soon after, we hear the door being opened. Nora, cheerfully humming, enters the room; she is dressed in outdoor clothes and carries a great number of packages, which she sets down on the table, right. She lets the door to the hall stand open and we see a Porter carrying a Christmas tree and a basket, which he hands to the Maid, who had opened the door for them.)

NORA: Be sure you hide the tree, Helene. We can't let the children see it before it's decorated tonight. (*To the Porter as she takes out her purse.*) How much—? Oh yes, I know, half a krone—here's one—no, keep the change.

(The Porter thanks her and leaves. Nora closes the door. She continues laughing softly to herself while she takes off her outdoor clothes. She takes a bag of macaroons from her pocket and eats a couple; then she walks cautiously and listens outside her husband's door.)

He's home, all right.

(Humming again, she goes over to the table, right.)

HELMER: (*From within the study.*) Do I hear a skylark singing out there?

NORA: (*Busy opening some packages.*) Yes you do.

HELMER: Is there by any chance a squirrel rummaging around?

NORA: Yes!

HELMER: When did the squirrel get home?

NORA: Just this second. (*She puts the bag of macaroons in her pocket and wipes her mouth.*) Come out here, Torvald, and look at what I've bought.

HELMER: Can't be disturbed! (*After a moment, he opens the door and looks in, his pen in his hand.*) Did you say bought? All that? Has the little spendthrift been out wasting money again?

NORA: Oh, Torvald—this year we really ought to let ourselves go a little bit. It's the first Christmas we haven't had to watch our money.

HELMER: But we still can't go around wasting it, you know.

NORA: Yes, Torvald, now we can afford to waste a little bit here and there. Isn't that right? Just a teeny little bit. Now that you've got such a big salary and we've got heaps and heaps of money coming in?

HELMER: Yes, after New Year's. And then it's three whole months before the first paycheck.

NORA: Fuff! We can borrow till then.

HELMER: Nora! (*Goes over to her and takes her playfully by the ear.*) Is that dizzy little head of yours spinning around again? Suppose I borrowed a thousand today, and you wasted it all on Christmas, and then on New Year's Eve I got hit in the head by a falling brick and lay there—

NORA: (*Covering his mouth.*) Ugh! Don't say awful things like that!

HELMER: Well, suppose it happened—what then?

NORA: If anything that awful happened, some silly loan would be the least of my worries.

HELMER: What about the people I'd borrowed from?

NORA: Them? Who cares about them! They're only strangers.

HELMER: Nora, Nora, you are such a woman! Seriously, Nora, you know what I think about these things. No debts! Never borrow! Some freedom's lost, and because of that some beauty too, from a home that's built on borrowing and debt. The two of us have managed to hold out bravely until now; and we'll stay the course for the little time remaining.

NORA: (*Goes over to the stove.*) All right, Torvald, whatever you want.

HELMER: (*Following.*) Now, now; the little songbird mustn't droop its wings. Right? Is the squirrel standing there sulking? (*Taking out his wallet.*) Nora, guess what I have?

NORA: (*Turning quickly.*) Money!

HELMER: There, see? (*Handing her some bills.*) For Heaven's sake, I know how much a house goes through at Chrismastime.

NORA: (*Counting.*) Ten—twenty—thirty—forty—Oh, thank you, thank you, Torvald. This will help me no end.

HELMER: It had certainly better.

NORA: Yes, yes, I'll make sure it does. But come here so I can show you what I've bought. And so cheap! Look—new clothes for Ivar, also a sword. Here's a horse and trumpet for Bob. And for Emmy, a doll and a doll bed. They're pretty plain, but she'll just tear them to pieces anyway before you know it. And here's some dress material and some handkerchiefs for the maids—even though old Anne-Marie really deserves a little more.

HELMER: And what's in that package there?

NORA: (*With a cry.*) No, Torvald! Not till tonight!

HELMER: Aha! But tell me, you little spendthrift, what did you think of for yourself?

NORA: For me? Oh, I don't need anything.

HELMER: You most certainly do. Tell me what you'd like most of all—within reason.

NORA: Oh, I really don't know. Yes—listen, Torvald—

HELMER: Well?

NORA: (*Fumbling with his button; not looking at him.*) If you want to give me something, you could—you could—

HELMER: Well, say it.

NORA: (*Quickly.*) You could give me money, Torvald. Only what you can spare; then one of these days I could buy something with it.

HELMER: No, but Nora—

NORA: Yes, do it, Torvald, darling. I'm begging you. And I'll hang the money in pretty gilt paper on the tree. Wouldn't that be lovely?

HELMER: What do we call those little birds that are always spending their money?

NORA: Spendthrifts—yes, I know, I know. But let's do what I say, Torvald; then I'll have time to think about what I really need. That's pretty practical, isn't it?

HELMER: (*Smiling.*) Absolutely—if you could only hold on to the money I give you, and if you actually bought something for yourself with it. But it will go for the house, for a lot of things we don't need, and I'll just have to shell out again.

NORA: Oh, Torvald—

HELMER: Can't be denied, my dear little Nora. (*Puts his arm around her waist.*) Spendthrifts are sweet; but they go through an awful lot of money. It's unbelievable how expensive it is to keep a spendthrift.

NORA: Oh, fuff—how can you say that? I save absolutely everything I can.

HELMER: (*Laughing.*) Yes, that's true—everything you *can*. But the trouble is, you *can't*.

NORA: (*Humming and smiling with quiet complacency.*) Hmm. You just can't imagine what kinds of expenses larks and squirrels have, Torvald.

HELMER: You are a strange little one. Just like your father was. You'll try anything you can think of to get hold of some money; but the moment you get some, it slips through your fingers. You never know what you've done with it. But you are what you are. It's in your blood—these things are hereditary, Nora.

NORA: I wish I'd inherited a lot of Papa's qualities.

HELMER: Well I don't want you to be anything but what you are: my sweet little songbird. But listen—I'm getting the distinct impression—you've got a sort of a—what can I call it—a kind of a guilty look today.

NORA: I do?

HELMER: You certainly do. Look me straight in the eye.

NORA: (*Looking at him.*) Well?

HELMER: (*Wagging his finger.*) Our sweet tooth wouldn't have been running wild in town today, would it?

NORA: No, what makes you think that?

HELMER: You're sure that sweet tooth didn't make a little stop at the bakery?

NORA: No, Torvald, I swear—

HELMER: Didn't nibble a little candy?

NORA: No, absolutely not.

HELMER: Not even munched on a macaroon or two?

NORA: No, Torvald, honestly, I promise—

HELMER: Now, now—of course I'm only joking.

NORA: (*Going to the table, right.*) I'd never dream of going against you.

HELMER: No, I know that. And after all, you've given me your word. (*Goes to her.*) Well, you keep your little Christmas secrets to yourself, then, my dearest Nora. I guess everything will be revealed this evening when we light the tree.

NORA: Did you remember to invite Doctor Rank?

HELMER: No—there's no need; it's taken for granted. But I'll ask him again when he stops in this morning. I've ordered the very best wine. Nora, you can't imagine how excited I am about tonight.

NORA: Me too! And the children are just going to love it!

HELMER: Ah, it's so marvelous to have a secure position and a comfortable income. Isn't it fun just to think about that?

NORA: Oh, it's wonderful!

HELMER: Do you remember last Christmas? Three whole weeks beforehand, you locked yourself up every evening, till way past midnight, making flowers for the Christmas tree, and all the other little surprises you had for us. Uch—I've never been so bored in my whole life.

NORA: I wasn't bored at all.

HELMER: (*Smiling.*) But it didn't amount to much after all, Nora.

NORA: Oh, are you going to tease me with that again? I couldn't help it that the cat came in and tore everything to bits.

HELMER: No, that's right, you couldn't, my poor little Nora. You worked so hard to make us happy, that's the main thing. But it's good that those hard times are behind us.

NORA: Yes, it's really wonderful.

HELMER: Now I don't have to sit here all alone boring myself, and you don't have to torture your precious eyes and your delicate little fingers—

NORA: (*Clapping her hands.*) No, is that true, Torvald, I really don't have to? How wonderful to hear that! (*Takes his arm.*) Now I'll tell you what I thought we should do—as soon as Christmas is over—(*The door bell rings.*) Oh, that doorbell. (*Tidying up the room.*) That means a visitor—what a bore!

HELMER: I'm not at home to visitors, remember that.

MAID: (*In the doorway.*) Madam, there's a strange lady here to see you.

NORA: Show her in.

MAID: (*To Helmer.*) And the Doctor arrived at the same time.

HELMER: He went straight to my study?

MAID: Yes, sir, he did.

(*Helmer goes into his room. The Maid shows Mrs. Linde, dressed in traveling clothes, into the room and closes the door after her.*)

MRS. LINDE: (*Timidly and somewhat hesitantly.*) Good day, Nora.

NORA: (*Uncertainly.*) Good day—

MRS. LINDE: You don't recognize me.

NORA: No; I don't know—I think—(*Bursting out.*) Kristine! Is it really you?

MRS. LINDE: Yes it is.

NORA: Kristine! How could I not recognize you? But then how could I—? (*Quieter.*) You've changed, Kristine.

MRS. LINDE: Yes, I expect I have. In nine—ten—long years—

NORA: Is it that long? Yes, that's right. Oh, the last eight years have been happy ones, believe me. And now you've come to town as well. Made the long trip in winter. That was brave.

MRS. LINDE: I just got here this morning on the steamer.

NORA: To enjoy yourself at Christmas, of course. That's a lovely idea! Yes, enjoy ourselves—we will certainly do that. But take off your coat. You're not too cold? (*Helps her.*) That's it; now let's settle down and be cozy here by the stove. No, take the armchair there. I'll sit here in the rocking chair. (*Gripping her hands.*) Yes, now you look more like yourself again; it was just those first few moments—you have gotten a bit paler, Kristine—and maybe a little thinner.

MRS. LINDE: And much, much older, Nora.

NORA: Well, maybe a little older, a tiny little bit; but not too much. (*Drawing back, suddenly serious.*) Oh, I can't believe how thoughtless I am, sitting here chattering—Kristine, can you forgive me?

MRS. LINDE: What do you mean, Nora?

NORA: (*Quietly.*) Poor Kristine, you're a widow.

MRS. LINDE: Yes, for three years now.

NORA: I knew it of course, I read it in the paper. Oh Kristine, you have to believe me, I was always going to write you at the time, but I kept putting it off, and things kept getting in the way.

MRS. LINDE: Nora, dear, I understood completely.

NORA: No, it was horrible of me. You poor thing, it must have been so hard for you—and he didn't leave you anything to live on?

MRS. LINDE: No.

NORA: And no children?

MRS. LINDE: No.

NORA: So, nothing at all.

MRS. LINDE: No—not even a sense of grief to hold on to.

NORA: (*Looking at her in disbelief.*) Kristine, how is that possible?

MRS. LINDE: (*Smiles sadly, stroking Nora's hair.*) Ah, sometimes it happens that way, Nora.

NORA: So completely alone. That must be terribly sad for you. I have three lovely children—you can't see them right now, they're out with Anne-Marie. But now you have to tell me everything.

MRS. LINDE: No, no, I'd rather hear about you.

NORA: No, you have to go first. Today I'm not going to be selfish. Today I'm only going to think about you. But I have to tell you *one* thing. Did you hear about the great luck we just had?

MRS. LINDE: No, what is it?

NORA: My husband has been made manager of the Bank.

MRS. LINDE: Your husband? That is lucky!

NORA: Isn't it? The law is such a chancy business, especially when you won't take the ugly cases. Torvald would never do that, of course, and I agree with him completely. So you can imagine how happy we are! He starts at the Bank right after New Year's, and then he'll be getting a huge salary and lots of commissions. From now on we'll be able to live quite differently—we can actually do what we want. Oh, Kristine, I feel so light and happy! Isn't it lovely to have lots of money, and not have to worry about anything?

MRS. LINDE: It's lovely just to have enough.

NORA: No, not just enough, but lots and lots of money!

MRS. LINDE: (*Smiling.*) Nora, Nora, haven't you gotten over that yet? You were such a spendthrift in school.

NORA: (*Laughing softly.*) Yes, Torvald still says the same thing. (*Wagging her finger.*) But "Nora, Nora" hasn't been as wild as you all think. We haven't exactly been in a position where I could waste any money. We've both had to work.

MRS. LINDE: You too?

NORA: Yes, odd jobs—sewing, embroidery, work like that— (*Casually.*) and also other things. You know Torvald left the government when we got married; he saw he'd never be promoted, and he needed to earn more money than before. In that first year he worked himself to the bone, always looking for extra income, day and night. But he couldn't keep it up, and he got deathly sick. The doctor said he absolutely had to move south.

MRS. LINDE: Didn't you stay a whole year in Italy?

NORA: That's right. It wasn't that easy to get away, as you can imagine. Ivar had just been born. But we had to go, there was no question about it. Ah, it was a wonderful trip, and it saved Torvald's life. But it was incredibly expensive.

MRS. LINDE: I believe you.

NORA: Four thousand, eight hundred kroner. That's a lot of money.

MRS. LINDE: It's just lucky you had it when the emergency came up.

NORA: Well, I can tell you, we had to get it from Papa.

MRS. LINDE: So that's how. That was about the time your father died, I think.

NORA: Yes, Kristine, it was right then. Just think, I couldn't go and be with him. I stayed right here and waited every day for little Ivar to come into the world. And I had my poor, sick Torvald to take care of. Dear, sweet Papa! I never saw him again, Kristine. That was the saddest time in my whole marriage.

MRS. LINDE: I know how much he meant to you. But then you left for Italy?

NORA: Yes, we had the money then, and the doctors insisted. So we left in a month.

MRS. LINDE: And your husband came back completely cured?

NORA: Right as rain!

MRS. LINDE: But—the doctor—?

NORA: What do you mean?

MRS. LINDE: I thought the maid said the man who came in with me was a doctor.

NORA: Yes, Doctor Rank. He's not here on a house call, he's our best friend—he comes by at least once a day. No, Torvald hasn't been sick a day since then. And the children are strong and sound and so am I. (*Jumping up and clapping her hands.*) Oh God, oh God, Kristine, it's so wonderful to live and be happy! But I'm being hateful here, only talking about myself. (*Sits on a stool close by Kristine and lays her arms on her knees.*) Please don't be mad at me! Tell me something—is it really true that you didn't love your husband? So why did you marry him?

MRS. LINDE: My mother was still alive, but she was bedridden and couldn't take care of herself; and I also had to look after my two younger brothers. I couldn't justify refusing his offer.

NORA: No, no, you were right. He was rich at the time, wasn't he?

MRS. LINDE: He was pretty well-off, I think. But the business wasn't very solid, Nora: when he died it all went to pieces, nothing was left.

NORA: And then—?

MRS. LINDE: Well, I had to do what I could for myself—a little shop, a few students, whatever else I could find. These last three years have been like one long workday without a break. But now it's over, Nora. My poor mother doesn't need me anymore, she's gone. And the boys are working now, they're on their own.

NORA: You must feel such relief—

MRS. LINDE: No, not at all. Only inexpressibly empty. Nothing more to live for. (*Stands uneasily.*) So I couldn't stand it any longer out in that little backwater. It's got to be easier here to find something to do, something to keep my mind working. If only I could be lucky enough to find a steady job, some office work—

NORA: But Kristine, that's so exhausting, and you're tired enough to begin with. You'd be better off if you could get away to a spa for a while.

MRS. LINDE: (*Going over to window.*) I don't have a Papa to send me on a trip, Nora.

NORA: (*Getting up.*) Oh, don't be mad at me!

MRS. LINDE: Nora, dear, don't you be mad at me. That's the worst thing about this situation of mine; it leaves you with so much bitterness. You've got nothing to work for, but you still have to watch out for every opportunity. You have to live, so you become selfish. When you told me your news, I was more excited for my own sake than yours.

NORA: Why? Oh, I see—you mean maybe Torvald can do something for you.

MRS. LINDE: That's exactly what I was thinking.

NORA: And so he will, Kristine! Leave it to me—I'll suggest it so beautifully, so beautifully—find something charming that he'll really appreciate. Oh, I can't wait to help you.

MRS. LINDE: You're so kind, Nora, to take such an interest in me—doubly kind, since you don't know much about life's hardships yourself.

NORA: I—? Don't know much—?

MRS. LINDE: (*Smiling.*) Well, good Lord, a little sewing and things like that—you're such a child, Nora.

NORA: (*Tosses her head, walks across the room.*) You shouldn't be so sure about that.

MRS. LINDE: Oh?

NORA: You're like everyone else. You all think I'm not capable of anything serious—

MRS. LINDE: Now, now—

NORA: That I've never been put to the test in the cold, hard world.

MRS. LINDE: Nora, you've just been telling me all about your troubles.

NORA: Fuff! Trifles! (*Quietly.*) I haven't told you the big thing.

MRS. LINDE: What big thing? What do you mean?

NORA: You look down on me an awful lot, Kristine, but you really shouldn't. You're proud that you've worked so hard for your mother all these years.

MRS. LINDE: I don't look down on anyone. But it's true that I'm proud—and happy—that I was given the chance to ease my mother's sorrow in her last days.

NORA: And when you think about what you've done for your brothers, you're proud of that as well.

MRS. LINDE: I think I'm entitled to that.

NORA: So do I. But now you'll hear, Kristine. I also have something to be proud and happy about.

MRS. LINDE: I don't doubt it. But how do you mean?

NORA: Let's talk quietly. What if Torvald heard? He mustn't, not for anything in the world. Nobody can find out about this, nobody but you.

MRS. LINDE: What is it?

NORA: Come over here. (*Pulls her down on the sofa beside her.*) Now then: here's what I have to be proud and happy about. I saved Torvald's life.

MRS. LINDE: Saved—? How did you save—?

NORA: I told you about the trip to Italy. Torvald would never have survived if he hadn't gone down there—

MRS. LINDE: Yes, well, your father gave you all the money you needed—

NORA: (*Smiling.*) Yes, that's what Torvald and everyone else believe, but—

MRS. LINDE: But—?

NORA: Papa never gave anything. I got the money myself.

MRS. LINDE: You? That was a lot of money.

NORA: Four thousand, eight hundred kroner. What do you say to that?

MRS. LINDE: But Nora, how was that possible? Did you win the lottery?

NORA: (*Disdainfully.*) The lottery. (*Snorting.*) What kind of art would *that* have taken?

MRS. LINDE: Then where did you get it from?

NORA: (*Humming and smiling secretively.*) Hmm; tra la la la la!

MRS. LINDE: Because you certainly couldn't have borrowed it.

NORA: Oh? Why not?

MRS. LINDE: No, a wife can't get a loan without her husband's permission.

NORA: (*Tossing her head.*) Well, but a wife with a head for business, a wife who knows how to be a little clever—

MRS. LINDE: Nora, I just don't understand—

NORA: And you don't need to. Nobody said anything about *borrowing* the money. Maybe I got it some other way. (*Throwing herself back on the sofa.*) Maybe I got it from one of my admirers. When you're as alluring as I am—

MRS. LINDE: You're crazy.

NORA: I've got you really curious now, haven't I?

MRS. LINDE: Listen to me, Nora: you haven't done anything foolish, have you?

NORA: (*Sitting up again.*) Is it foolish to save your husband's life?

MRS. LINDE: I think it's foolish that without his knowledge you—

NORA: But that's just it—he mustn't know anything! Good Lord, can't you see that? He can never know how bad off he was. The doctors came to *me* to say his life was in jeopardy—that only a trip south could save him. At first I tried to coax him into it—I told him how lovely it would be to take a trip abroad like other young wives—then I begged and cried—I said he should be kind and indulge a woman in my condition—and I hinted that he could easily take out a loan. That really set him off, Kristine. He told me I was being frivolous, and that it was his duty as a husband not to indulge my every whim and caprice—I think that's what he called them. Well, well, I thought, saved you must be and saved you shall be—and that's when I came up with my plan.

MRS. LINDE: Didn't your husband ever find out that the money wasn't your father's?

NORA: Never. Papa died right after that. I thought about letting him in on it and asking him not to say anything. But with him lying there so sick—and finally it wasn't necessary.

MRS. LINDE: And you've never confided in your husband?

NORA: No, for heaven's sake, how can you even imagine that? He's so strict about those things. And besides, Torvald's a man—he'd be so humiliated if he knew he owed me anything. It could even spoil our relationship; it would be the end of our beautiful, happy home.

MRS. LINDE: So you'll never tell him?

NORA: (*Reflectively, half-smiling.*) Yes, maybe someday; years from now, when I can't count on my looks any more. Don't laugh! I mean when Torvald's not as attracted to me as he is now—when my dancing and dressing-up and reciting for him don't interest him any more. Then it'll be good to have something to fall back on. (*Breaking off.*) Dumb, dumb, dumb! That'll never happen. So what do you think of my big secret, Kristine? I can do things after all, can't I? But as you can imagine, it's been a big worry for me. It hasn't been that easy to make the payments on time. So I had to save a little, here and there, whenever I could. I couldn't really take anything out of the housekeeping budget, because Torvald has to live in a certain style. And I couldn't scrimp on the children's clothes; I used up whatever I got for them—the angels!

MRS. LINDE: Poor Nora! So it came out of your allowance?

NORA: Yes, of course. But then it was mostly my problem. Whenever Torvald gave me money for new clothes or whatever, I'd only use half; I always bought the simplest, cheapest things. I'm lucky that everything looks good on me, so Torvald never noticed. But it made me sad sometimes, Kristine—because it's so nice to dress up now and then, isn't it?

MRS. LINDE: Yes it is.

NORA: But I found other ways to make some money too. Last winter I was lucky enough to get a big copying job to do. So I shut myself in and wrote every evening till late at night. Ah, I'd get so tired, so tired—but it was also great fun, sitting and working and earning money like that. Almost like being a man.

MRS. LINDE: How much have you managed to pay off like that?

NORA: Well, I can't really say exactly. This kind of account is very hard to keep track of. I only know that I've paid back everything I can scrape together. A lot of times I didn't know which way to turn. (*Smiling.*) I'd sit here and imagine that a rich old man had fallen in love with me.

MRS. LINDE: What? Which man?

NORA: Oh, come on! And that he'd just died and when they read his will, there it was in big letters: "My entire fortune is to be paid in cash, immediately, to the delightful Mrs. Nora Helmer."

MRS. LINDE: But Nora, who is he?

NORA: Good Lord, don't you get it? There never was any such person; it was just something I'd sit here and dream about when I couldn't think of any other way to get the money. But now it doesn't matter, the old bore can go back where he came from; I don't need him or his will, because my troubles are over. Oh, God, it's so lovely to think of, Kristine! Carefree! To be carefree, completely carefree! To run around and play with the children; to make everything in the house warm and beautiful, just the way Torvald likes it! Then maybe we can travel a little. Maybe I'll get down to the ocean again. Oh yes, it is so wonderful to live and be happy!

(*The bell rings in the hallway.*)

MRS. LINDE: (*Rising.*) The bell—maybe I should go.

NORA: No, stay here. It won't be for me. It's probably for Torvald.

MAID: (*From the hall doorway.*) Excuse me, ma'am. There's a gentleman here to speak with the lawyer.

NORA: With the Bank Manager, you mean.

MAID: Yes, with the Bank Manager. But I didn't know if—since the Doctor's in there—

NORA: Who is the gentleman?

KROGSTAD: (*From the doorway.*) It's me, Mrs. Helmer.

(*Mrs. Linde starts, checks herself, and turns toward the window.*)

NORA: (*A step towards him, tense, in a low voice.*) You? What is it? What do you want to talk to my husband about?

KROGSTAD: Bank matters—more or less. I have a minor position on the bank staff, and I hear your husband is our new chief.

NORA: And so it's—

KROGSTAD: Just dry business, Mrs. Helmer. Absolutely nothing else.

NORA: Then would you please be good enough to step into his study?

(*She nods indifferently and shuts the hallway door; then she goes and tends the stove.*)

MRS. LINDE: Nora—who was that man?

NORA: That was a lawyer named Krogstad.

MRS. LINDE: So it really was him.

NORA: Do you know that man?

MRS. LINDE: I used to know him—a long time ago. He was a law clerk for a while up in our area.

NORA: Yes, that's right, he was.

MRS. LINDE: He certainly has changed.

NORA: He had a very unhappy marriage.

MRS. LINDE: And now he's a widower?

NORA: With several children. There we go, now it's burning. (*She closes the stove door and moves the rocking chair a little to the side.*)

MRS. LINDE: He's got himself involved in all kinds of businesses, they say.

NORA: Oh yes? Probably; I really wouldn't know. But let's not think about business—it's so boring!

(*Doctor Rank comes out from Helmer's study.*)

RANK: (*Still in the doorway.*) No, no, Torvald: I don't want to be in the way; I'd just as soon go talk to your wife for a while. (*Closing the door and noticing Mrs. Linde.*) I'm sorry—I'm in the way here too.

NORA: You certainly are not. (*Introducing him.*) Doctor Rank, Mrs. Linde.

RANK Ah ha! That's an oft-mentioned name in this house. I think I passed you on the stairs when I arrived.

MRS. LINDE: Yes, I don't handle stairs very well.

RANK: Ah ha—are you having some kind of trouble?

MRS. LINDE: Probably just overwork.

RANK: Nothing more? So you've probably come to town to catch your breath in the holiday parties.

MRS. LINDE: I'm looking for a job.

RANK: Is that the prescription for overwork?

MRS. LINDE: One has to live, Doctor.

RANK: Yes, there's general agreement on that point.

NORA: Oh, come on now, Doctor Rank, you want to live as much as anyone.

RANK: Yes, I really do. Wretched as I am, I really want to stretch my torment to the limit. All my patients feel the same way. And it's the same with the morally diseased—right now there's a terminal moral case in there with Helmer—

MRS. LINDE: (*Quietly.*) Ah—!

NORA: Who's that?

RANK: Oh, just a certain lawyer Krogstad, no one you'd know anything about. His character, my ladies, is rotten right down to the roots—but even he began making speeches—as if it were self-evident—that he had to *live.*

NORA: Oh? What did he want to talk to Torvald about?

RANK: I don't know for sure. All I heard was something about the bank.

NORA: I didn't know Krog—that this lawyer Krogstad had anything to do with the bank.

RANK: Yes, he's got some kind of position down there. (*To Mrs. Linde.*) I don't know if you have, in your part of the country, any of these moral detectives, these investigators who go around sniffing out moral corruption and then get their victims into a safe place where they can keep them under constant surveillance—it's a lucrative business these days. The healthy ones get left out in the cold—no room for them!

MRS. LINDE: And yet it's the sick ones who need to be brought inside.

RANK: (*Shrugs his shoulders.*) There you have it. That's the philosophy that's turning our whole world into a hospital.

(*Nora, lost in thought, breaks into quiet laughter, clapping her hands.*)

RANK: Why do you laugh? Do you really know what the world is?

NORA: What do I care about the boring old world? I was laughing at something else—something terribly funny. Tell me, Doctor Rank, all those people who work at the bank—are they all under Torvald now?

RANK: Is *that* what's so terribly funny to you?

NORA: (*Smiling and humming.*) Never mind! Never mind! (*Walking around the room.*) Yes, it is extremely amusing that we—that Torvald has so much influence over so many people. (*Takes a bag from her pocket.*) Doctor Rank, how about a little macaroon?

RANK: Ah ha! Macaroons! I thought they were illegal here.

NORA: Yes, but Kristine gave me these—

MRS. LINDE: What? I—?

NORA: Now, now, now, don't worry. How could you know that Torvald made a law against them? You see, he's afraid they'll rot my teeth. But, fuff—just this once—don't you agree, Doctor Rank? There you are! (*She pops a macaroon into his mouth.*) You too, Kristine. And I'll have one too, just a little one—or two at the most. (*Walking around again.*) Yes, now I am really tremendously happy. There's just one last thing in the world I have a tremendous desire to do.

RANK: Oh? What's that?

NORA: I have this tremendous desire to say something so that Torvald can hear it.

RANK: So why can't you say it?

NORA: No, I don't dare. It's too horrible.

MRS. LINDE: Horrible?

RANK: Well, then, maybe you'd better not. But with us—can't you? What do you want to say so Torvald can hear?

NORA: I have a tremendous desire to say: To hell with everything!

RANK: Are you crazy?

MRS. LINDE: For heaven' sake, Nora.

RANK: Say it—here he is.

NORA: (*Hiding the macaroons.*) Shh, shh, shh!

(*Helmer enters from his study, hat in hand and overcoat on his arm.*)

NORA: Well, my dear, are you through with him?

HELMER: Yes, he just left.

NORA: Let me introduce you—this is Kristine, who's just come to town.

HELMER: Kristine? I'm sorry, but I don't know—

NORA: Mrs. Linde, Torvald dear, Mrs. Kristine Linde.

HELMER: Oh, I see. A childhood friend?

MRS. LINDE: Yes, we knew each other back then.

NORA: And just think, she made the long trip here just to talk to you.

MRS. LINDE: Well, actually, I didn't—

NORA: Kristine, you see, is extremely good at office work, and so she's tremendously eager to place herself under the direction of a capable man so that she can learn even more than she—

HELMER: Very sensible, Mrs. Linde.

NORA: So that when she heard you'd been made bank manager—there was a bulletin about it in all the papers—she started out as fast as she could, and—it's true, isn't it, Torvald? You could do something for Kristine for my sake, yes?

HELMER: It's not completely out of the question. You are, I suppose, a widow?

MRS. LINDE: Yes.

HELMER: And you have experience in office work?

MRS. LINDE: Yes, quite a bit.

HELMER: Well then, it's entirely possible that I can offer you a position—

NORA: (*Clapping her hands.*) You see, you see!

HELMER: You appeared at a lucky moment, Mrs. Linde.

MRS. LINDE: How can I thank you—

HELMER: Not at all necessary. (*Puts on overcoat.*) But today I'll have to ask you to excuse me—

RANK: Wait—I'll go with you.

(*Rank gets his fur coat from the hall and warms it at the stove.*)

NORA: Don't be out long, Torvald my dear.

HELMER: Just an hour, no more.

NORA: Are you leaving too, Kristine?

MRS. LINDE: (*Putting on her outdoor things.*) Yes, now I've got to find myself a room.

HELMER: Then maybe we can all walk together for a while.

NORA: (*Helping her.*) It's so boring that we don't have space here, but it's just impossible for us to—

MRS. LINDE: Don't even think of it! Goodbye, Nora, and thank you for everything.

NORA: Goodbye for now. But I'll see you again this evening. You too, Doctor Rank. What? If you feel well? Of course you will! Wrap yourself up nice and warm.

(*They all go out together into the hall. Children's voices are heard on the stairs.*)

NORA: There they are! There they are!

(*She runs to open the front door. Anne-Marie, their nanny, enters with the children.*)

NORA: Come in, come in! (*Bends down and kisses them.*)

Oh, you sweet little darlings! Look at them, Kristine, aren't they lovely!

RANK: No loitering out here in the draft!

HELMER: Let's go, Mrs. Linde; this place is unbearable now for anyone but mothers.

(*Doctor Rank, Helmer, Mrs. Linde go down the stairs. The nursemaid goes into the living room with the children. Nora goes in also, after shutting the door to the hallway.*)

NORA: You look so clean and healthy! Your cheeks are all red! Like apples and roses. (*The children chatter away to her throughout the following.*) Was it fun? That's great. Really? You pulled both Emmy and Bob on the sled? My goodness, both of them together! You're a clever boy, Ivar. Here, let me hold her for a little while, Anne-Marie. My sweet little doll-baby! (*Takes the smallest child from Anne-Marie and dances with her.*) Yes, yes, mommy will dance with Bob too. What? A snowball fight? Oh, I wish I was there with you! No, don't bother, I'll undress them myself, Anne-Marie. Yes, let me do it, it's so much fun. Go in for a while—you look frozen. There's warm coffee for you on the stove. (*Anne-Marie goes into the room on the left. Nora takes off the children's outdoor clothes and throws them around while the children all talk at the same time.*) Is that so? A great big dog came running after you? But it didn't bite? No, dogs never bite lovely little doll-babies. Stop peeking into the packages, Ivar! What is it? Oh, wouldn't you like to know? No, it's something awful! Well? Do you want to play? What'll we play? Hide-and-seek. Yes, let's play hide-and-seek. Bob, you hide first. Me? All right, I'll hide first.

(*She and the children play, laughing and shouting, in the living room and the adjoining room to the right. At last Nora hides*) *under the table; the children come storming in, searching, not finding her; then, hearing her muffled laughter, rush to the table, lift the tablecloth, and discover her. A storm of delight. Meanwhile, there has been a knocking at the front door; no one has noticed it. Now the door half-opens, and Krogstad appears. He waits a little while the game continues.)*

KROGSTAD: I beg your pardon, Mrs. Helmer.

NORA: (*Turns, with a stifled cry, half jumps up.*) Ah! What do you want?

KROGSTAD: Excuse me. The front door was open—somebody must have forgotten to shut it.

NORA: (*Rising.*) My husband's not here, Mr. Krogstad.

KROGSTAD: I know that.

NORA: Well—what do you want?

KROGSTAD: A word with you.

NORA: With—? (*To the children, quietly.*) Go in with Anne-Marie. No, the strange man won't hurt Mama. When he's gone we can play some more. (*She leads the children in to the room on the left and closes the door after them. Now, tense and nervous.*) You want to speak with me?

KROGSTAD: Yes, I do.

NORA: Today—? But it's not the first of the month yet—

KROGSTAD: No, it's Christmas eve. It's up to you how much Christmas cheer you'll have.

NORA: What do you want? Today I can't possibly—

KROGSTAD: We won't talk about that right now. It's something else. I suppose you have a moment?

NORA: Well, yes; all right—though—

KROGSTAD: Good. I was sitting over at Olsen's Restaurant and I saw your husband going down the street—

NORA: Oh yes.

KROGSTAD: With a lady.

NORA: So?

KROGSTAD: I wonder if you'll allow me to ask if that lady was Mrs. Linde?

NORA: Yes.

KROGSTAD: Just arrived in town?

NORA: Yes, today.

KROGSTAD: She's a good friend of yours?

NORA: Yes, she is. But I can't see—

KROGSTAD: I also knew her at one time.

NORA: I'm aware of that.

KROGSTAD: Really? That's what I thought. Well then, let me get right to the point: Is Mrs. Linde getting a job at the bank?

NORA: Why do you think you can cross-examine me, Mr. Krogstad? You, who's just one of my husband's employees? But since you ask, you might as well know: yes, Mrs. Linde got a job. And I arranged it all for her, Mr. Krogstad. Now you know.

KROGSTAD: As I thought.

NORA: *(Pacing the floor.)* Oh, I should hope that one always has a little bit of influence. Just because one is a woman, it doesn't follow that—when one is in an inferior position, Mr. Krogstad, one ought to be very careful with somebody who—

KROGSTAD: Who has influence?

NORA: Exactly.

KROGSTAD: *(Changing tone.)* Mrs. Helmer, would you be good enough to use your influence on my behalf?

NORA: What? What do you mean?

KROGSTAD: Would you be kind enough to make sure that I keep my inferior position at the bank?

NORA: What do you mean? Who's trying to take it away from you?

KROGSTAD: Oh, you don't have to play the innocent with me. I understand perfectly well that your friend doesn't want to run the risk of seeing me again; and now I also understand who to thank for being let go.

NORA: But I promise you—

KROGSTAD: Yes, yes, yes. But here's the point: there's still time, and I'd advise you to use your influence to prevent it.

NORA: But, Mr. Krogstad, I have no influence at all.

KROGSTAD: No? I thought a minute ago you said—

NORA: I didn't mean it that way. What makes you think I've got any sort of influence over my husband in things like that?

KROGSTAD: Oh, I've known your husband since we were students together—and I don't believe our Bank Manager has any more will power than any other married man.

NORA: You talk like that about my husband and I'll show you the door.

KROGSTAD: The lady has courage.

NORA: I'm not afraid of you any more. Soon after New Year's I'll be done with the whole business.

KROGSTAD: Now listen to me, Mrs. Helmer. If it becomes necessary, I'll fight to the death for my little job at the bank.

NORA: Yes, it looks that way.

KROGSTAD: And not just for the money—that's the least of my concerns. It's something else—well, all right—you know, of course, like everyone else, that some years ago I was guilty of an indiscretion.

NORA: I think I heard something about it.

KROGSTAD: The case never came to trial, but even so every door was closed to me. So I had to go into the sort of business you're familiar with. I had to find something—and I think I can say that I've been far from the worst in that line of work. But now I want to put all of it behind me. My sons are growing up. For their sake I want to win back as much respect as I can in the community. That position in the bank was the first rung in the ladder for me. Now your husband wants to kick me right back off the ladder and into the mud again.

NORA: But for God's sake, Mr. Krogstad, it's just not in my power to help you.

KROGSTAD: That's because you don't have the will to do it—but I can force you to.

NORA: You wouldn't tell my husband that I owe you money?

KROGSTAD: Hmm—what if I did?

NORA: That would be shameful. *(Choking with tears.)* That secret—my pride and my joy—if he learned about it in such a horrible way—learned it from you—. You'd put me through such an incredibly unpleasant scene—

KROGSTAD: Only unpleasant?

NORA: *(Vehemently.)* Just try it! It'll only be worse for you. Because then my husband will really get to see what kind of man you are, and you'll have no chance of keeping your job.

KROGSTAD: I asked you if all you were afraid of was this unpleasant scene here at home?

NORA: If my husband finds out about it, of course he'll pay you off immediately, and we'd have nothing more to do with you.

KROGSTAD: *(A step nearer.)* Listen, Mrs. Helmer: either you've got a terrible memory or a very shaky grasp of business. Let me get a few facts straight for you.

NORA: How do you mean?

KROGSTAD: When your husband was sick, you came to me for four thousand, eight hundred kroner.

NORA: I didn't know where else to go.

KROGSTAD: I promised to get it for you—

NORA: And you did.

KROGSTAD: I promised to get it for you on certain conditions. At the time you were so wrapped up in your husband's illness, that I suppose you didn't think through all the details. Maybe I'd better remind you of them. Now: I promised to get you the money based on a note that I drafted.

NORA: Yes, which I signed.

KROGSTAD: Very good. But below your signature I added some lines to the effect that your father would guarantee the loan. Your father was to sign there.

NORA: Was to—? He signed it.

KROGSTAD: I left out the date. Your father was supposed to date his own signature. Do you remember that?

NORA: Yes, I think so—

KROGSTAD: Then I handed the note over to you so you could mail it to your father. Isn't that the case?

NORA: Yes.

KROGSTAD: And of course you did that right away—because only about five, six days later, you brought me the note, with your father's signature. And then you got your money.

NORA: Well? Haven't I been meeting my payments?

KROGSTAD: Yes, more or less. But to return to the question: that was a difficult time for you, wasn't it, Mrs. Helmer?

NORA: Yes, it was.

KROGSTAD: Your father was very ill, I believe.

NORA: He was very near the end.

KROGSTAD: He died soon after that?

NORA: Yes.

KROGSTAD: Tell me, Mrs. Helmer, do you by any chance recall the date of your father's death? Which day of the month, I mean.

NORA: Papa died on the twenty-ninth of September.

KROGSTAD: Quite correct; I've already confirmed that. That brings us to an oddity that I simply cannot account for.

NORA: What kind of oddity? I don't understand—

KROGSTAD: Here's the oddity, Mrs. Helmer: your father countersigned the note three days after his death.

NORA: How? I don't understand—

KROGSTAD: Your father died on the twenty-ninth of September. But look at this. Here your father has dated his signature "October 2nd." Isn't that odd, Mrs. Helmer? (*Nora is silent.*) Can you explain it to me? (*Nora remains silent.*) Here's another remarkable thing: the date "October 2nd" and the year are not written in your father's hand, but in a hand that I ought to know. Now, that could be explained; your father forgot to date his signature, and someone else did it for him, somewhat carelessly, before anyone knew of his death. Nothing wrong with that. Everything hinges on the signature. And that *is* genuine, isn't it, Mrs. Helmer? It really was your father himself who signed his name there?

NORA: (*After a short silence, throws back her head and looks firmly at him.*) No, it wasn't. *I* signed Papa's name.

KROGSTAD: Listen, Mrs. Helmer—do you understand that this is a dangerous confession?

NORA: Why? You'll get your money soon enough.

KROGSTAD: Can I ask you—why didn't you send the note to your father?

NORA: Impossible. Papa was so sick. If I had asked him for his signature, I'd have had to tell him what the money was for. I just couldn't tell him, in his condition, that my husband was dying. It was just impossible.

KROGSTAD: Then it would have been better for you to give up the trip.

NORA: No, impossible again. That trip was to save my husband's life. I couldn't give that up.

KROGSTAD: But didn't it occur to you that you were committing a fraud against me?

NORA: I couldn't worry about that. I certainly wasn't concerned about you. I could hardly stand you, making up all those cold conditions when you knew perfectly well how much danger my husband was in.

KROGSTAD: Mrs. Helmer, you obviously don't have any idea what you've implicated yourself in. But let me tell you this: what I once did was nothing more, and nothing worse, and it destroyed me.

NORA: You? Are you trying to get me to believe that you risked everything to save your wife?

KROGSTAD: Laws don't much care about motives.

NORA: Then they must be very bad laws.

KROGSTAD: Bad or not, if I produce this paper in court, you'll be judged by those laws.

NORA: I don't believe it. Doesn't a daughter have the right to spare her dying father from worry and anxiety? Shouldn't a wife have the right to save her husband's life? I don't know the law very well, but I'm sure it must say somewhere in there that these things are legal. You must be a very bad lawyer, Mr. Krogstad.

KROGSTAD: Maybe so. But business—this kind of business we're in—don't you think I know something about that? Good. Do what you want. But hear this: if I get thrown down a second time, you're coming with me. (*He bows and goes out through the hall door.*)

NORA: (*Stands for a moment, reflecting, then tosses her head.*) Nonsense! He's trying to frighten me! I'm not all that naïve. (*Starts gathering up the children's clothes, but soon stops.*) But—? No, impossible. I did it out of love.

CHILDREN: (*In the doorway, left.*) Mama, the strange man's going down the street.

NORA: Yes, I know. But don't mention the strange man to anyone. You hear? Not even Papa.

CHILDREN: No, Mama. Now can we play again?

NORA: No, no. Not now.

CHILDREN: But Mama, you promised.

NORA: Yes, but right now I can't. Go inside; I've got too much to do. Go in, go in, my dear, sweet little ones. (*She herds them carefully into the room and closes the door after them. She sits on the sofa, takes up her embroidery, makes some stitches, but soon stops.*) Helene! Let me have the tree in here. (*Goes to the table at left and opens a drawer, pauses again.*) No, that's completely impossible!

MAID: (*With the spruce tree.*) Where should I put it, Ma'am?

NORA: There—in the middle of the floor.

MAID: Anything else?

NORA: No, thank you. I have what I need.

(*The Maid, having set the tree down, goes out.*)

NORA: (*Busy decorating the tree.*) Candles here, flowers here—that horrible man! Talk, talk, talk. Nothing's going to happen. The Christmas tree will be just lovely. I'll do anything you want me to, Torvald—I'll sing for you, dance for you—

(*Helmer, with a packet of papers under his arm, comes in through the hall.*)

NORA: Ah! Back already?

HELMER: Yes. Has someone been here?

NORA: Here? No.

HELMER: That's strange. I just saw Krogstad going out the door.

NORA: Really? Oh, of course. Krogstad was here for a moment.

HELMER: Nora, I can see it in your eyes, he's been here asking you to put in a good word for him.

NORA: Yes.

HELMER: And you were going to pretend it was your own idea. You'd pretend he'd never been here. Did he ask you to do that as well?

NORA: Yes, Torvald, but—

HELMER: Nora, Nora, you could go along with that? Do business with that sort of person, and make promises to him? And then, on top of it all, tell me a lie!

NORA: A lie?

HELMER: Didn't you tell me no one had been here? (*Wagging his finger.*) My little songbird mustn't ever do a thing like that again. A songbird needs a clean beak to chirp with. No false notes. (*Takes her by the waist.*) Isn't that the way it should be? Yes, of course it is. So let's not talk about it any more. (*Sits by the stove.*) Ah, it's so snug and cozy here.

NORA: (*Working on the tree; after a short pause.*) Torvald!

HELMER: Yes?

NORA: I'm terribly excited about the Stenborg's party the day after tomorrow.

HELMER: And I'm terribly curious to see what you'll surprise me with.

NORA: Oh, that stupid nonsense!

HELMER: What?

NORA: I can't find anything I like; everything seems so pointless, so idiotic.

HELMER: Is that what little Nora thinks?

NORA: (*Behind his chair, her arms on its back.*) Are you very busy, Torvald?

HELMER: Well—

NORA: What are those papers?

HELMER: Bank business.

NORA: Already?

HELMER: I've convinced the retiring manager to give me full authority to make changes in personnel and procedure. I'll have to use Christmas week for that. I want everything in order for the New Year.

NORA: So that's why this poor Krogstad—

HELMER: Hm.

NORA: (*Still leaning on the back of his chair, stroking the hair on his neck.*) If you weren't so busy, I would ask you for a terribly big favor.

HELMER: Let's hear it. What can it be?

NORA: No one has your good taste. I really want to look my best at the costume party. Torvald, couldn't you take over from me and advise me what to wear and how to design my costume?

HELMER: So our little rebel's ready for a cease-fire?

NORA: Yes, Torvald. I can't get anywhere without your help.

HELMER: All right. I'll think about it. We'll come up with something.

NORA: How sweet of you! (*Goes over to the Christmas tree; pause.*) These red flowers are so pretty—But tell me, was what that Krogstad did really such a crime?

HELMER: He forged people's names. Do you know what that means?

NORA: Maybe he did it out of need.

HELMER: Yes, or thoughtlessness, like so many others. And I wouldn't condemn a man categorically because of one isolated incident.

NORA: No, you wouldn't, would you, Torvald?

HELMER: Men can often redeem themselves by openly confessing their guilt and accepting their punishment.

NORA: Punishment?

HELMER: But Krogstad didn't do that. He got himself off the hook with tricks and loopholes. That's what's corrupted him.

NORA: Do you think that would—?

HELMER: Imagine what life is like for a man like that: he has to lie and dissemble and cheat everyone he meets—has to wear a mask in front of his nearest and dearest—yes, even his wife and children. And the children—that's the most terrible part of it.

NORA: Why?

HELMER: Because an atmosphere so filled with lies brings pestilence and disease into every corner of a home. Every breath the children take carries the infection.

NORA. (*Closer behind him.*) Are you sure about that?

HELMER: Ah, my dear, I'm a lawyer—I've seen it often enough. Almost everyone who turns bad as a youth has had a compulsive liar for a mother.

NORA: Why just—a mother?

HELMER: Usually you can trace it to the mother, but fathers have the same effect; it's something every lawyer knows. And yet this Krogstad has been living at home, poisoning his children with lies and deceit; that's why I call him morally corrupt. And that's why my sweet little Nora must promise me not to plead his case. Your hand on that. Now, now, what's this? Give me your hand.

There. That's settled. And let me tell you, it would be impossible for me to work with him; I literally feel sick when I'm around someone like that.

NORA: (*Withdraws her hand and goes over to the other side of the Christmas tree.*) It's so hot in here! And I've got so much to pull together!

HELMER: (*Rising and gathering his papers.*) Yes, I've got to try to get through some of these before dinner. I'll also give some thought to your costume. And I might also be thinking about something to hang on the tree in gilt paper—. (*Lays his hand on her head.*) Oh, my sweet little songbird. (*He goes into his room and closes the door.*)

NORA: (*Softly, after a silence.*) No, no! It's not true. It's impossible. It just can't be possible.

ANNE-MARIE: (*In doorway, left.*) The children are asking if they can come in to Mama.

NORA: No, no, no, don't let them in here with me! You stay with them, Anne-Marie.

ANNE-MARIE: Very well, Ma'am.

NORA: (*Pale with terror.*) Harm my children—! Poison my home? (*Short pause; she tosses her head.*) It's not true. It could never be true!

END OF ACT ONE

ACT TWO

The same room. In the corner by the piano stands the Christmas tree, stripped, bedraggled, with its candle-stumps all burned down. Nora's outdoor clothing lies on the sofa.

(Nora, alone, walks restlessly around the room. Finally she stands by the sofa and picks up her coat.)

NORA: *(Dropping the coat again.)* Somebody's coming! *(Goes to the door, listens.)* No, nobody there. Naturally—nobody's coming on Christmas day—or tomorrow either. But maybe— *(She opens the door and looks out.)* No, nothing in the mailbox—perfectly empty. *(Comes forward.)* Oh, nonsense! Of course he wasn't serious about it. Nothing like that could happen. After all, I have three small children.

(Anne-Marie, carrying a large carton, comes in from the room on the left.)

ANNE-MARIE: Well, I finally found the box of masquerade costumes.

NORA: Thanks. Put it on the table.

ANNA-MARIE: *(Does so.)* But it's a terrible mess.

NORA: Ah, I wish I could rip them into a million pieces.

ANNE-MARIE: Lord bless us—they can be fixed up again. Just have a little patience.

NORA: Yes, I'll go and get Mrs. Linde to help.

ANNE-MARIE: You're not going out again now? In this horrible weather? Mrs. Nora will catch cold—get sick.

NORA: Worse things could happen. How are the children?

ANNE-MARIE: The poor little things are playing with their Christmas presents, but—

NORA: Are they always asking for me?

ANNE-MARIE: They're so used to having their Mama with them.

NORA: Yes, Anne-Marie, but I can't be with them as much as before.

ANNE-MARIE: Well, little children get used to anything.

NORA: Do you think so? Do you think they'd forget their Mama if she were really gone?

ANNE-MARIE: Lord help us—gone?

NORA: Listen—tell me, Anne-Marie—I've wondered about this a lot— how could you ever, in your heart of hearts, stand to give your child away to strangers?

ANNE-MARIE: But I just had to when I became little Nora's wetnurse.

NORA: Yes, but how could you actually do it?

ANNE-MARIE: When I could get such a good place? A poor girl in trouble has to jump at a chance like that. Because that slick good-for-nothing wouldn't do anything for me.

NORA: But your daughter's completely forgotten you.

ANNE-MARIE: Oh no, not really. She wrote to me when she was confirmed, and when she got married.

NORA: (*Clasps her around the neck.*) Dear old Anne-Marie—you were a good mother for me when I was little.

ANNE-MARIE: Poor little Nora, with me as her only mother.

NORA: And if my little ones didn't have a mother, I know that you— stupid, stupid, stupid! (*Opening the carton.*) Go to them. Right now I have to—tomorrow you'll see how beautiful I look.

ANNE-MARIE: Yes, Mrs. Nora will be the most beautiful woman at the party.

(*Anne-Marie goes into the room on the left.*)

NORA: (*Begins to unpack the box, but soon throws the whole thing aside.*) Ah, if I had the nerve to go out. If only nobody would come. If only nothing happened here at home in the meantime. Stupid talk; nobody's coming. Just don't think. I have to brush out this muff. Beautiful gloves, beautiful gloves. Get it out, get it out! One, two, three, four, five, six, (*Screams.*) Oh, here they come. (*Goes toward the door, but stops, irresolute. Mrs. Linde comes in from the hall where she has removed her outdoor clothes.*) So it's you, Kristine. No one else out there? I'm glad you're here.

MRS. LINDE: I heard you were asking for me.

NORA: Yes, I happened to be passing by. I need your help with something. Come sit with me by the sofa. Look at this. There's going to be a costume party tomorrow over at Consul Stenborg's, and Torvald wants me to go as a Neapolitan fisher girl and dance the tarantella—I learned it in Capri.

MRS. LINDE: Well, well—you're giving a real performance?

NORA: Yes, Torvald says I should. Look—here's my costume. Torvald had it made for me down there. But it's all torn now and I just don't know—

MRS. LINDE: We'll get that fixed up in no time; the trimmings are just coming loose here and there, that's all. Needle and thread? There, now we have what we need.

NORA: This is so nice of you.

MRS. LINDE: (*Sewing.*) So you're going in disguise tomorrow, Nora? You know what? I'll come by for a minute and look at you when you're all dressed up. You know I've completely forgotten to thank you for the lovely evening yesterday.

NORA: (*Gets up and crosses the floor.*) Oh, I don't think it was as nice yesterday as it usually is. You should have gotten here a little earlier, Kristine. Torvald really knows how to make a home charming and elegant.

MRS. LINDE: So do you, just as much, I'd say. You're not your father's daughter for nothing. Tell me—is Doctor Rank always so depressed?

NORA: No, yesterday he was particularly low. But he's got a very serious illness—tuberculosis of the spine, poor man. You know his father was a disgusting creature who kept mistresses and things like that—that's how poor Doctor Rank got to be so sickly.

MRS. LINDE: (*Dropping her sewing to her lap.*) Nora, my dear, how do you know about these things?

NORA: (*Walking around.*) Fuff. When you've had three children you end up meeting some women who know a little about medicine, and they tell you a few things.

MRS. LINDE: (*Sewing again; short silence.*) Does Doctor Rank come to the house every day?

NORA: Every single day. He's Torvald's best friend ever since they were children, and he's my good friend too. Doctor Rank sort of belongs to the house.

MRS. LINDE: But tell me this—is he honest? I mean, doesn't he like to tell people what they want to hear?

NORA: No, not at all. What makes you think that?

MRS. LINDE: When you introduced us yesterday he said he'd heard my name here so often—but then I noticed that your husband didn't have any idea who I was. So how could Doctor Rank—

NORA: That's right, Kristine. Torvald is so unbelievably devoted to me—he says he wants me all to himself. When we were first married he'd get jealous if I so much as mentioned any of my old friends from back home. So, of course, I stopped. But with Doctor Rank I can talk about all those things, because he enjoys hearing about them.

MRS. LINDE: Listen to me, Nora: in many ways you're still a child. I'm quite a bit older than you and I have a little more experience. Let me tell you something: you should put an end to all this with Doctor Rank.

NORA: What should I put an end to?

MRS. LINDE: All of it, I think. Yesterday you said something about a rich admirer who was going to give you money—

NORA: Yes, but unfortunately he doesn't exist. So what?

MRS. LINDE: Is Doctor Rank rich?

NORA: Yes.

MRS. LINDE: No one to care for?

NORA: No, no one—but—?

MRS. LINDE: And he comes by every day?

NORA: Yes, that's what I told you.

MRS. LINDE: How can such a cultivated man be so obvious?

NORA: I really don't understand you.

MRS. LINDE: Don't play games, Nora. Don't you think I know who lent you the money?

NORA: Are you out of your mind? How can you even think that? A good friend of ours, who comes over here every single day! That would have been horrible!

MRS. LINDE: So it really wasn't him?

NORA: No, I promise you. I would never have thought of that—anyway, he didn't have any money to lend back then—he inherited it all later.

MRS. LINDE: Well, that was just as well for you, I think.

NORA: No, I would never have thought of asking Doctor Rank. Even though I'm sure that if I did—

MRS. LINDE: But of course you wouldn't.

NORA: No, of course not. I can't imagine how it would be necessary. On the other hand, I'm sure that if I even mentioned it to him—

MRS. LINDE: Behind your husband's back?

NORA: I've got to get out of this other thing—that's also behind his back. I've really got to get out of that.

MRS. LINDE: Yes, that's what I said yesterday. But—

NORA: (*Walking up and down.*) A man can deal with these things so much better than a woman—

MRS. LINDE: Your own husband can, yes.

NORA: Nonsense. (*Stopping.*) When you pay back everything you owe you get your note back.

MRS. LINDE: That's right.

NORA: And you can tear it up in a hundred thousand pieces and burn it—that disgusting piece of paper!

MRS. LINDE: (*Looking straight at her, putting the sewing down, rising slowly.*) Nora—you're hiding something from me.

NORA: Can you see that?

MRS. LINDE: Something's happened since yesterday morning. Nora, what is it?

NORA: (*Going to her.*) Kristine! (*Listens.*) Ssh! Torvald's home. Look—go in there with the children for a while. Torvald can't stand to see people sewing. Let Anne-Marie help you.

MRS. LINDE: (*Gathering some of her things.*) Yes, all right, but I'm not leaving before we talk all this through. (*She goes into the room at left; at the same time, Helmer comes in from the hall.*)

NORA: (*Goes to meet him.*) Oh, I've been waiting for you, Torvald my dear.

HELMER: Was that the dressmaker?

NORA: No, it's Kristine; she's helping me with my costume. You know, I think I'm going to outdo myself this time.

HELMER: Yes, that was a pretty good idea I had, wasn't it?

NORA: Brilliant. But wasn't it also nice of me to agree to it?

HELMER: (*Taking her under the chin.*) Nice of you? Agreeing with your husband? All right, you crazy thing, I know you didn't mean it that way. But I don't want to disturb you; I suppose you'll want to try it on

NORA: Will you be working?

HELMER: Yes. (*Shows her a bundle of papers.*) See. I've been down to the bank – (*He is about to go into his study.*)

NORA: Torvald.

HELMER: Yes.

NORA: If your little squirrel were to beg you ever so nicely for something—?

HELMER: Well?

NORA: Would you do it?

HELMER: First, of course, I'd need to know what it is.

NORA: The squirrel would romp around and do tricks if you'd be sweet and say yes.

HELMER: Come on, what is it?

NORA: The lark would sing high and low in every room—

HELMER: So what, she does that anyway.

NORA: I'd pretend I was a fairy child and dance for you in the moonlight, Torvald.

HELMER: Nora, I hope this isn't that same business from this morning.

NORA: (*Coming closer.*) Yes, Torvald, please, I beg you!

HELMER: You really have the nerve to drag that up again.

NORA: Yes, yes, you've got to do what I say; you've got to let Krogstad keep his job in the bank.

HELMER: But Nora, I'm giving his job to Mrs. Linde.

NORA: That's very sweet of you; but can't you get rid of another clerk, someone besides Krogstad?

HELMER: I can't believe how stubborn you're being! Just because you went ahead and made a foolish promise to speak up for him, now I'm supposed to—

NORA: That's not why, Torvald. It's for your own sake. That man writes articles for some horrible newspapers; you've said so yourself. He can do you an awful lot of harm. I'm scared to death of him—

HELMER: Aha—I understand. You're frightened of the old memories.

NORA: What do you mean by that?

HELMER: You're thinking about your father.

NORA: That's right. Remember how those horrible people wrote about Papa in the papers and slandered him so terribly. I believe they'd have gotten him fired if the government hadn't sent you up there to investigate and if you hadn't been so kind and fair to him.

HELMER: My little Nora, there is a considerable difference between your father and me. Your father's public life was not exactly beyond reproach—but mine is. And that's how I plan to keep it for as long as I hold my position.

NORA: Oh, you can never tell what spiteful people might do. It could be so nice and quiet and happy in our home—so peaceful and carefree—you and me and the children, Torvald—

HELMER: And precisely by continuing to plead for him like this you're making it impossible for me to keep him on. It's already known around the bank that I'm letting Krogstad go. What if the rumor got around that the new bank manager was letting himself be overruled by his wife—

NORA: Yes, so what?

HELMER: Oh, of course—as long as our little rebel here gets her way— I should make myself look silly in front of my whole staff—make people think I can be influenced by all kinds of outside pressures—you can bet that would come back to haunt me soon enough. Besides—there's one thing that makes it impossible to have Krogstad in the bank as long as I'm the manager.

NORA: What's that?

HELMER: I might be able to overlook his moral failings if I had to—

NORA: Yes, Torvald, isn't that right?

HELMER: And I hear he's quite good at his job too. But he was a boyhood friend of mine—one of those stupid friendships you get into without thinking, and end up regretting later in life. I might just as well tell you—we're on a first name basis. And that tactless idiot makes no secret of it in front of people. The opposite, in fact—he thinks it entitles him to take a familiar tone with me, so he's always coming out with "Hey Torvald—Torvald, can I talk to you, Torvald—" and I can tell you I find it excruciating. He'll make my life at the bank completely intolerable.

NORA: Torvald, you can't be serious.

HELMER: Oh? Why not?

NORA: No, because these are such petty things.

HELMER: What are you saying? Petty? Do you think I'm petty?

NORA: Not at all, Torvald, and that's just the reason—

HELMER: All right; you call me petty, I might as well be just that. Petty! Very well! Now we'll put a stop to all of this. (*Goes to the door and calls.*) Helene!

NORA: What are you doing?

HELMER: (*Searching through his papers.*) A decision. (*The Maid enters.*) See this letter? Find a messenger right away and have him deliver it. Quickly. The address is on the envelope. There—here's some money.

MAID: Yes sir. (*She leaves with the letter.*)

HELMER: (*Tidying up his papers.*) So that's that, my little Miss Stubborn.

NORA: (*Breathless.*) Torvald, what was that letter?

HELMER: Krogstad's notice.

NORA: Get it back, Torvald! There's still time. Oh, Torvald, get it back! Do it for my sake—for your own sake—for the children's sake! Listen, Torvald, do it! You don't realize what can happen to all of us.

HELMER: Too late.

NORA: Yes, too late.

HELMER: Nora, I forgive you for being nervous about this, even though you're really insulting me. Yes, you are. Isn't it insulting to think that *I* would be afraid of what some hack journalist might do for revenge? But I forgive you, all the same, because it shows so beautifully how much you love me. That's how it should be, my own darling Nora. Come what may! When things get tough, I've got the courage—and the strength, you can believe it. I'm the kind of man who can take it all on himself.

NORA: (*Terrified.*) What do you mean by that?

HELMER: The whole thing, like I said.

NORA: (*Resolutely.*) You'll never have to do that, never.

HELMER: Good—so we'll share it, Nora, as man and wife. That's the way it should be. (*Fondling her.*) Happy now? Well, well, well—enough of those frightened dove's eyes. It's nothing but empty fantasy. Now you should run through your tarantella and try the tambourine. I won't hear a thing in the office, so you can make all the noise you want. (*Turning in the doorway.*) And when Rank comes, tell him where he can find me. (*He nods to her, goes to his study with his papers, and closes the door behind him.*)

NORA: (*Distracted with fear, standing as though glued to the spot, whispering.*) He's really going to do it. He will do it. He'll do it in spite of everything—No, never, never in this world! Anything but that—escape! A way out— (*The bell rings in the hall.*) Doctor Rank! Anything but that! Whatever else happens!

(*She brushes her hands over her face, pulls herself together and goes to open the door in the hall. Doctor Rank is standing outside hanging up his fur coat. During the following, it begins to grow dark.*)

NORA: Doctor Rank, I recognized your ring. But you can't see Torvald quite yet; I think he's busy.

RANK: And you?

NORA: (*While he comes into the room and she closes the door after him.*) Oh, as you know perfectly well, I always have an hour to spare for you.

RANK: Thanks. I shall make use of it as long as I can.

NORA: What do you mean? As long as you can?

RANK: Yes, does that worry you?

NORA: Well, it's such a strange way to talk. Is anything going to happen?

RANK: Something that I've been expecting for a long time. But I didn't think it would come so soon.

NORA: (*Gripping his arm.*) What have you found out? Doctor Rank, you have to tell me!

RANK: (*Sitting by the stove.*) It's all over. There's no point in lying to myself.

NORA: (*Breathing easier.*) Is it you—?

RANK: Who else? I'm the worst of all my patients, Mrs. Helmer. Over the last few days I've done a general audit of my internal account. Bankrupt. Within a month I'll probably be rotting in the churchyard.

NORA: Oh, really. What a horrible thing to say.

RANK: It *is* a horrible thing. But the worst of it all is the horror beforehand. There's one more examination to go; when I've done that I'll know when the disintegration will begin. There is something I want to ask you. Helmer is so sensitive; he can't stand to be around anything ugly. I won't let him come to my sickroom.

NORA: Oh, but Doctor Rank—

RANK: I won't allow him in there. Under any circumstances. I'll lock the door to him. As soon as I'm absolutely certain of the worst, I'll send you my card with a black cross on it; then you'll know that it's begun.

NORA: No, you are completely unreasonable today. And I especially wanted you to be in a really good mood.

RANK: When I hold death in my hands? And to suffer like this for someone else's guilt? Is there any justice in that? In every family—every single one—somehow this inexorable retribution is taking its course.

NORA: (*Stopping her ears.*) La la la la la! Cheer up! Cheer up!

RANK: Yes, finally even I can only laugh at the whole thing. My poor, innocent back has to pay for my father's career as a lascivious lieutenant.

NORA: (*By the table to the left.*) Was he that addicted to asparagus and *pâté de foie gras?*

RANK: Yes, and truffles.

NORA: Truffles, yes. And also oysters, I believe.

RANK: Yes, oysters, oysters, of course.

NORA: And port and champagne too. It's so sad that all these delicious things have to go and attack our bones.

RANK: Especially when they attack the unfortunate bones that never got the slightest pleasure from them.

NORA: Ah, yes—that's the greatest sadness of all.

RANK: (*Looks searchingly at her.*) Hmm—

NORA: (*Shortly after.*) Why did you smile?

RANK: No, no—you laughed.

NORA: No, you smiled, Doctor Rank!

RANK: (*Getting up.*) You're an even bigger flirt than I thought!

NORA: I'm full of crazy ideas today.

RANK: So it seems.

NORA: (*With both hands on his shoulders.*) Dear, dear Doctor Rank: for Torvald and me, you simply will not die.

RANK: Oh, you'll soon get over that loss. Those who go away are soon forgotten.

NORA: (*Looking anxiously at him.*) Do you think so?

RANK: You make new relationships, and then—

NORA: Who makes new relationships?

RANK: Both you and Helmer will, after I'm gone. You're well on your way already, I'd say. What was that Mrs. Linde doing here last night?

NORA: Come on now—you're not telling me you're jealous of poor Kristine?

RANK: Yes I am. She'll be my successor here in this house. When my time is up, I'll bet that woman will—

NORA: Ssh—don't talk so loud—she's in there.

RANK: Again today! There, you see?

NORA: She's just fixing my costume. Good Lord, you're unreasonable today. (*Sits on the sofa.*) Now be nice, Doctor Rank. Tomorrow you'll see how beautifully I'll dance—and you can imagine I'm doing it just for you—yes, for Torvald too, of course. (*Takes various things out of a carton.*) Doctor Rank, sit here. I want to show you something.

RANK: (*Sitting.*) What is it?

NORA: Look here. Look!

RANK: Silk stockings.

NORA: Flesh-colored. Lovely, aren't they? It's so dark in here now, but in the morning—no, no, no, only the feet. Oh, well, you might as well go ahead and look higher up.

RANK: Hmm.

NORA: What's this critical stare? Don't you think they'll fit?

RANK: I couldn't possibly have an accurate opinion on that.

NORA: (*Glancing at him for a moment.*) Shame on you. (*Hits him lightly on the ear with the stockings.*) That's what you get. (*Puts them away again.*)

RANK: And what other splendors do I get to see?

NORA: Not a thing—you're being bad. (*She hums a little and rummages through her things.*)

RANK: (*After a short pause.*) When I'm sitting here like this, so close to you, I can't imagine—I can't begin to comprehend—what would have become of me if I had never found my way to this house.

NORA: (*Smiling.*) Yes, I believe you really enjoy being here with us.

RANK: (*Quietly, looking ahead.*) And to have to leave it all behind—

NORA: Nonsense, you're not leaving us behind.

RANK: (*As before.*) And to think that nothing remains after you're gone—no little gesture of gratitude—hardly even a passing regret—just a vacant place that the first person who comes along can fill.

NORA: And what if I were to ask you now for—? No—

RANK: For what?

NORA: For a great proof of your friendship.

RANK: Yes, yes?

NORA: I mean a tremendously big favor—

RANK: Would you really let me be so happy, just this once?

NORA: You have no idea what it is.

RANK: All right—so tell me.

NORA: No, Doctor Rank, I can't. It's too big, too unreasonable. It's advice, and help, and a great service too.

RANK: So much the better. I can't imagine what you mean. But keep talking. Don't you have confidence in me?

NORA: Yes, in you before anyone else. You're my best and truest friend, you know that. That's why I can tell you. All right, Doctor Rank: there's something you've got to help me prevent. You know how intensely, how indescribably deeply Torvald loves me—he'd give his life for my sake without a moment's thought.

RANK: (*Bending toward her.*) Nora—do you think he's the only one?

NORA: (*With a slight start.*) Who—?

RANK: Who would gladly give his life for you?

NORA: (*Heavily.*) I see.

RANK: I promised myself that you'd know before the end. I'll never find a better chance than this. Yes, Nora, now you know. And you also know that you can trust me like nobody else.

NORA: (*Rises and speaks, evenly and calmly.*) Let me through

RANK: (*Makes way for her, but remains seated.*) Nora—

NORA: (*In the hall doorway.*) Helene, bring in the lamp. (*She goes over to the stove.*) Ah, dear Doctor Rank, that was really awful of you.

RANK: (*Rising.*) That I've loved you just as much as anyone? Was *that* awful?

NORA: No, but that you felt you had to tell me. That was just not necessary.

RANK: What do you mean? You mean that you knew—?

(*The Maid enters with the lamp. sets it on the table, and goes out again.*)

RANK: Nora—Mrs. Helmer—I'm asking you. Did you know?

NORA: Oh, how do I know what I knew or didn't know? I can't say. How could you be so clumsy, Doctor Rank! When everything was so nice.

RANK: Well, in any case now you know that I'm at your service with body and soul. So please go on.

NORA: (*Looking at him.*) After this?

RANK: Please, please tell me what it is.

NORA: Now I can't tell you anything.

RANK: Yes, yes. Don't torment me like this. Let me do whatever is humanly possible for you.

NORA: You can't do anything for me now. In fact, I really don't need any help. You'll see—it was just my imagination. It really is. Of course! (*Sits in the rocking chair, looks at him, smiling.*) Well, you are a piece of work, Doctor Rank. Don't you think you should be a little ashamed, now that the lamp is here?

RANK: No, not really. But maybe I'd better go—for good?

NORA: No, you certainly will not do that. Of course you'll keep coming here just like before. You know perfectly well that Torvald can't do without you.

RANK: Yes, but what about you?

NORA: Oh, I always enjoy your visits very much.

RANK: That's exactly what set me off on the wrong track. You're an enigma to me. I've often felt you'd almost rather be with me than with Helmer.

NORA: Well, you see, there are the people you love the most, and the people you'd almost rather be with.

RANK: Ah yes, you're on to something there.

NORA: When I was at home, of course I loved Papa the most. But I always had the most fun sneaking into the maids' rooms, because they never tried to teach me anything; and they always had so much fun talking to each other.

RANK: Ah—so *they're* the ones that I've replaced.

NORA: (*Jumping up and going to him.*) Oh, dear Doctor Rank, I didn't mean that at all. But you can see that with Torvald it's a lot like it was with Papa—

(*The Maid enters from the hall.*)

MAID: Ma'am. (*Whispers and hands Nora a card.*)

NORA: (*Glancing at the card.*) Ah! (*Puts it in her pocket.*)

RANK: Something wrong?

NORA: No, no, not at all. It's just—it's about my new costume.

RANK: How could that be? Your costume's in there.

NORA: Oh, yes—that one. But this is a different one, I ordered it— Torvald can't find out—

RANK: Aha—there's our great secret.

NORA: That's right. Go on in to him. He's working in the inner room. Keep him there as long as—

RANK: Don't worry—he won't get by me. (*He goes into Helmer's study*)

NORA: (*To the Maid.*) And he's waiting in the kitchen?

MAID: Yes, he came up the back stairs.

NORA: Did you tell him somebody was here?

MAID: I did, but that didn't help.

NORA: He won't go away?

MAID: No, he won't leave until he's talked to you.

NORA: Let him come in then; but quietly. Helene, not a word of this to anyone; it's a surprise for my husband.

MAID: Oh, yes, I understand. (*She goes out.*)

NORA: This terrible thing is really happening. It's coming no matter what. No, no, no. It can't happen. It must not happen.

(*She goes and bolts Helmer's door. The Maid opens the hall door for Krogstad and closes it after him. He's dressed in traveling clothes, a fur coat, overshoes, and a fur cap.*)

NORA: (*Goes toward him.*) Talk quietly—my husband's home.

KROGSTAD: I don't care.

NORA: What do you want from me?

KROGSTAD: Some answers.

NORA: Quick, then. What?

KROGSTAD: You know, of course, I got my notice.

NORA: I couldn't stop it, Mr. Krogstad. I fought for you as hard as I could, but it was no use.

KROGSTAD: Does your husband really love you so little? He knows what I can do to you, and he still dares—

NORA: How can you imagine he knows about it?

KROGSTAD: No, I didn't think he did. It's not like my fine Torvald Helmer to show that kind of strength.

NORA: Mr. Krogstad, I demand respect for my husband.

KROGSTAD: Good Lord, of course, all due respect. But since the lady has kept all this so carefully hidden, might I ask if you've also come to understand a little better than yesterday what you've actually done?

NORA: Better than you could ever teach me.

KROGSTAD: Yes, I'm such a terrible lawyer—

NORA: What do you want with me?

KROGSTAD: Just to see how things are with you, Mrs. Helmer. I couldn't stop thinking about you all day. A cashier, a hack journalist, a—well, a man like me also has a little of what is commonly called heart, you know.

NORA: Then show it. Think of my little children.

KROGSTAD: Have you or your husband given any thought to mine? But that's not the issue right now. I just wanted to tell you that you don't need to take this business too seriously. For the time being I'm not taking any action.

NORA: Oh, that's true, I was sure of it.

KROGSTAD: The whole thing can be settled amicably. No one else needs to know about it, just the three of us.

NORA: My husband can never find out.

KROGSTAD: How can you stop that? Can you pay off the balance?

NORA: No, not right now.

KROGSTAD: Maybe you can find a way to raise the money in a few days?

NORA: No way that I'd use.

KROGSTAD: Well, it wouldn't do you any good anyway. Even if you were standing there with a pile of cash in your hands you still wouldn't get your note back.

NORA: Tell me what you're going to do with it.

KROGSTAD: Just keep it—just hold it in my custody. No one else needs to know anything about it. So if you happen to be thinking of some desperate remedy—

NORA: Which I am.

KROGSTAD: If you're thinking of running away from home—

NORA: Which I am.

KROGSTAD: Or something worse—

NORA: How did you know?

KROGSTAD: Then give it up right now.

NORA: How could you know I was thinking of *that?*

KROGSTAD: Most of us think of *that* to begin with. I thought about it too—but I didn't have the courage.

NORA: (*Lifelessly.*) I don't either.

KROGSTAD: (*Relieved.*) That's true?

NORA: I don't have it; I don't have it.

KROGSTAD: It'd be pretty silly anyway. As soon as the first big storm blows over—I have here in my pocket a letter to your husband—

NORA: Which tells everything?

KROGSTAD: As nicely as possible.

NORA: (*Quickly.*) He must never get that letter. Tear it up. I'll get the money somehow.

KROGSTAD: Excuse me, Mrs. Helmer, but I think I just told you—

NORA: I'm not talking about what I owe you. Just let me know how much you demand from my husband and I'll get you the money.

KROGSTAD: I'm not demanding any money from your husband.

NORA: So what then?

KROGSTAD: I'll tell you. I want to get back on my feet, Mrs. Helmer; I want to move up. And your husband is going to help me. For the last year and a half I haven't gone near anything disreputable—all the time fighting to make ends meet—but I was happy to work my way up, step by step. Now I'm being driven out again and I'm not in a very forgiving mood. I'm ready to climb, I tell you. I'll get back in the bank, and in a higher position than before. Your husband will set me up.

NORA: He'll never do that!

KROGSTAD: He'll do it. I know him; he won't even dare to argue. And once I'm in there with him, you'll see how it goes. In a year I'll be the manager's right-hand man. Nils Krogstad will be running that bank, not Torvald Helmer.

NORA: You'll never live to see that.

KROGSTAD: You think you might—

NORA: Now I have the courage.

KROGSTAD: Forget it—a pampered, spoiled woman like you?

NORA: You'll see—you'll see.

KROGSTAD: Under the ice, maybe? Down in the freezing black water? Floating up in the spring, ugly, unrecognizable, your hair falling out—

NORA: You don't frighten me.

KROGSTAD: You don't frighten me either. People don't do such things, Mrs. Helmer. Besides, what would be the point? I'd have him in my pocket just the same.

NORA: After—? Even when I'm no longer—?

KROGSTAD: Are you forgetting? In that case I'll be in charge of your reputation. (*Nora stares speechless at him.*) Well, I've warned you. Don't do anything stupid. When Helmer gets my letter, I'll wait for a word from him. Just keep in mind that it's your husband who has forced me back onto these old roads of mine. I'll never forgive him for that. Goodbye, Mrs. Helmer. (*He goes out through the hallway.*)

NORA: (*Goes to the hall door, opens it a fraction, and listens.*) Gone. He didn't leave the letter. No, no, no, that would be impossible! (*Opening the door farther.*) What? He's waiting outside. Not going downstairs. Changing his mind? Maybe he'll—?

(*A letter drops into the mailbox; then Krogstad's footsteps are heard receding as he walks downstairs. Nora, with a stifled cry, runs across the room to the sofa table; short pause.*)

NORA: In the mailbox. (*Creeps cautiously to the hall door.*) Lying there. Torvald, Torvald—no saving us now!

(*Mrs. Linde enters with the costume from the room at the left.*)

MRS. LINDE: Well, I think that's it for the repairs. Should we try it—

NORA: (*In a low, hoarse voice.*) Kristine, come here.

MRS. LINDE: (*Throws the dress onto the sofa.*) What's the matter—you're upset!

NORA: Come here. See that letter? There—see it, through the window in the mailbox?

MRS. LINDE: Yes, I see it.

NORA: It's from Krogstad.

MRS. LINDE: Nora—Krogstad's the one who lent you the money!

NORA: Yes. And now Torvald will know everything.

MRS. LINDE: Believe me, Nora, that's best for both of you.

NORA: There's more to it. I forged a signature.

MRS. LINDE: Oh for heaven's sake—

NORA: I'm just telling you this, Kristine, so that you can be my witness.

MRS. LINDE: What do you mean, witness? How can I—?

NORA: If I were to lose my mind—that could easily happen—

MRS. LINDE: Nora!

NORA: Or if anything else happened to me, if I couldn't be here—

MRS. LINDE: Nora, you're beside yourself!

NORA: And if someone wanted to try to take the whole thing onto himself, all the blame, you see—

MRS. LINDE: Yes, but how can you think—

NORA: You've got to swear it isn't true, Kristine. I'm in my perfect mind; I understand exactly what I'm saying; and I'm telling you: no one else knew about it. I did it all alone. Remember that.

MRS. LINDE: I will. But I don't understand any of it.

NORA: How could you understand? A wonderful thing is about to happen.

MRS. LINDE: Wonderful?

NORA: Yes, a wonderful thing. But also terrible, Kristine, and it just can't happen, not for all the world.

MRS. LINDE: I'm going to talk to Krogstad right away.

NORA: Don't: he'll only hurt you some way.

MRS. LINDE: Once upon a time he'd have gladly done anything for me.

NORA: Him?

MRS. LINDE: Where does he live?

NORA: How should I know? Wait— (*Searches her pocket.*) Here's his card. But what about the letter, the letter—?

HELMER: (*In his study, knocking on the door.*) Nora!

NORA: (*Screams in panic.*) What is it? What do you want?

HELMER: Now, don't be frightened. We're not coming in. The door's locked; are you trying on your costume?

NORA: Yes, I'm trying it on. I'm going to be so beautiful, Torvald.

MRS. LINDE: (*Having read the card.*) He lives right around the corner.

NORA: Yes, but that's no help. We're lost. The letter's in the box.

MRS. LINDE: Your husband has the key?

NORA: Always.

MRS. LINDE: Krogstad will have to ask for his letter back unopened— he'll have to find some excuse—

NORA: But this is the time when Torvald usually—

MRS. LINDE: Stall him. Go in there and stay with him. I'll get back as fast as I can. (*She goes out hurriedly through the hall door. Nora goes to Helmer's door and opens it, looking in.*)

NORA: Torvald!

HELMER: Well—can I finally come back into my own living room? Come on, Rank, now we'll get to see—(*In the doorway.*) But—?

NORA: What, Torvald my dear?

HELMER: Rank had me all set for a great dress parade.

RANK: (*In the doorway.*) That's what I was expecting, but I guess I was wrong.

NORA: No one gets to bask in my full glory until tomorrow.

HELMER: But Nora, you look so tired. Have you been practicing too hard?

NORA: No, I haven't practiced at all yet.

HELMER: You know it's essential—

NORA: Absolutely essential. But I can't possibly do it without your help; I've forgotten everything.

HELMER: We'll get it back quick enough.

NORA: Yes, take care of me right to the end, Torvald. Do you promise? Ah, I'm so nervous. That big party—you have to give up everything for me tonight. Not one bit of business, don't even go near your work. All right, Torvald. Promise?

HELMER: I promise. Tonight I'll be completely at your service—you helpless little thing. Hmm—just one item to take care of first— (*Goes toward the hall door.*)

NORA: What do you want out there?

HELMER: Just seeing if there's any mail.

NORA: No, no, Torvald, don't do that!

HELMER: What now?

NORA: Torvald, please, there's nothing there.

HELMER: Just let me have a look. (*About to go; Nora, at the piano, plays the opening notes of the tarantella. Helmer stops at the door.*)

NORA: I can't dance tomorrow if I don't rehearse with you.

HELMER: (*Going to her.*) Nora, are you really so frightened of it?

NORA: Tremendously frightened. Let's rehearse right now; there's still time before dinner. Oh, Torvald, sit down and play for me. Show me how it goes; direct me, like you always do.

HELMER: I'd be glad to, if you want.

(*Nora snatches the tambourine out of the box, and also a long, multi-colored shawl which she drapes around herself; then she springs forward and calls out.*)

NORA: Play for me! Now I'll dance!

(*Helmer plays and Nora dances; Doctor Rank stands behind Helmer and watches.*)

HELMER: (*Playing.*) Slower, slower—

NORA: I can't help it.

HELMER: Not so violent, Nora!

NORA: That's how it has to be.

HELMER: (*Stopping.*) No, no—that's not it at all.

NORA: (*Laughing, swinging the tambourine.*) What did I tell you?

RANK: Let me play for her.

HELMER: (*Getting up.*) Yes, good idea. That way I can be a better teacher.

(*Rank sits at the piano and plays. Nora dances with increasing wildness. Helmer has placed himself by the stove, continually directing dancing instructions to her; she seems not to hear him; her hair loosens and falls over her shoulders; she doesn't notice, but keeps on dancing. Mrs. Linde enters.*)

MRS. LINDE: (*As though spellbound in the doorway.*) Ah—!

NORA: (*Still dancing.*) See, Kristine, what fun!

HELMER: But Nora, you're dancing as if your life were at stake.

NORA: It is, it is!

HELMER: Rank, stop. This is absolute madness. Stop it!

(*Rank stops playing and Nora suddenly comes to a halt.*)

HELMER: (*Goes to her.*) I would never have believed this—you've forgotten everything I taught you.

NORA: (*Throwing down the tambourine.*) As you can see.

HELMER: Some extra work's in order here.

NORA: Yes, you see how important it is. You've got to keep teaching me right up to the last minute. Promise, Torvald?

HELMER: Depend on it.

NORA: You can't even think—today or tomorrow—about anything but me—don't open any letters, don't even touch the mailbox—

HELMER: Ah—you're still afraid of that man.

NORA: Yes, yes, that too.

HELMER: Nora, I can see it in your face, there's a letter from him out there.

NORA: I don't know. I think there is. But you can't read things like that now; there can't be anything horrible between us till all this is over.

RANK: (*Softly to Helmer.*) You shouldn't go against her.

HELMER: The child will have its way. But tomorrow night—after you've danced—

NORA: Then you're free.

MAID: (*In the doorway, right.*) Ma'am, dinner's on the table.

NORA: We'll have champagne, Helene.

MAID: Very good, ma'am. (*Goes out.*)

HELMER: Hey, hey—a whole banquet?

NORA: Yes—a champagne supper right through till dawn! (*Calling out.*) And some macaroons, Helene—lots of them—just this once.

HELMER: (*Taking her hands.*) There, there, there—not so wild, not so scared—be my little skylark again.

NORA: Oh, yes, I certainly will. But go to dinner—you too, Doctor Rank. Kristine, I need you to help me with my hair.

RANK: (*Softly as they go.*) There wouldn't be anything—anything on the way?

HELMER: No, my friend, not a thing; nothing more than these silly fears I've been telling you about. (*They go out, right.*)

NORA: Well?

MRS. LINDE: Gone to the country.

NORA: I saw it in your face.

MRS. LINDE: He gets back tomorrow night. I left him a note.

NORA: You shouldn't have done that. You can't stop it now. Behind it all there's this great joy—waiting for a wonderful thing to happen.

MRS. LINDE: What are you waiting for?

NORA: You can't understand that. Go in with them—I'll be there in a minute.

(*Mrs. Linde goes into the dining room. Nora stands for a moment as if to compose herself; then she looks at her watch.*)

NORA: Five. Seven hours to midnight. Then twenty-four hours to the next midnight. Then the tarantella will be done. Twenty four plus seven—thirty-one hours to live.

HELMER: (*In the doorway, right.*) What happened to the skylark?

NORA: (*Going to him with open arms.*) Here's your skylark!

END OF ACT TWO

ACT THREE

*Same room. The sofa-table, with chairs around it, has been moved
to the middle of the room. A lamp is burning on the table. The
door to the hall stands open. Dance music can be heard from the
apartment above.*

(*Mrs. Linde is sitting by the table, desultorily turning the pages of
the book; she attempts to read but seems unable to fix her
attention. Once or twice she listens, tensely, for a sound at the
door.*)

MRS. LINDE: Not here yet. And it's now or never. If he'd only— (*Listens
again.*) Ah—there he is. (*She goes out into the hall and cautiously
opens the outer door; quiet footsteps are heard on the stairs. She
whispers.*) Come in. Nobody's here.

KROGSTAD: (*In the doorway.*) I found a note from you at home. What
does it mean?

MRS. LINDE: I had to talk to you.

KROGSTAD: Oh yes? And it had to be here, in this house?

MRS. LINDE: My place is impossible—there's no private entrance to my
room. Come in; we're all alone. The maid's asleep and the
Helmers are at a party upstairs.

KROGSTAD: (*Comes into the room.*) Well, well, well—so the Helmers
are dancing tonight. How about that?

MRS. LINDE: Why shouldn't they?

KROGSTAD: True enough—why shouldn't they.

MRS. LINDE: Well, Krogstad, let's talk.

KROGSTAD: Do the two of us have anything more to talk about?

MRS. LINDE: We have a lot to talk about.

KROGSTAD: I wouldn't have thought so.

MRS. LINDE: No, because you've never really understood me.

KROGSTAD: What was there to understand, more than the usual thing?
A heartless woman sends a man packing as soon as she gets a
better offer.

MRS. LINDE: Do you think I'm that heartless? Do you think it was easy
for me to break up with you?

KROGSTAD: Wasn't it?

MRS. LINDE: Krogstad, did you really think that?

KROGSTAD: Then how could you have written to me that way?

MRS. LINDE: I couldn't do anything else. If I had to make the break, it
was my duty to try to stamp out whatever feelings you had for me.

KROGSTAD: (*Clenching his hands.*) So that was it! And this—all this for money's sake!

MRS. LINDE: Don't forget that I had a helpless mother and two little brothers. We couldn't wait for you, Krogstad; your prospects were so cloudy then.

KROGSTAD: Maybe. But you had no right to abandon me for somebody else's sake.

MRS. LINDE: Yes—I don't know. I've asked myself over and over if I had any right to do that.

KROGSTAD: (*More quietly.*) When I lost you I felt the ground dissolve under my feet. Look at me: I'm a man adrift on a wreck.

MRS. LINDE: Help could be close by.

KROGSTAD: It was—until you appeared and blocked the way.

MRS. LINDE: I didn't know, Krogstad. I only learned today that I'm replacing you at the bank.

KROGSTAD: Since you say so, I believe it. But now you know—so won't you pull out?

MRS. LINDE: No, because that wouldn't do you the least bit of good.

KROGSTAD: Oh, who cares? I'd do it anyway.

MRS. LINDE: I've learned to act rationally. Life, and bitter necessity, have taught me that.

KROGSTAD: And life has taught me not to believe in empty phrases.

MRS. LINDE: Then life has taught you a very rational lesson. But you do believe in deeds, don't you?

KROGSTAD: What do you mean?

MRS. LINDE: You said that you were like a man adrift, standing on a wreck.

KROGSTAD: I said that with good reason.

MRS. LINDE: Well I'm a woman adrift, I'm hanging on to a wreck as well.

KROGSTAD: That was your choice.

MRS. LINDE: There was no other choice at the time.

KROGSTAD: So?

MRS. LINDE: Krogstad, what if these two shipwrecks could reach across to one another?

KROGSTAD: What are you saying?

MRS. LINDE: Two on one raft stand a better chance than each one alone.

KROGSTAD: Kristine!

MRS. LINDE: Why do you suppose I came to town?

KROGSTAD: Were you really thinking about me?

MRS. LINDE: For me to go on living, I need to work. All my life, as long as I can remember, I've worked—it's given me my only real joy. But now I'm completely alone in the world, completely empty and desolate. Working for yourself—well, there's no joy in that. Krogstad: give me someone and something to work for.

KROGSTAD: I don't believe all this. This is just some hysterical feminine urge for self-sacrifice.

MRS. LINDE: Have you ever known me to be hysterical?

KROGSTAD: Can you really mean all this? Do you know about my past—the whole story?

MRS. LINDE: Yes.

KROGSTAD: And you know what people think of me here?

MRS. LINDE: You hinted just now that you thought you could have been a different person with me.

KROGSTAD: I know that for sure.

MRS. LINDE: Couldn't it still happen?

KROGSTAD: Kristine—you're serious about this? Yes, you are. I can see it in you. Do you have the courage as well?

MRS. LINDE: I need someone to be a mother to, and your children need a mother. The two of us need each other. Krogstad, I have faith in you, in what's there deep down in your heart. I could risk anything together with you.

KROGSTAD: (*Seizing her hands.*) Thank you, Kristine, thank you—now I know I can bring myself up in people's eyes—ah, I forgot—

MRS. LINDE: (*Listening.*) The tarantella! Go, go, go!

KROGSTAD: What's going on?

MRS. LINDE: Do you hear the music up there? When it's over, they'll be down.

KROGSTAD: All right, I'll go. It's all pointless. Of course you don't know what I've done with the Helmers.

MRS. LINDE: Yes, Krogstad, I know all about it.

KROGSTAD: And you still have the courage to—

MRS. LINDE: I know very well how far despair can drive a man like you.

KROGSTAD: If I could only undo what I've done!

MRS. LINDE: That's easy. Your letter's still in the mailbox.

KROGSTAD: Are you sure?

MRS. LINDE: Absolutely. But—

KROGSTAD: (*Looks searchingly at her.*) Is that what this is all about? Would you save your friend at any price? Tell me honestly, tell me straight—is that it?

MRS. LINDE: Krogstad: when you've sold yourself *once* for someone else's sake, you don't do it a second time.

KROGSTAD: I'll demand my letter back.

MRS. LINDE: No, no.

KROGSTAD: Yes, of course I will. I'll stay here until Helmer comes down; I'll tell him to give me back my letter—that it's only about my dismissal—that he shouldn't read it.

MRS. LINDE: No, Krogstad. Don't take back your letter.

KROGSTAD: But wasn't that exactly why you got me over here?

MRS. LINDE: Yes, in the first panic. But in the twenty-four hours between then and now, I've seen some incredible things in this house. Helmer has to learn everything; this awful secret has to come to light; those two have to come to a clear understanding—they can't go on with all this hiding, all these lies.

KROGSTAD: Well, if you're willing to take the risk—. But there's one thing I can do right away.

MRS. LINDE: (*Listening.*) Hurry! Go, go! The dance is over. We're not safe another second!

KROGSTAD: I'll wait for you downstairs.

MRS. LINDE: Yes, do that. You'll have to see me home.

KROGSTAD: This incredible happiness—I've never felt anything like it! (*He goes out by the front door; the door between the living room and the hall stays open.*)

MRS. LINDE: (*Tidies the room a little and gets her outer garments ready.*) What a change! What a change! People to work for, to live for—a home to make. That's something worth doing. If only they'd come soon. (*Listens.*) Ah—there they are. Get dressed.

(*Helmer's and Nora's voices are heard outside; a key is turned and Helmer leads Nora almost forcibly into the hall. She is wearing the Italian costume with a large black shawl over it; he's in evening dress with an open black domino over it.*)

NORA:: (*Still in the doorway, resisting.*) No, no, no, not in there! I'm going up again. I don't want to leave so early!

HELMER: But Nora, my dearest—

NORA: Oh, I beg you, I implore you, from the bottom of my heart Torvald—just one more hour!

HELMER: Not another minute, Nora my sweet. You know we had an agreement. Come on now, into the drawing room; you're catching cold out here. (*He leads her gently into the drawing room against her resistance.*)

MRS. LINDE: Good evening.

NORA: Kristine!

HELMER: Well, Mrs. Linde—here so late?

MRS. LINDE: Yes, forgive me. I really wanted to see Nora in her costume.

NORA: So you've been sitting here waiting for me?

MRS. LINDE: Yes, I didn't get here in time—you'd all gone upstairs. And I just thought I couldn't leave without seeing you.

HELMER: (*Taking off Nora's shawl.*) Well, get a good look at her. I think she's worth looking at. Isn't she lovely, Mrs. Linde?

MRS. LINDE: Yes, I have to say—

HELMER: Isn't she incredibly lovely? That was the general consensus at the party, too—but also incredibly stubborn, the sweet thing. What to do about that? Would you believe it, I almost had to use force to get her down here.

NORA: Ah, Torvald, you're going to regret that you didn't let me have my way just a half-hour more.

HELMER: Hear that, Mrs. Linde? She danced her tarantella to thunderous applause—well deserved applause, too—even though there was something a little too naturalistic about the whole thing—I mean, something that went beyond the strict requirements of art. But so what? The main thing is, she was a success—a tremendous success. Should I let her stay around after that? Spoil the effect? No, thank you! I took my lovely Capri girl—my capricious little Capri girl, I could say—on my arm; made a quick trip around the ballroom—a curtsy to all sides—and as they say in novels, the lovely apparition vanished. Exits are tremendously important, Mrs. Linde—they should always be effective; but that's what I can't get Nora to see. Uch, it's hot in here. (*Throws his domino on a chair and opens the door to his room.*) What? it's dark—oh, yes, of course—excuse me— (*Goes in and lights candles.*)

NORA: (*Whispering quickly and breathlessly.*) Well?

MRS. LINDE: (*Quietly.*) I talked to him.

NORA: And—?

MRS. LINDE: Nora, you have to tell your husband everything.

NORA: (*Dully.*) I knew it.

MRS. LINDE: You've got nothing to worry about from Krogstad—but you have to speak out.

NORA: I won't do it.

MRS. LINDE: Then the letter will.

NORA: Thank you, Kristine. Now I know what I have to do. Sssh!—

HELMER: (*Coming in again.*) Now, Mrs. Linde—have you had a chance to admire her?

MRS. LINDE: Yes, and now I'll say good night.

HELMER: So soon? Is this yours, this knitting?

MRS. LINDE: (*Taking it.*) Oh yes.

HELMER: So you also knit.

MRS. HELMER: Yes.

HELMER: Know what? You should embroider instead.

MRS. HELMER: Really? Why?

HELMER: Much prettier. Want to see? You hold the embroidery like this with your left hand, and guide the needle with your right—like this—lightly, in and out, in a sweeping curve—right?

MRS. LINDE: I suppose so—

HELMER: Now knitting, on the other hand—so ugly to watch—see here, the arms jammed together, the needles going up and down—there's something Chinese about it. Ah—that was a tremendous champagne up there.

MRS. LINDE: Well, Nora, good night! And no more stubbornness!

HELMER: Well said, Mrs. Linde!

MRS. LINDE: Good night, Mr. Helmer.

HELMER: (*Following her to the door.*) Good night, good night. I hope you're all right getting home. I would, of course—but you don't have far to go. Good night, good night. (*She leaves; he closes the door after her and comes in again.*) Well, well. We finally got her out the door. What an incredible bore that woman is.

NORA: Aren't you tired, Torvald?

HELMER: No, not a bit.

NORA: Not sleepy at all?

HELMER: Absolutely not—in fact, I'm exhilarated! You, on the other hand, are looking very tired and sleepy.

NORA: Yes, I'm tired. I'll go to sleep soon.

HELMER: See, see! I was right! It was time to go home.

NORA: Oh, everything you do is right.

HELMER: (*Kisses her on the brow.*) Now my little lark is talking like a real person. Say—did you notice how lively Rank was tonight?

NORA: Was he? I didn't get to talk to him.

HELMER: I barely did myself, but I haven't seen him in such a good mood in a long time. (*Looks at Nora a while, then comes closer to her.*) Hmm—my God, it's glorious to be back in our own home again, completely alone with you—you enchanting young woman!

NORA: Don't look at me like that, Torvald!

HELMER: Shouldn't I look at my most precious possession? All this magnificence, and it's mine, mine alone, completely and utterly mine!

NORA: You shouldn't talk this way to me tonight.

HELMER: (*Following her.*) The tarantella's still in your blood. I understand. And that makes me want you even more. Listen! Now the guests are beginning to leave. (*More softly.*) Nora—soon the whole house will be silent.

NORA: I hope so.

HELMER: Yes, my own darling Nora, that's right. Ah—do you know why, whenever I'm out at a party with you—do you know why I barely speak to you, why I keep my distance, hardly even shoot you a stolen glance? Do you know why I do that? Because I'm imagining you're my secret lover, my young, secret sweetheart, and that no one in the room guesses there's anything going on between us.

NORA: Oh yes, yes, yes—I know you're always thinking of me.

HELMER: And when it's time to go, and I place the shawl over your smooth young shoulders, around this wonderful curve of your neck—then I pretend you're my young bride, that we've come straight from the wedding, that I'm bringing you home for the first time, alone with you for the first time, completely alone with you, you young, trembling, delicious—ah, I've done nothing but long for you all night! When I saw you doing the tarantella—like a huntress, luring us all to your trap—my blood started to boil. I couldn't stand it any longer. That's why I got you down here so early—

NORA: Get away, Torvald! Please get away from me. I don't want all this.

HELMER: What are you saying? Still playing the lark with me, Nora? You want, you don't want? Aren't I your husband?

(*There's a noise outside.*)

NORA: (*Startled.*) Did you hear that?

HELMER: (*Going to the door.*) Who's there?

RANK: (*Outside.*) Just me. May I come in for a moment?

HELMER: (*Softly, irritated.*) What can he possibly want now? (*Aloud.*)

Just a second. (*Goes to the door and opens it.*) I'm so glad you didn't pass us by on your way out.

RANK: I thought I heard voices, and I really wanted to stop in. (*Looking around.*) Oh, yes—the old haunts. What a warm little nest you've got here.

HELMER: Speaking of which, you were having a pretty warm time upstairs—almost hot, I'd say.

RANK: Absolutely. And why not? You have to get the most out of life—everything you can, anyway, for as long as you can. That was excellent wine.

HELMER: And the champagne!

RANK: You thought so too? My thirst for it was amazing—even to me.

NORA: Torvald also had his share of champagne tonight.

RANK: Oh yes?

NORA: Yes, and that makes him so entertaining.

RANK: And why shouldn't you enjoy an evening like this after a productive day?

HELMER: Productive? I can't exactly say that for myself.

RANK: (*Slaps him on the back.*) Ah, but you see, I can!

NORA: Doctor Rank, it sounds like you've done some medical research today.

RANK: That's right.

HELMER: Oh come on—here's little Nora talking about medical research!

NORA: And may I congratulate you on the results?

RANK: Yes indeed.

NORA: Were they good?

RANK: The best kind—for doctor and patient alike—certainty.

NORA: (*Quickly, inquisitively.*) Certainty.

RANK: Absolute certainty. So haven't I earned a festive night out?

NORA: Yes, Doctor Rank, you have.

HELMER: I'm all for that—as long as the morning after's not too bad.

RANK: Well, you never get something for nothing in this world.

NORA: Doctor Rank, do you like masquerade balls?

RANK: Oh yes—especially when the disguises are good and strange—

NORA: So tell me. At the next one, how should the two of us appear?

HELMER: You little noodlehead! You're already on to the next one?

RANK: The two of us? I can tell you that: you'll go as Charmed Life—

HELMER: All right, but what's the costume for that?

RANK: Your wife can go just as she always is.

HELMER: Well said. Now have you decided on something for yourself?

RANK: Yes, Helmer, my mind's made up.

HELMER: Well?

RANK: At the next masquerade, I will be—invisible.

HELMER: That's pretty funny.

RANK: I hear there's a hat—a huge, black hat—called the Hat of Invisibility. You put it on, and no one on earth can see you.

HELMER: (*Stifling a grin.*) Oh, yes, of course.

RANK: But I've forgotten what I really came for. Helmer, how about a cigar—a dark Havana.

HELMER: With pleasure. (*Holds out the case to him.*)

RANK: Thanks. (*Takes one and cuts the tip.*)

NORA: Let me give you a light.

RANK: Thank you. (*She holds the match as he lights the cigar.*) Now, good-bye.

HELMER: Old friend—good-bye, good-bye.

NORA: Sleep well, Doctor.

RANK: Thank you for that wish.

NORA: Now wish me the same.

RANK: Wish you?—All right, if you want—sleep well. And thanks for the light. (*He exits, nodding to both of them.*)

HELMER: (*Quietly.*) He's drunk.

NORA: (*Vaguely.*) Maybe.

(*Helmer takes his keys from his pocket and goes out into the hall.*)

NORA: What are you doing, Torvald?

HELMER: I've got to empty the mailbox—it's so full, there's no room for the morning papers.

NORA: Are you working tonight?

HELMER: You know I'm not. What's this? Someone's been fiddling with the lock.

NORA: The lock?

HELMER: Yes, definitely. Who could it be? I can't believe the maids—? Wait, here's a broken hairpin—Nora, this is yours—

NORA: (*Quickly.*) Then it must be the children.

HELMER: Well you've really got to break them of that. Hmm—there we go, finally got it open. (*Takes out the contents and shouts into the kitchen.*) Helene? Helene—put out the hall lamp. (*He comes back into the room and shuts the door. He holds the letters in his hand.*) Look—see how it piled up? (*Sorts through them.*) What's this?

NORA: (*By the window.*) The letter! No, no, Torvald!

HELMER: Two cards, from Rank.

NORA: From Doctor Rank?

HELMER: (*Looking at them.*) Doctor Rank, Physician and Surgeon. They were on top. He must have dropped them in as he left.

NORA: Is there anything on them?

HELMER: There's a black cross over the name. Look. That's gruesome. It's like he's announcing his own death.

NORA: That's exactly what he's doing.

HELMER: What? Did he tell you anything?

NORA: Yes. He said that when these cards arrived, it meant he's saying goodbye to us. Now he'll shut himself in and die.

HELMER: My poor friend. Of course I knew I wouldn't have him for long. But so soon—and now he's hiding himself away like a wounded animal.

NORA: If it has to happen, it's best to let it happen quietly. Isn't that right, Torvald?

HELMER: (*Pacing up and down.*) He'd grown to be a part of us. I don't think I can imagine myself without him. His loneliness—his suffering was like a cloudy background to our sunlit happiness. Well, maybe it's best this way—at least for him. (*Stands still.*) And maybe for us too, Nora. Now we only have each other. (*Puts his arms around her.*) Ah, you—my darling wife. I don't think I'll ever be able to hold you close enough. You know, Nora—so many times I've wished that you were in some terrible danger, so I could risk my life, my blood, everything, everything for you.

NORA: (*Tears herself free and says firmly and resolutely.*) Read your mail now, Torvald.

HELMER: No, not tonight. Tonight I want to be with you—

NORA: With your friend's death on your mind?

HELMER: You're right. We're both a little shaken by this. This ugliness has come between us—thoughts of death and decay. We have to try to get rid of them; until then, we go our separate ways.

NORA: (*Her arms around his neck.*) Torvald—good night! Good night!

HELMER: (*Kissing her forehead.*) Good night, little songbird. Sleep well, Nora. Now I'll read the mail. (*He goes in with the letters, shuts the door behind him.*)

(*Nora, with wild eyes, fumbles around, seizes Helmer's domino, wraps it around herself, and whispers quickly, hoarsely, spasmodically.*)

NORA: Never see him again—never, never, never. (*Throws the shawl over her head.*) Never see the children again either—not even the children—never, never—the icy black water—the bottomless—that—if only it weren't all over—now he has it, he's reading it now—no, no, not yet. Torvald, goodbye, children, goodbye— (*She starts to go into the hall; at the same moment Helmer flings open his door and stands there, an open letter in his hand.*)

HELMER: Nora!

NORA: (*Screams.*) Ahh—!

HELMER: What is this? Do you know what's in this letter?

NORA: Yes. Yes I know. Let me go. Let me out!

HELMER: (*Holding her back.*) Where are you going?

NORA: (*Trying to break loose.*) Don't try to save me, Torvald!

HELMER: (*Staggers back.*) It's true?! What he said is the truth? Horrible! No—it's impossible—this can't be true.

NORA: It is true. I have loved you more than anything in the world.

HELMER: Don't start with your silly excuses.

NORA: (*Taking a step toward him.*) Torvald!

HELMER: You miserable—what have you done?

NORA: Let me go. You won't have to take the blame for me. You're not going to take it on yourself.

HELMER: No more playacting! (*Locking the hall door.*) You'll stay right here and explain yourself. Do you understand what you've done? Answer me! Do you understand?

NORA: (*Looking fixedly at him, her face hardening.*) Yes. Now I'm beginning to understand everything.

HELMER: (*Pacing up and down.*) Ah!—what a rude awakening for me! For eight years—my pride and joy, a hypocrite, a liar, —even worse, a criminal! There's so much ugliness at the bottom of all this—indescribable ugliness! Uccch! (*Nora remains silent, looking fixedly at him.*) I should have seen it coming. Every one of your father's disgusting values—quiet!—every disgusting value is coming out in you. No religion, no morals, no sense of duty—this is my punishment for being so easy on him up there. I did it for your sake; and you repay me like this!

NORA: Yes, like this.

HELMER: You've destroyed my happiness. My whole future—thrown away! It's horrible when you think about it. I'm totally at the mercy of some amoral animal who can do whatever he wants with me—demand anything he wants, order me around, command me however he pleases, and I can't so much as squeak in protest. And this is how I'll go down, right to the bottom, all for the sake of some frivolous woman.

NORA: When I'm gone from this world, then you'll be free.

HELMER: Stop playacting! You sound like your father—he always had one of those phrases on the tip of his tongue. How would it help me if you were gone from this world, as you put it? Not in the least. He can still reveal everything, and if he does I'd be suspected of being an accomplice to your crimes! People might think I was behind it all, that it was my idea! And I have you to thank for all this—after I've carried you along, taken you and led you by the hand ever since we were married. Do you understand what you have done to me.

NORA: (*Coldly and calmly.*) Yes.

HELMER: I can't grasp this—it's just unbelievable to me. But we have to try to set things right. Take off that shawl. I said take it off! I've got to find some way to appease him—this thing has to be covered up, whatever it costs. As for you and me, things will seem just like before. For public consumption only, of course. You'll stay in the house, that's understood. But I can't trust you to bring up the children. Oh God—to have to say that to the one I—even now—well, that's over. After today there's no happiness, only holding the wreckage together, the scraps and shards— (*The doorbell rings. Helmer starts.*) What's that? It's so late! Is this it? Is he going to—? Nora, hide yourself! Say you're sick. (*Nora stands motionless. Helmer goes and opens the hall door.*)

MAID: (*Half dressed in the hall doorway.*) A letter for Mrs. Helmer.

HELMER: Give it here. (*Takes the letter and closes the door.*) Yes, it's from him. You're not getting it. I'll read it myself.

NORA: Read it.

HELMER: (*By the lamp.*) I hardly dare. It could be the end for both of us. I've got to know. (*Tears open the letter; scans a few lines; looks at an enclosed paper and gives a cry of joy.*) Nora! (*Nora looks enquiringly at him.*) Nora! No, let me read it again—yes, yes, it's true. I'm saved! Nora, I'm saved!

NORA: And I?

HELMER: You too, of course. We're both saved, both of us. See? He sent you back your note—he writes that he's sorry and ashamed—that a happy change in his life—oh, what does it matter what he writes? We're saved, Nora! Now no one can hurt you. Oh, Nora, Nora—no: first, let's get all this ugliness out of here. Let me see. (*Glances at the note for a moment.*) No, I won't look at it. It'll be nothing more than a dream I had. (*He tears both letters in pieces and throws them both into the stove, watching them burn.*) So, nothing left. He wrote that ever since Christmas eve—God, these must have been three terrible days for you, Nora.

NORA: I have fought a hard battle these last three days.

HELMER: And suffered, not seeing any way out but—no, we won't think about this ugly thing any more. We'll just rejoice and keep telling ourselves "it's over—it's all over." Do you hear me, Nora? It seems like you haven't quite got it yet—it's over! What's this about, this cold stare? Ah, poor little Nora, I understand—you can't bring yourself to believe I've forgiven you. But I have, Nora, I swear. I've forgiven everything. I know perfectly well that you did all this out of love for me.

NORA: That's true.

HELMER: You've loved me like a wife should love her husband. You just couldn't judge how to do it. But do you think that makes me love you any the less, because you couldn't manage by yourself? No, no—just lean on me. I'll counsel you, I'll direct you. I wouldn't be much of a man if this female helplessness didn't make you doubly attractive to me. Forget what I said in those first few terrible moments, when I thought I was going to lose everything. I've forgiven you, Nora—I swear, I've forgiven you.

NORA: Thank you for your forgiveness. (*She goes out through the door on the right.*)

HELMER: No, stay— (*Looking in.*) What are you doing?

NORA: Taking off my costume.

HELMER: (*By the open door.*) Yes, do that. Try to calm down, collect your thoughts, my little, shivering songbird. If you need protection, I have broad wings to shelter you with. (*Walks around near the door.*) Oh, Nora—our home is so snug, so cozy. This is your nest, where I can keep you like a dove that I've snatched, unharmed, from the falcon's claws; I'll bring peace and rest to your beating heart. Little by little it will happen, Nora, believe me. Tomorrow, this will all seem different to you; and soon everything will be back to normal. I won't need to keep saying I forgive you—you'll feel it, you'll know it's true. How could you ever think I could bring myself to disown you, or even punish you? You don't know how a man's heart works, Nora. There's something indescribably sweet and satisfying for a man in knowing he's forgiven his wife—forgiven her from the bottom of his heart. It's as if he possesses her doubly now—as if she were born into the world all over again—and she becomes, in a way, his wife and his child at the same time. And that's what you'll be for me from now on, you little, helpless, confused creature. Don't be frightened of anything—just open your heart to me and I'll be both your conscience and your will. What's this—? You've changed your dress?

NORA: Yes, Torvald, I've changed my dress.

HELMER: But why now, so late?

NORA: I'm not sleeping tonight.

HELMER: But Nora, dear—

NORA: (*Looking at her watch.*) It's not all that late. Sit down, Torvald. We have a great deal to talk about together. (*She sits at one end of the table.*)

HELMER: Nora—what's going on? That hard expression—

NORA: Sit down. This will take time. I have a lot to say to you.

HELMER: (*Sits at table directly opposite her.*) You're worrying me, Nora. I don't understand you.

NORA: No, that's just it. You don't understand me. And I have never understood you—not until tonight. No—no interruptions. You have to hear me out. We're settling accounts, Torvald.

HELMER: What do you mean by that?

NORA: (*After a short silence.*) Doesn't *one* thing strike you about the way we're sitting here?

HELMER: What might that be?

NORA: We've been married for eight years. Doesn't it strike you that this is the first time that the two of us—you and I, man and wife— have ever talked seriously?

HELMER: Well—"seriously"—what does that mean?

NORA: In eight whole years—no, longer—right from the moment we met, we haven't exchanged one serious word on one serious subject.

HELMER: Should I constantly be involving you in problems you couldn't possibly help me solve?

NORA: I'm not talking about problems. I'm saying that we've never sat down together and seriously tried to get to the bottom of anything.

HELMER: But Nora, dearest—would you have wanted that?

NORA: Yes, of course, that's just it. You've never understood me. A great wrong has been done me, Torvald. First by Papa, then by you.

HELMER: What! By us—who've loved you more than anyone in the world.

NORA: (*Shaking her head.*) You've never loved me. You just thought it was a lot of fun to be in love with me.

HELMER: Nora, how can you say that?

NORA: It's a fact, Torvald. When I was at home with Papa, he told me all his opinions; so of course I had the same opinions. And if I had any others, I kept them hidden, because he wouldn't have liked that. He called me his doll-child, and he played with me like I played with my dolls. Then I came to your house—

HELMER: What kind of way is that to describe our marriage?

NORA: (*Undisturbed.*) I mean, I went from Papa's hands into yours. You set up everything according to your taste; so of course I had the same taste, or I pretended to, I'm not really sure. I think it was half-and-half, one as much as the other. Now that I look back on it, I can see that I've lived like a beggar in this house, from hand to mouth; I've lived by doing tricks for you, Torvald. But that's how you wanted it. You and Papa have committed a great sin against me. It's your fault that I've become what I am.

HELMER: Nora—this is unreasonable, and it's ungrateful! Haven't you been happy here?

NORA: No, never. I thought so, but I never really was.

HELMER: Not—not happy!

NORA: No, just having fun. You've always been very nice to me. But our home has never been anything but a playpen. I've been your doll-wife here, just like I was Papa's doll-child at home. And my children, in turn, have been my dolls. It was fun when you came and played with me, just like they had fun when I played with them. That's what our marriage has been, Torvald.

HELMER: There's some truth in this—as exaggerated and hysterical as it is. But from now on, things will be different. Playtime is over: now the teaching begins.

NORA: Who gets this teaching? Me or the children?

HELMER: Both you and the children, my dearest Nora.

NORA: Ah, Torvald: you're not the man to teach me how to be a good wife to you.

HELMER: You can say that!

NORA: And me—how can I possibly teach the children?

HELMER: Nora!

NORA: Didn't you say that yourself, not too long ago? You didn't dare trust them to me?

HELMER: In the heat of the moment! How can you take that seriously?

NORA: Yes, but you spoke the truth. I'm not equal to the task. There's another task I have to get through first. I have to try to teach myself. And you can't help me there. I've got to do it alone. And so I'm leaving you.

HELMER: (*Springing up.*) What did you say?

NORA: If I'm going to find out anything about myself—about everything out there—I have to stand completely on my own. That's why I can't stay with you any longer.

HELMER: Nora, Nora!

NORA: I'll leave right away. Kristine can put me up for tonight—

HELMER: You're out of your mind! I won't allow it—I forbid you!

NORA: It's no use forbidding me anything any more. I'll take what's mine with me. I won't take anything from you, now or later.

HELMER: What kind of madness is this?

NORA: Tomorrow I'm going home—back to my old hometown, I mean. It'll be easier for me to find something to do up there.

HELMER: You blind, inexperienced creature!

NORA: I have to try to get some experience, Torvald.

HELMER: Abandon your home, your husband, your children! Do you have any idea what people will say?

NORA: I can't worry about that. I only know what I have to do.

HELMER: It's grotesque! You're turning your back on your most sacred duties!

NORA: What do you think those are—my most sacred duties?

HELMER: I have to tell you? Aren't they to your husband and children?

NORA: I have other duties, equally sacred.

HELMER: No you don't! Like what?

NORA: Duties to myself.

HELMER: You're a wife and mother, first and foremost.

NORA: I don't believe that any more. I believe that, first and foremost, I'm a human being—just as much as you—or at least I should try to become one. I'm aware that most people agree with you, Torvald, and that your opinion is backed up by plenty of books. But I can't be satisfied any more with what most people say, or what's written in the books. Now I've got to think these things through myself, and understand them.

HELMER: What don't you understand about your place in your own home? Don't you have an infallible teacher for questions like this? Don't you have your religion?

NORA: Oh, Torvald, I really don't know what religion is.

HELMER: What are you saying?

NORA: I only know what Pastor Hansen said when I was confirmed. He told me that religion was this and that and the other thing. When I get away from here, when I'm alone, I'll look into that subject too. I'll see if what Pastor Hansen said is true—or at least, if it's true for me.

HELMER: These things just aren't right for a young woman to be saying. If religion can't get through to you, let me try your conscience. You do have some moral feeling? Or—answer me—maybe not?

NORA: Well, Torvald, it's not easy to answer that. I really don't know. I'm actually quite confused about these things. I only know that my ideas are totally different from yours. I find out that the law is not what I thought it was—but I can't get it into my head that the law is right. A woman has no right to spare her dying father's feelings, or save her husband's life! I just can't believe these things.

HELMER: You're talking like a child. You don't understand the society you live in.

NORA: No, I don't. But now I'm going to find out for myself. I've got to figure out who's right—the world or me.

HELMER: You're ill, Nora—you have a fever. I almost think you're out of your mind.

NORA: I've never been so clear—and so certain—about so many things as I am tonight.

HELMER: You're clear and certain that you'll desert your husband and children?

NORA: Yes, I will.

HELMER: There's only one explanation left.

NORA: What is it?

HELMER: You no longer love me.

NORA: No. That's precisely it.

HELMER: Nora!—you can say that!

NORA: Oh, it hurts so much, Torvald. Because you've always been so kind to me. But I can't help it. I don't love you any more.

HELMER: (*Struggling to control himself.*) Are you also clear and certain about that?

NORA: Yes, absolutely clear and certain. That's why I can't live here any more.

HELMER: Can you tell me how I lost your love?

NORA: Yes, I can. It was this evening, when the wonderful thing didn't happen—then I saw that you weren't the man I thought you were.

HELMER: Say more—I'm not following this.

NORA: I've waited so patiently for ten years now—good Lord. I know that these wonderful things don't come along every day. Then this disaster broke over me, and I was absolutely certain: now the wonderful thing is coming. While Krogstad's letter was lying out there, I never imagined you'd give in to his terms, even for a minute. I was so certain you'd say to him: tell your story to the whole world! And when that was done—

HELMER: Yes, then what? When I'd given my wife up to shame and disgrace—!

NORA: When that was done, I was completely certain that you would step forward and take everything on yourself—you'd say "I am the guilty one."

HELMER: Nora!

NORA: You're thinking that I'd never accept such a sacrifice from you? No, of course I wouldn't. But what good would my protests be over yours? *That* was the wonderful thing I was hoping for, and in terror of. And to prevent it, I was willing to end my life.

HELMER: I'd work for you night and day, Nora—gladly—suffer and sacrifice for your sake. But no one gives up his honor for the one he loves.

NORA: That's exactly what millions of women have done.

HELMER: Oh—! You're thinking and talking like an ignorant child.

NORA: Maybe. But you don't think—or talk—like the man I could choose to be with. When your big fright was over—not the danger I was in, but what might happen to you—when that threat was past, then it was like nothing happened to you. I was just what I was before, your little songbird, your doll, and you'd have to take care of it twice as hard as before, since it was so frail and fragile. In that moment, Torvald, it dawned on me that I'd been living with a stranger—that I'd borne three children with him—. Aah—I can't stand the thought of it! I could tear myself to pieces.

HELMER: (*Heavily.*) I see. I see. A gulf has really opened up between us. But Nora, can't we fill it in somehow?

NORA: The way I am now, I'm no wife for you.

HELMER: I can transform myself—I have the strength for it.

NORA: Maybe—if your doll is taken away from you.

HELMER: To live without—without you! Nora, I can't bear the thought of it!

NORA: All the more reason it has to happen. (*Having gone in to the right, she returns with her outdoor clothes and a little travelling bag which she sets on a chair by the table.*)

HELMER: Nora, Nora, not now! Wait until tomorrow.

NORA: (*Puts on her coat.*) I can't spend the night in a strange man's house.

HELMER: Can't we live here like brother and sister?

NORA: (*Tying her hat.*) You know very well how long that would last. (*Throws her shawl around her.*) Goodbye, Torvald. I won't see the children. They're in better hands than mine, that much I know. The way I am now, I can't do anything for them.

HELMER: But some day, Nora—some day—?

NORA: How do I know? I have no idea what will become of me.

HELMER: But you're my wife, right now and always, no matter what becomes of you.

NORA: Listen, Torvald; when a wife deserts her husband's house, as I'm doing now, I've heard that the law frees him from any responsibility to her. And anyway, I'm freeing you. From everything. Complete freedom on both sides. See, here's your ring. Give me mine.

HELMER: Even that.

NORA: Even that.

HELMER: Here it is.

NORA: So. Well, now it's finished. I'm putting the keys here. As far as the household goes, the maids know all about it—better than I do. Tomorrow, after I'm gone, Kristine will come and pack the things I brought from home. I'll have them sent.

HELMER: All finished, all over! Nora—will you never think about me after this?

NORA: Of course I'll think about you often—and the children, and the house—.

HELMER: Could I write to you, Nora?

NORA: No, never. You can't do that.

HELMER: But I'll have to send you—

NORA: Nothing; nothing.

HELMER: —help you, if you need—

NORA: No. I'm telling you, I accept nothing from strangers.

HELMER: Nora—can't I ever be anything more than a stranger to you?

NORA: (*Taking her travelling bag.*) Oh, Torvald—not unless the most wonderful thing of all were to happen—

HELMER: Name it—what is this most wonderful thing?

NORA: It's—both you and I would have to transform ourselves to the point that—oh, Torvald, I don't know if I believe in it any more—

HELMER: But I will. Name it! Transform ourselves to the point that—

NORA: That our living together could become a marriage. Goodbye. (*She goes through the hall door.*)

HELMER: (*Sinking down into a chair by the door and burying his face in his hands.*) Empty. She's not here. (*A hope flares up in him.*) The most wonderful thing of all—?

(*From below, the sound of a door slamming shut.*)

END OF PLAY

GHOSTS

GHOSTS was originally produced March 27- May 17, 1992 at the Alliance Studio under the direction of Chris Coleman. The cast was as follows in order of appearance:

Regina Engstrand . . . . Susie Spear
Jakob Enstrand . . . . Al Hamacher
Pastor Manders . . . . Jeremiah Sullivan
Mrs. Helene Alving . . . . Mavourneen Dwyer
Osvald Alving. . . . . Dikran Tulaine

Ghosts

ACT ONE

*A spacious garden room, with a door in the left wall and two
doors in the wall on the right. In the middle of the room a round
table surrounded by chairs; on the table lie books, magazines and
newspapers. In the foreground to the left, a window, near it a little
sofa with a sewing table in front of it. In the background, the room
is continued in an open and somewhat smaller garden room or
conservatory, which ends in a wall of large glass panes. In the
right wall of the garden room is a door that leads down into the
garden. Through the glass wall can be glimpsed a gloomy fjord
landscape, veiled by steady rain.*

*(Engstrand is standing by the garden door. His left leg is somewhat
deformed; under the sole of his boot he has a wooden block.
Regina, with an empty flower-sprayer in her hands, prevents him
from coming any nearer.)*

REGINA: *(In a low voice.)* What do you want? Stay right where you are.
You're soaking wet.

ENGSTRAND: It's Our Lord's rain, my child.

REGINA: It's the devil's rain, that's what it is.

ENGSTRAND: For Christ's sake, Regina—the things you say! *(He limps a
couple of steps into the room.)* But here's what I wanted to tell
you.

REGINA: Don't stomp around with that foot of yours! The young
master is upstairs sleeping.

ENGSTRAND: Sleeping now? In broad daylight?

REGINA: None of your business.

ENGSTRAND: I went out on a binge last night . . .

REGINA: I can believe *that.*

ENGSTRAND: Yes, for we humans are weak, my child.

REGINA: We certainly are.

ENGSTRAND: And this world's full of temptations, you see—but by God,
I made it to work at five–thirty this morning just the same.

REGINA: Yes, yes, but now you have to get out of here. I won't stay
here rendezvousing with you.

ENGSTRAND: What aren't you doing?

REGINA: I don't want anyone to find you here. So—get going.

ENGSTRAND: I'm damned if I'll go before I get to talk to you. This afternoon I'll finish up at the schoolhouse, and then I'll scoot back to town on the night boat.

REGINA: *(Mutters.)* Nice trip.

ENGSTRAND: Thanks for that, my child. Tomorrow they'll be dedicating the orphan asylum, and you know they'll throw a huge party with—you know—lots of drinking: and no one will be able to say that Jakob Engstrand can't keep himself clear of temptation.

REGINA: Ha!

ENGSTRAND: Yes, because, there'll be a lot of important people here tomorrow. Pastor Manders is expected from town.

REGINA: He's coming today.

ENGSTRAND: There, you see? I'll be damned if I'll give him any reason to say a word against me. You understand?

REGINA: Aha! So *that's* it!

ENGSTRAND: What do you mean, that's it?

REGINA: What are you trying to trick the Pastor into this time?

ENGSTRAND: Shh, you're crazy. Would I trick the Pastor into anything? No, no: Pastor Manders is much too good to me. But that's what I wanted to talk to you about, see—I'm going home tonight.

REGINA: The sooner the better, as far as I'm concerned.

ENGSTRAND: Yes, but I want you with me, Regina.

REGINA: *(Her mouth open.)* You want me with you? What are you saying?

ENGSTRAND: I'm saying I want you back home with me.

REGINA: *(Scornfully.)* You'll never get me back there. Not in this life.

ENGSTRAND: We'll soon see about that.

REGINA: You bet we'll see. *Me*, who's been brought up by a lady like Mrs. Alving; a chamberlain's wife? Who's been treated almost like part of the family? I should run home to *you*? To a house like that? Uch!

ENGSTRAND: What the hell is this? Talking back to your own father, you little bitch?

REGINA: *(Muttering, without looking at him.)* You've said often enough that I'm no concern of yours.

ENGSTRAND: Puh! You're not going to worry about *that*—

REGINA: Haven't you often cursed me. Called me a—*fi donc*!

ENGSTRAND: No, God help me, I've never used such an ugly word.

REGINA: I remember perfectly well what word you used.

ENGSTRAND: Yes, well, only when I was a little—this world is full of temptations, Regina.

REGINA: Uch!

ENGSTRAND: When your mother nagged me like she did I had to find a way to get back at her. The way she played the fine lady! *(Imitating her.)* "Let me go, Engstrand! Leave me alone! I've served three years in the household of Chamberlain Alving of Rosenvold!" Jesus, God, she never could shut up about the fact that the captain was made a chamberlain while she was in service there.

REGINA: Poor Mother. You drove her to her death quick enough.

ENGSTRAND: Oh yes, oh yes. I'm guilty of everything.

REGINA: Uff! And then that leg of yours!

ENGSTRAND: What's that you're saying, my child?

REGINA: *Pied de mouton.*

ENGSTRAND: Is that English?

REGINA: Yes.

ENGSTRAND: It's good you've learned a few things; that'll come in handy now, Regina.

REGINA: *(After a short silence.)* What did you want with me in town?

ENGSTRAND: Can you even ask what a Father might want with his only child? Aren't I a lonely, deserted widower?

REGINA: Don't give me that crap. Why do you want me there?

ENGSTRAND: All right. I'll tell you. I'm thinking of trying something new.

REGINA: *(Cynically.)* Again? It never amounts to anything.

ENGSTRAND: Ah, but this time you'll see, Regina—may the devil have me for dinner if—

REGINA: *(Stamps her foot.)* Stop swearing!

ENGSTRAND: Shhh, shhh! You're absolutely right, my child. Let me just say this: I've saved quite a bit of money from this orphanage job.

REGINA: Really? That'll be nice for you.

ENGSTRAND: And after all, what can you spend it on out here in the country?

REGINA: So. What about it?

ENGSTRAND: So, I got the idea to put that money into something that will pay. Some sort of establishment for seamen.

REGINA: Oh God.

ENGSTRAND: A really classy establishment, you understand. Not some flea–bag hotel for sailors. No, damn it. This place will be for ship's captains and mates—the best people, you see?

REGINA: And I'm supposed to—?

ENGSTRAND: You get to help out, you know what I mean? As you can imagine, it would do wonders for appearances. You wouldn't have a hell of a lot to do, my girl. In fact you could do exactly as you pleased.

REGINA: Oh come on!

ENGSTRAND: Because you have to have women around the place, that's clear as day. You want some entertainment in the evenings, some singing and dancing and so on. See, these are wayfaring seamen who range the world's oceans. *(Coming closer.)* Don't be stupid now and get in your own way, Regina. What'll become of you out here? What good will all that education do you? Helping with the children in the new orphanage—is that really right for you? Do you really want to work yourself to death for those god–awful little brats?

REGINA: No: if what I really wanted—it could happen. It could happen.

ENGSTRAND: What could happen?

REGINA: Never mind. So you've saved a lot of money?

ENGSTRAND: Altogether, probably about seven, eight hundred kroner.

REGINA: Not bad.

ENGSTRAND: It's enough to get started, my girl.

REGINA: What about giving me a little of that money?

ENGSTRAND: No, by God, that's out of the question.

REGINA: Not even enough to buy material for a stupid dress?

ENGSTRAND: Just come into town with me and you'll have plenty of dresses.

REGINA: Ffft. I could manage that on my own if I wanted to.

ENGSTRAND: Ah, but it's much better with a father's guiding hand, Regina. Right now I can get a nice house on Little Harbor Street. They don't want too much of a deposit, and it could make a perfect seamen's establishment, you see.

REGINA: But I don't want to live with you! I don't want anything to do with you! Now go!

ENGSTRAND: You sure as hell wouldn't have to stay with me very long, my girl. Especially if you knew how to market yourself—as good-looking a thing as you've turned into these last couple of years.

REGINA: Me—?

ENGSTRAND: It wouldn't be long before a mate—maybe even a cap-tain—

REGINA: Forget that. Sailors have no *savoir vivre*.

ENGSTRAND: What don't they have?

REGINA: I know all about sailors, thank you. I'm not marrying one.

ENGSTRAND: So forget about marrying them. The other way can pay off just as well. *(More confidentially.)* Him—the Englishman—the one with the yacht—he paid three hundred dollars, and she was no prettier than you.

REGINA: *(Going for him.)* Get out of here!

ENGSTRAND: *(Retreating.)* Hey, hey—you aren't going to hit me now, are you?

REGINA. Aren't I? Talk that way about Mother, and you bet I'll hit you! Get out of here! *(Drives him toward the garden door.)* And don't slam the door—young Mr. Alving—

ENGSTRAND: Is sleeping, I know. It's amazing how much you worry about young Mr. Alving—*(Lowering his voice.)* Ah ha! It wouldn't happen to be *him* that's—?

REGINA: Out, out, out! You're crazy, I tell you! No, don't go that way. Pastor Manders is coming. Go down the kitchen stairs.

ENGSTRAND: *(Towards the right.)* Yes, yes, I'm going. But you have a talk with the one coming there. He's the man to tell you what a child owes her father. And I am your father, all the same. I can prove it in the parish register.

(He goes out through the door that Regina has opened for him and closes it after himself. Regina quickly looks at herself in the mirror, fans herself with a handkerchief and straightens her collar, then busies herself with flowers. Pastor Manders, in an overcoat, carrying an umbrella and with a small traveling bag on a strap over his shoulder, enters through the garden door into the conservatory.)

PASTOR MANDERS: Good day, Miss Engstrand.

REGINA: *(Turning in happy surprise.)* Well, good day, Pastor! Is the steamer here already?

PASTOR MANDERS: It's just in. *(Comes into the room.)* The weather's been terrible lately.

REGINA: *(Following him.)* It's a blessing for the farmers, Pastor.

PASTOR MANDERS: Yes, of course. You're right. We townspeople don't remember that often enough. *(He begins to take off his overcoat.)*

REGINA: Oh, can't I help you? There we go. You're all wet! I'll just hang this in the hall. Now your umbrella—I'll set it so it can dry.

(*She goes out with the things through the other door on the right. Pastor Manders sets his traveling bag and hat down on a chair. Meanwhile Regina returns.*)

PASTOR MANDERS: It is really good to be indoors. So—everything's in readiness here?

REGINA: Yes, thank you.

PASTOR MANDERS: I imagine you're awfully busy getting ready for tomorrow.

REGINA: Oh, yes. There's a lot to do.

PASTOR MANDERS: And Mrs. Alving's at home, I trust?

REGINA: Heavens, yes. She's upstairs right now giving the young master some hot cocoa.

PASTOR MANDERS: I heard down at the pier that Osvald's home.

REGINA: Yes, he came the day before yesterday. We didn't expect him 'til today.

PASTOR MANDERS: And in fine fettle, I hope.

REGINA: Yes, thanks, he certainly is. Of course, he's awfully tired after his trip. He came all the way from Paris without a break—I mean, he made the whole trip on the same train. I think he's sleeping now, so we should be just a little quieter.

PASTOR MANDERS: Shhh, we'll be so, so quiet.

REGINA: (*Moving an armchair up to the table.*) And please sit down, Pastor, make yourself at home.

(*He sits. She slips a footstool under his feet.*)

REGINA: There! Is the Pastor comfortable now?

PASTOR MANDERS: Thanks, thanks. I'm perfectly comfortable. (*Looking at her.*) You know, Miss Engstrand, I really think you've grown since I saw you last.

REGINA: You think so, Pastor? The mistress says I've filled out too.

PASTOR MANDERS: Filled out? Well, perhaps a bit. Quite appropriately.

(*A short silence.*)

REGINA: Should I tell the mistress—?

PASTOR MANDERS: Thank you, there's no hurry. Now tell me, my dear Regina, how are things with your father out here?

REGINA: He's doing very well, thank you, Pastor.

PASTOR MANDERS: He came to see me last time he was in town.

REGINA: Did he really? He's always so pleased when he can speak with the Pastor.

PASTOR MANDERS: And you make sure to see him every day?

REGINA: Me? Oh, of course, whenever I get the time to—

PASTOR MANDERS: Your father does not have a very strong personality, Miss Engstrand. He really needs a guiding hand—

REGINA: Yes. That's probably true.

PASTOR MANDERS: Someone around him he can turn to, whose judgment he can count on. He confessed that to me quite openly last time he came to see me.

REGINA: Yes, he said something like that to me too. But I don't know if Mrs. Alving could do without me—especially now, when we've got to take care of the new orphanage. And I owe her so much, she's always been so kind to me.

PASTOR MANDERS: Remember a daughter's duty, my dear girl. Naturally, we would have to get Mrs. Alving's consent—

REGINA: But I'm not sure it would be exactly right for me, at my age, to keep house for a single man.

PASTOR MANDERS: What? Miss Engstrand, we're talking about your own father!

REGINA: Yes, maybe, but all the same. If only it was a good house, and a really respectable man—

PASTOR MANDERS: But, my dear Regina—

REGINA: One that I could feel affection for, and look up to as if I were his daughter—

PASTOR MANDERS: Yes, but my dear, good child—

REGINA: In that case, I'd gladly go back to town. It's so lonely out here—and you yourself know, Pastor, what it's like to be all alone in the world. I think I can say that I'm ready, willing, and able. Doesn't the Pastor know of anyplace for me?

PASTOR MANDERS: I? I certainly do not know . . .

REGINA: But dear, dear Pastor—please think of me, anyway, if there ever—

PASTOR MANDERS: *(Getting up.)* I certainly will, Miss Engstrand.

REGINA: Yes, because if—

PASTOR MANDERS: Would you perhaps be so kind as to get Mrs. Alving?

REGINA: Right away, Pastor.

(She goes out to the left. Pastor Manders walks up and down the room a few times, stands for a while at the back of the room with his hands behind his back and looks out at the garden. Soon, he approaches the table, takes a book, looks at the title page, and begins inspecting others.)

PASTOR MANDERS: Hm. Well, well!

(Mrs. Alving comes in through the door at left. She is followed by Regina, who immediately goes out through the door right.)

MRS. ALVING: *(Holding out her hand.)* Welcome, Pastor.

PASTOR MANDERS: Good day to you, Mrs. Alving. Here I am, as promised.

MRS. ALVING: Punctual as ever.

PASTOR MANDERS: But you can imagine I was hard pressed to get away. All these blessed committees and councils I sit on—

MRS. ALVING: All the kinder of you to come so promptly. Now we can get through our business before lunch. But where's your bag?

PASTOR MANDERS: *(Hastily.)* My things are down at the general store. I'm staying there tonight.

MRS. ALVING: *(Suppressing a smile.)* You really can't be persuaded to spend the night in my house?

PASTOR MANDERS: No, no, thanks just the same. I'll stay down there like I usually do. It's so convenient for the return trip.

MRS. ALVING: Well, you'll do what you want. But I really think that a pair of old folks like us—

PASTOR MANDERS: Good heavens, how you joke! But of course you're overflowing with joy today. There's the celebration tomorrow, and you've got Osvald home.

MRS. ALVING: Yes, imagine how lucky I am! He hasn't been home in more than two years. And he's promised to stay with me all winter.

PASTOR MANDERS: Has he really? That's a gracious son you have there—I can imagine that life in Rome or Paris offers other sorts of attractions.

MRS. ALVING: Yes, but here at home, you see, he has his mother. Ah, my dear, blessed boy—still a place in his heart for his mother.

PASTOR MANDERS: It would be a great sadness if separation and the pursuit of a thing like art could dull his natural feelings.

MRS. ALVING: Yes, you could say that. But there's no fear of that with him. I can't wait to see if you'll recognize him. He'll be down shortly. Right now he's resting a little on the sofa upstairs. But sit down, my dear Pastor.

PASTOR MANDERS: Thanks. So it's a good time, then, to—?

MRS. ALVING: Yes, absolutely. *(She sits at the table.)*

PASTOR MANDERS: Good. Let me show you—*(He goes over to the chair where his traveling bag is lying, takes a sheaf of papers out of it, sits on the opposite side of the table and searches for a clear space for the papers.)* Now—first we have—*(Breaking off.)* Tell me, Mrs. Alving, how did these books get here?

MRS. ALVING: These books? I'm reading them.

PASTOR MANDERS: You read this kind of thing?

MRS. ALVING: Of course I do.

PASTOR MANDERS: Do you think this kind of reading makes you any happier or better?

MRS. ALVING: I think I've become more confident, yes.

PASTOR MANDERS: That's extraordinary. In what way?

MRS. ALVING: Well, I find that I'm much clearer and surer about so many of the things I've been working out on my own. That's what's so odd, Pastor Manders, there's nothing really new in these books. Nothing but what most people already think and believe. But most people aren't ready to confront these things, or even acknowledge them.

PASTOR MANDERS: But my God! Do you seriously believe that most people—?

MRS. ALVING: Yes, I truly believe that.

PASTOR MANDERS: But not here in this country—among us?

MRS. ALVING: Oh, yes—among us as well.

PASTOR MANDERS: Well—I must say I—

MRS. ALVING: What do you have against these books anyway?

PASTOR MANDERS: I hope you don't think I spend my time researching these kinds of publications.

MRS. ALVING: Then I guess you don't really know what you're condemning.

PASTOR MANDERS: I have read more than enough *about* these writings to condemn them.

MRS. ALVING: What about your own judgment?

PASTOR MANDERS: Dear lady, there are innumerable instances in life when you must rely on others for your judgments. That's the way this world works, and it's for the best. How else would society function?

MRS. ALVING: Well, well. Maybe you're right.

PASTOR MANDERS: Otherwise, I couldn't deny that there can be a considerable fascination in these writings. And I can't really blame you for wanting to get acquainted with the intellectual currents which we hear about as they spread through the wider world—where you've let your son wander for so long. But—

MRS. ALVING: But—?

PASTOR MANDERS: *(Lowering his voice.)* But you don't have to talk about it, Mrs. Alving. You're not obliged to offer everyone who wanders in a catalog of your library—or a summary of your private thoughts.

MRS. ALVING: No, of course not—I think that's true.

PASTOR MANDERS: Just consider your obligations to this children's home, which you decided to build at a time when your thinking about spiritual matters was profoundly different from what it is now—as I understand it, in any case.

MRS. ALVING: Yes, yes. I admit that completely—but about the children's home—

PASTOR MANDERS: That's what we're here to talk about, yes. All the same—prudence, dear lady. Now let's get down to business. *(Opens folder and takes out some papers.)* You see these?

MRS. ALVING: The deeds?

PASTOR MANDERS: All of them, in perfect order. You can't imagine how hard it's been to get them ready in time. I actually had to press for them—the authorities are almost painfully scrupulous when they have a decision to make. Anyway, here they are. *(Leafing through the papers.)* Here is the deed of conveyance for the property known as Solvik, within the Rosenvold estate, along with the new buildings: the schoolhouse, teacher's dormitory and chapel. And here is the authorization for the bequest, and for the by-laws of the asylum. Would you like to see?— *(He reads.)* "By-Laws of the Children's Home to be known as the 'Captain Alving Memorial.' "

MRS. ALVING: *(Looks at the papers for a long time.)* So there it is.

PASTOR MANDERS: I chose "Captain" instead of "Chamberlain." "Captain" seemed less pretentious.

MRS. ALVING: Whatever you think.

PASTOR MANDERS: And here's the bankbook showing the interest on the capital endowment set aside for operating expenses.

MRS. ALVING: Thank you—but would you mind holding on to it?

PASTOR MANDERS: I'd be happy to. I think we should leave the money in the bank for now, even though the interest isn't very attractive—four percent with six months notice for withdrawal. If we came across a good mortgage investment—naturally it would have to be a first mortgage and absolutely secure—then we could get together and discuss it in more detail.

MRS. ALVING: Yes, yes, Pastor Manders, you're the expert on all that.

PASTOR MANDERS: In any case, I'll keep my eyes open. There's just one thing, though, that I've been meaning to ask you several times.

MRS. ALVING: And what might that be?

PASTOR MANDERS: Should the Memorial buildings be insured or not?

MRS. ALVING: Of course they should be insured.

PASTOR MANDERS: Wait a moment, Mrs. Alving. Let's examine the matter a little more closely.

MRS. ALVING: I have insurance for everything—the buildings, their contents, my crops and livestock—

PASTOR MANDERS: Obviously. On your own possessions. I do the same thing, of course. But here, you see, it's a different matter. The Memorial is, as it were, to be consecrated to a high purpose.

MRS. ALVING: Yes, but what if—

PASTOR MANDERS: Speaking for myself, I can't honestly think of the slightest objection to insuring ourselves fully.

MRS. ALVING: No, that's what I think, too.

PASTOR MANDERS: But how would that sit with public opinion around here? You're a better judge of that than I.

MRS. ALVING: Hmm. Public opinion . . .

PASTOR MANDERS: Is there a significant body of important opinion—I mean really important opinion—that might object?

MRS. ALVING: What do you mean by really important opinion?

PASTOR MANDERS: I was thinking mostly of people whose influence—whose position—make it hard to avoid giving their opinions a certain weight.

MRS. ALVING: You could find quite a few like that who might object to this—

PASTOR MANDERS: There, you see! In town we have any number of them. Just think of my colleagues and their flocks. It would be terribly easy for them to infer that neither you nor I had sufficient faith in Divine Providence.

MRS. ALVING: But you know for yourself that you're—

PASTOR MANDERS: Yes, yes, I know, I know—I have a clear conscience, true enough. But even so we might not be able to avoid a damaging appearance, and that could easily interfere with the work of the Memorial.

MRS. ALVING: If that were to happen, then—

PASTOR MANDERS: Nor can I quite set aside the difficult—I think I can even say painful position I would probably be put in. There's a lot of interest in this institution in the town's leading circles. It benefits the town as well, of course, and there's hope that it will lead to a major reduction in our community welfare taxes. Since I've been your adviser on the business side of things, I'm afraid those fanatics would turn on me first and foremost.

MRS. ALVING: You shouldn't be subjected to that.

PASTOR MANDERS: Not to mention the attacks in the press—

MRS. ALVING: Enough, Pastor—the matter is settled.

PASTOR MANDERS: Then you don't want any insurance?

MRS. ALVING: No, we'll do without.

PASTOR MANDERS: *(Leaning back in his chair.)* But if an accident were to happen—one never knows. Would you be able to guarantee—?

MRS. ALVING: No, absolutely not—I can tell you that right now.

PASTOR MANDERS: Well then, Mrs. Alving. This really is a grave responsibility we're taking upon ourselves.

MRS. ALVING: But do you think we have any other choice?

PASTOR MANDERS: No, that's just it. We can't do anything else. We shouldn't leave ourselves open to censure—and we have no right to stir up indignation in the community.

MRS. ALVING: You certainly shouldn't, anyway, in your position.

PASTOR MANDERS: I think we really can count on having luck on our side in this project—even a kind of special dispensation.

MRS. ALVING: Let's hope so, Pastor Manders.

PASTOR MANDERS: So, we'll leave things as they are?

MRS. ALVING: Certainly.

PASTOR MANDERS: Good. As you wish. *(Makes a note.)* And so—no insurance.

MRS. ALVING: You know, it's odd that you happened to bring this up today of all days—

PASTOR MANDERS: I've often intended to—

MRS. ALVING: Because yesterday we almost had a fire down there.

PASTOR MANDERS: What?

MRS. ALVING: Well, it didn't amount to much. Some wood shavings in the carpenter's shop caught fire.

PASTOR MANDERS: Where Engstrand works?

MRS. ALVING: Yes—they say he's pretty careless with matches.

PASTOR MANDERS: He has so much on his mind, that man—so many tribulations. But God be praised, I hear he's making an effort now to lead an irreproachable life.

MRS. ALVING: Really? Who told you that?

PASTOR MANDERS: He himself. And he's a good worker, too.

MRS. ALVING: As long as he's sober.

PASTOR MANDERS: Ah, that unfortunate weakness! But he tells me he's driven to it because of his leg. The last time he was in town—it was very moving—he came up to me and thanked me so sincerely for getting him this job here, so he could be with Regina.

MRS. ALVING: He doesn't see that much of her.

PASTOR MANDERS: Oh yes—he speaks with her every day. He told me so himself.

MRS. ALVING: Well, maybe so.

PASTOR MANDERS: He's convinced that he needs someone to hold him back when temptation looms. That's what's so lovable about Jakob Engstrand—the way he comes to you, helpless, reproaching himself and confessing his trespasses. The last time he saw me—listen, Mrs. Alving, if it were absolutely necessary for him to have Regina home with him again—

MRS. ALVING: *(Rising quickly.)* Regina!

PASTOR MANDERS: Then you mustn't stand against the idea.

MRS. ALVING: But I am against it—completely against it! And besides, Regina will have a position with the Memorial.

PASTOR MANDERS: Remember that he is her father, no matter what.

MRS. ALVING: And I know just exactly the kind of father he's been to her. No, she'll never get my consent to go back with him.

PASTOR MANDERS: *(Rising.)* My dear lady, don't take it so violently. I'm sorry to see you misjudge Jakob Engstrand so completely. It's almost as if you were frightened—

MRS. ALVING: *(More calmly.)* Never mind. I have taken Regina into my house, and she'll stay in my house. *(Listens.)* Shh, Pastor Manders, let's not talk about this any more. *(Joy lights up her face.)* Listen! Osvald's coming downstairs. Now we'll concentrate on him.

(Osvald Alving, in a light overcoat, hat in hand and smoking a large meerschaum pipe, enters through the door, left.)

OSVALD: *(Remains standing in the doorway.)* Oh, excuse me, I thought you were in the study. *(Comes forward.)* Good morning.

PASTOR MANDERS: *(Staring.)* That's extraordinary!

MRS. ALVING: Yes, what do you have to say about him now, Pastor Manders?

PASTOR MANDERS: I'd say—I'd say—but is it really—?

OSVALD: Yes, it really is the Prodigal Son, Pastor.

PASTOR MANDERS: My dear young friend—

OSVALD: Well, the homecoming son, then.

MRS. ALVING: Osvald remembers when you had so much against his becoming a painter.

PASTOR MANDERS: To mortal eyes, many a step can well seem perilous that later—ah, welcome, welcome home! Really, my dear Osvald—I suppose I may still use your first name?

OSVALD: Of course, what else would you call me?

PASTOR MANDERS: Good. What I meant was—my dear Osvald—you mustn't think that I condemn everything artists stand for. I assume there must be quite a few who can preserve their inner selves unstained in that way of life.

OSVALD: Let's hope so.

MRS. ALVING: *(Beaming with pleasure.)* I know one who has preserved an unstained self both inside and out. All you have to do is look at him, Pastor.

OSVALD: *(Pacing up and down.)* Yes, yes, Mother—that's enough.

PASTOR MANDERS: Without a doubt, there's no denying it. And you've already begun to make a name for yourself. The papers have mentioned you quite a bit, and always in glowing terms. Although I have to say that lately there hasn't been as much.

OSVALD: *(Near the conservatory.)* I haven't been painting much recently.

MRS. ALVING: A painter needs to rest now and then, like everyone else.

PASTOR MANDERS: Yes, I understand—to prepare himself, to gather strength for some really big project.

OSVALD: Yes. Mother, are we eating soon?

MRS. ALVING: In half an hour. He's got a good appetite, thank God.

PASTOR MANDERS: And a taste for tobacco, too.

OSVALD: I found Father's pipe upstairs in the bedroom, so—

PASTOR MANDERS: Aha! That's it then.

MRS. ALVING: What?

PASTOR MANDERS: When Osvald came through that door there with the pipe in his mouth, it was as if I saw his father alive again.

OSVALD: Really?

MRS. ALVING: How can you say that? Osvald takes after me.

PASTOR MANDERS: Yes, but there's a line there, around the corners of the mouth, something about the lips, that brings Alving back to mind—at least when he's smoking.

MRS. ALVING: No, absolutely not. I think Osvald's mouth reminds me more of a priest's.

PASTOR MANDERS: Yes, yes, many of my colleagues have a similar expression.

MRS. ALVING: Put the pipe down now—I don't want smoking in here.

OSVALD: *(Does so.)* Gladly. I just wanted to try it—because I smoked it once before, as a child.

MRS. ALVING: You did?

OSVALD: Yes. I was very small at the time. And I remember I came up to Father's room one evening when he was feeling happy and good.

MRS. ALVING: Oh, you don't remember anything from those years.

OSVALD: Oh yes—I remember it clearly. He took me and sat me on his knee and let me smoke his pipe. "Smoke it, boy," he said— "smoke it down deep, boy." And I smoked as much as I could, until I felt myself going pale and my forehead broke out in huge drops of sweat. Then he laughed so uproariously—

PASTOR MANDERS: Extraordinary.

MRS. ALVING: It's just something he dreamt.

OSVALD: No, Mother, I definitely didn't dream it. Don't you remember? You came in then and carried me to the nursery. I got sick, and I saw you were crying. Did Father often play jokes like that?

PASTOR MANDERS: As a young man he was so full of the joy of life.

OSVALD: And yet he was able to accomplish so much in the world—so much that was good and useful, even dying as young as he did.

PASTOR MANDERS: Yes, it's a fact that you've inherited the name of an energetic and worthy man, Osvald Alving. Let's hope it will be an inspiration to you—

OSVALD: It ought to be.

PASTOR MANDERS: It was nice of you to come home for these celebrations in his honor.

OSVALD: It's the least I can do for Father.

MRS. ALVING: And the nicest thing of all is how long I'll get to keep him.

PASTOR MANDERS: Yes, I hear you'll be staying all winter.

OSVALD: I'll be staying indefinitely, Pastor. Oh, it's wonderful to come home again.

MRS. ALVING: *(Beaming.)* Yes, isn't that true?

PASTOR MANDERS: *(Looking at him sympathetically.)* You went out into the world very early, Osvald.

OSVALD: Yes, I did. I wonder sometimes if it wasn't too early.

MRS. ALVING: Not at all. It's good for a bright boy. Especially when he's an only child. He shouldn't be kept at home to be spoiled by his mother and father.

PASTOR MANDERS: That's a highly debatable point, Mrs. Alving. The ancestral home is and always will remain a child's rightful place.

OSVALD: Now I'm in total agreement with the Pastor.

PASTOR MANDERS: Just look at your own son. Yes, we can talk about this in front of him. What has the result been for him? He's twenty–six or twenty–seven and he's never had the chance to see what a respectable home is like.

OSVALD: I beg your pardon, Pastor, but you're quite mistaken about that.

PASTOR MANDERS: Really? I thought you lived almost exclusively among artists.

OSVALD: I did, yes.

PASTOR MANDERS: Mostly among younger artists.

OSVALD: Yes, that's right.

PASTOR MANDERS: But I thought most of those people didn't have the means to support a home and family.

OSVALD: Many of them lack the means to get married, Pastor.

PASTOR MANDERS: That's what I'm saying.

OSVALD: But they can still have a home. And one or two do—very respectable, very pleasant homes.

(*Mrs. Alving, following closely, nods but says nothing.*)

PASTOR MANDERS: I'm not talking about bachelor's houses. When I say home, I mean a real family home where a man lives with his wife and his children.

OSVALD: Yes, or with his children and their mother.

PASTOR MANDERS: (*Startled, claps his hands.*) But merciful—!

OSVALD: Well?

PASTOR MANDERS: Lives with—his children's mother?

OSVALD: Yes. What should he do—abandon her?

PASTOR MANDERS: So you're talking about illicit relationships! About those irresponsible, so-called "free marriages!"

OSVALD: I've never noticed anything especially irresponsible about the way these people live together.

PASTOR MANDERS: But how is it possible that young men and women of even moderately decent upbringing can bring themselves to live like that—in the public eye.

OSVALD: What should they do instead? A poor young artist—a poor young girl—getting married costs money. What should they do?

PASTOR MANDERS: What should they do? Well, Mr. Alving, I'll tell you what they should do. They should stay away from each other from the beginning, that's what they should do.

OSVALD: That kind of advice wouldn't get you very far with young, warm-blooded people in love.

MRS. ALVING: No, not too far.

PASTOR MANDERS: *(Persisting.)* And the authorities tolerate such things! It goes on openly, no one stops it! *(Facing Mrs. Alving.)* Didn't I have good reason to be worried about your son? Moving in circles where blatant immorality is the custom—where it's even claimed as a right?

OSVALD: Let me tell you something, Pastor. I've been a regular Sunday guest in some of these unconventional homes—

PASTOR MANDERS: On Sundays, no less!

OSVALD: Yes, when people should be enjoying themselves. And never once have I heard an offensive word, much less witnessed anything that could be called immoral. But do you know where I *have* encountered immorality among the artists?

PASTOR MANDERS: No, praise God!

OSVALD: Then I think I should enlighten you: I run into it whenever one of our exemplary husbands and fathers comes down there to get a close look at the other side of life—so they do us artists the honor of paying a visit to our humble cafés. What an education we're treated to then! Those gentlemen can teach us about places and things we never even dreamed of.

PASTOR MANDERS: What? You're claiming that respectable men from here at home would—?

OSVALD: Haven't you ever—when these respectable men come home again—haven't you heard them screaming about the rampant epidemic of immorality abroad?

PASTOR MANDERS: Naturally, of course—

MRS. ALVING: I've heard it too.

OSVALD: Well, they know what they're talking about. There are connoisseurs among them. *(Clutching his head.)* Ah!—this beautiful, glorious, free life out there—polluted like that!

MRS. ALVING: You mustn't excite yourself, Osvald, it's not good for you.

OSVALD: No, Mother, you're right. It's not healthy. It's this damn fatigue. I'll go for a little walk before we eat. I'm sorry, Pastor—I know you can't bring yourself to see that. But it just suddenly came over me and I had to say it. *(He goes out through the second door, right.)*

MRS. ALVING: My poor boy.

PASTOR MANDERS: Yes, you might well say that. So this is what's become of him.

(Mrs. Alving looks at him silently. Manders walks up and down.) He called himself the Prodigal Son. Alas, how true—how true. So what do you think of all this?

MRS. ALVING: I think every word Osvald said was right.

PASTOR MANDERS: *(Stops short.)* Right? Right! With those principles?

MRS. ALVING: Here—all by myself—I've come to think exactly the same way. But I've never dared to talk about it. All right, now my boy will speak for me.

PASTOR MANDERS: You are a pitiable woman, Mrs. Alving. Now I must speak to you seriously; no longer as your business adviser and executor, nor as the life-long friend of your husband and yourself. I stand before you as your priest: exactly the same one who stood before you in your life's most desperate hour.

MRS: ALVING: And what does the priest have to say to me?

PASTOR MANDERS: First, I will rouse your memory a little, Mrs. Alving. The moment is right for it. Tomorrow is the tenth anniversary of your husband's death; tomorrow a memorial will be unveiled in commemoration of that event; tomorrow I will speak to the whole assembled company—but today I want to speak to you alone.

MRS. ALVING: All right, Pastor. Speak!

PASTOR MANDERS: Do you remember how, after being married barely a year, you came to the outer edge of the abyss? How you left your house and home, fled your husband—yes, Mrs. Alving, fled—fled him and refused to go back to him, no matter how much he pleaded and begged you to?

MRS. ALVING: Have you forgotten how unbelievably miserable I was that first year?

PASTOR MANDERS: The spirit of rebellion makes us seek happiness here in this life; that's precisely its aim. But what claim have we human beings to happiness? No, Mrs. Alving, we must do our duty! And your duty was to stand by the man you had chosen, and to whom you were bound by sacred ties.

MRS. ALVING: You know very well what kind of life Alving was leading in those days—the debaucheries he was guilty of.

PASTOR MANDERS: I am all too aware of the rumors about him that were making the rounds. And I am the last person to condone his behavior then, insofar as the rumors had any truth to them. But a wife is not her husband's judge; your job was to bear, with a humble spirit, the cross that a higher will destined for you. Instead you rebelliously cast away the cross, abandoned the weak and faltering, whom you should have supported—went off and put your good name and reputation at risk—and nearly dragged other reputations into it as well.

MRS. ALVING: Others? I think you mean *one* other.

PASTOR MANDERS: It was exceedingly reckless of you to seek refuge with me.

MRS. ALVING: With our pastor—in the home of a good friend?

PASTOR MANDERS: For that reason especially. Thank the Lord your God that I found the necessary firmness—that I was able to turn you away from your hysterical intentions, and that it was granted me to lead you back to your duty, home to your lawful husband.

MRS. ALVING: Yes, Pastor Manders, that was certainly your work.

PASTOR MANDERS: I was but a humble instrument in the hand of a higher power. And from this moment—when I bent you to the yoke of duty and obedience—didn't there grow a great blessing which filled all the days of your life? Didn't I foretell all this? Didn't Alving turn away from his errors, exactly as a man must do, and live with you lovingly and blamelessly for the rest of his life? Didn't he become a benefactor to this district, lifting you up alongside him until you became a colleague in everything he did? And a true colleague you were, Mrs. Alving—*that* I'll give you. But now I come to the next great failure in your life.

MRS. ALVING: What do you mean by that?

PASTOR MANDERS: Just as you once shirked the duties of a wife, you've shirked those of a Mother in the same way.

MRS. ALVING: Ah—

PASTOR MANDERS: All your life you've been ruled by a disastrously rebellious spirit. Your longings have drawn you toward everything undisciplined and lawless. You would never tolerate the slightest restraint. You've recklessly and irresponsibly tossed aside every inconvenience in your life, like some package you could just put down at will. It didn't please you to be a wife any longer, and so you left your husband. Being a mother was too much trouble, and so you turned your child loose with strangers.

MRS. ALVING: Yes, that's true. That's what I did.

PASTOR MANDERS: And in so doing, you've become a stranger to him.

MRS. ALVING: No, no. That I am *not!*

PASTOR MANDERS: You *are.* You *must* be! And look at the state in which you got him back! Consider well, Mrs. Alving. You trespassed against your husband; this memorial you're raising to him shows you admit this in your heart. Now admit, as well, that you have trespassed against your son; there might still be time to turn him away from his errors. Turn away yourself—and save what can still be saved in him. For truly *(With raised forefinger.)*—truly, Mrs. Alving, you are a profoundly guilty woman. I've considered it my duty to tell you this. *(Silence.)*

MRS. ALVING: *(Slowly and deliberately.)* Now you've spoken, Pastor; and tomorrow you'll speak publicly, in my husband's memory. I won't be speaking tomorrow. But I'll speak a bit to you today just as you have spoken to me.

PASTOR MANDERS: Of course, you want to make excuses for your conduct—

MRS. ALVING: No, I'll just tell you something.

PASTOR MANDERS: Well?

MRS. ALVING: Everything you've just been saying about my husband and me and our life together after—as you put it—you led me back to the path of duty—none of that is based on even the slightest observation on your part. From that moment on, you— our everyday best friend—never again set foot in our house.

PASTOR MANDERS: You and your husband moved away from town—

MRS. ALVING: Yes, and you never came out here to see us while my husband was alive. Business finally forced you to visit me, since you had gotten involved with the Memorial.

PASTOR MANDERS: *(Softly and uncertainly.)* Helene—if this is meant as a reproach, I'd ask you to consider—

MRS. ALVING: The sensitivities of your calling, yes. And of course I was a runaway wife—you can't be too careful with senseless creatures like that.

PASTOR MANDERS: Dear—Mrs. Alving, that is a gross exaggeration.

MRS. ALVING: Yes, yes, yes, let it go. I just want to say this: when you pass judgment on my married life, you are basing it on nothing more than the common gossip of the time.

PASTOR MANDERS: What if that's true? What then?

MRS. ALVING: Now, Pastor Manders—now I'm going to tell you the truth. I swore to myself that you—and only you—would know it someday.

PASTOR MANDERS: And what is this truth?

MRS. ALVING: The truth is that my husband died just as debauched as he lived his whole life.

PASTOR MANDERS: *(Fumbling for a chair.)* What did you say?

MRS. ALVING: Just as debauched, after nineteen years of marriage—in his proclivities, anyway—as he was before you married us.

PASTOR MANDERS: But these youthful errors—these improprieties, dissipations if you will—you call these a debauched life?

MRS. ALVING: Those are the words our family doctor used.

PASTOR MANDERS: I don't understand you.

MRS. ALVING: You don't have to.

PASTOR MANDERS: I feel dizzy. Your entire marriage—all those years of life with your husband—were nothing more than wallpaper over an abyss!

MRS. ALVING: Nothing more. Now you know.

PASTOR MANDERS: This—I find I can't comprehend it. I cannot understand—can't grasp—how was it possible? How could something like that be kept quiet?

MRS. ALVING: That has been my struggle, day after day. When we had Osvald, I thought Alving was getting better—but that didn't last long. Now the struggle had to be redoubled, a life-and-death struggle to guarantee that no one would find out what kind of man my child's father was. And you know how charming Alving was. People couldn't help thinking well of him. He was one of those people whose real lives never get in the way of their reputations. But then, Manders—you have to know this too— then came the most disgusting thing of all.

PASTOR MANDERS: More disgusting than all this?

MRS. ALVING: I put up with everything as long as it was done in secret, away from the house. But when the sickness came right within our own four walls—

PASTOR MANDERS: What are you saying? Here!

MRS. ALVING: Yes, right here in our home. In there *(Points toward the first door on the right.)* in the dining room was where I first discovered it. I needed something inside, and the door was ajar. I heard our maid come up from the garden to water the plants in here—

PASTOR MANDERS: Then—?

MRS. ALVING: I heard Alving come in. I heard him saying something to her very softly. And then I heard *(With a short laugh.)*—oh, I can still hear it, so devastating and at the same time so ludicrous—I heard my own maid whisper: "Let go of me. Chamberlain Alving! Leave me alone!"

PASTOR MANDERS: That was terribly indiscreet of him! Oh, but it wasn't anything more than a momentary lapse, I'm sure, Mrs. Alving. Please, believe me.

MRS. ALVING: I soon found out what to believe. Chamberlain Alving had his way with the girl—and that affair had its consequences, Pastor Manders.

PASTOR MANDERS: *(As if turned to stone.)* And all that in this house! In this house!

MRS. ALVING: I've had to endure a lot in this house. To keep him home evenings—and nights—I had to join him over a bottle up in his room. I had to sit alone with him, toasting and drinking with him, listening to his obscene, nonsensical talk, had to drag him into bed with my bare hands—

PASTOR MANDERS: *(Shaken.)* That you could endure that!

MRS. ALVING: I endured it for my little boy. But when that last humiliation occurred—my own maid—then I swore to myself that this would be the end! And so I took power in this house—absolute power over him and everything else. Now I had a weapon against him, you see; he didn't dare object. Then I sent Osvald away. He was almost seven—he'd begun to notice things, and ask questions the way children do. And I couldn't bear that, Manders. I thought the child would be poisoned just by breathing the air in this polluted house. And now you can see why he never set foot here as long as his father lived. No one can possibly know what that has cost me.

PASTOR MANDERS: Your life has certainly tested you to the limit.

MRS. ALVING: I couldn't have survived without my work. Yes, I have worked—all these additions to the estate, all the improvements, all the innovations that Alving got credit for—do you think those were *his*? He, who'd lie on the sofa all day reading old government papers! No; now I'll tell you this too: I was the one who steered him in the right direction whenever he had a lucid moment, and I had to carry the whole weight when he went back to his "errors" or just collapsed in a spineless, miserable heap.

PASTOR MANDERS: And you are raising a memorial to such a man.

MRS. ALVING: You see the power of a bad conscience.

PASTOR MANDERS: A bad—? What do you mean?

MRS. ALVING: I was always haunted by the idea that the truth would someday come out and be believed. So the memorial was meant to kill all the rumors and rule out every doubt.

PASTOR MANDERS: That you've certainly done, Mrs. Alving.

MRS. ALVING: And there was one other reason. I was determined that Osvald, my own son, wouldn't get anything at all from his father's inheritance.

PASTOR MANDERS: Then it's Alving's fortune that—

MRS. ALVING: Yes. The amount I've contributed to this institution every year comes to the exact total that made lieutenant Alving such a good match at the time.

PASTOR MANDERS: Then—I understand—

MRS. ALVING: It was the market price. I don't want that money to touch Osvald's hands. My son will get everything from me, and me alone.

(*Osvald Alving comes through the second door, right. He has left his hat and coat outside.*)

MRS. ALVING: You're back again, dear? My dear, dear boy!

OSVALD: Yes, you can't do anything in this interminable rain! But we're eating soon, I hear—that's good news!

REGINA: (*With a package from the dining room.*) A package has just come for Mrs. Alving.

MRS. ALVING: (*With a glance at Pastor Manders.*) The choral parts for tomorrow, probably.

PASTOR MANDERS: Hmm.

REGINA: And the meal is served.

MRS. ALVING: Good. We'll be there in a moment. I'll just—(*Begins to open package.*).

REGINA: (*To Osvald.*) Will Mr. Alving have red or white wine?

OSVALD: Both, Miss Engstrand.

REGINA: *Bien.* Very well, Mr. Alving. (*She goes into the dining room.*)

OSVALD: I'll help her uncork the bottles. (*He also goes in, the door half-closing behind him.*)

MRS. ALVING: (*Having opened the package.*) Yes, that's right—the choir music, Pastor Manders.

PASTOR MANDERS: (*With folded hands.*) How I'll ever be able to give my speech tomorrow with a clear conscience, I don't—

MRS. ALVING: Oh, you'll find a way.

PASTOR MANDERS: *(Softly, so as not to be heard in the dining room.)* Yes, above all we can't risk any scandal—

MRS. ALVING: *(Quietly but firmly.)* No. And then this long, horrible farce will come to an end. From tomorrow on, it will be as if the dead had never lived in this house. There'll be no one here but my boy and his Mother.

(In the dining room, the sound of a chair being overturned. At the same time, Regina's voice in a sharp whisper.)

REGINA: Osvald! Are you crazy? Let me go!

MRS. ALVING: *(Starting in terror.)* Ah—

PASTOR MANDERS: *(Agitated.)* What's happening? What *is* it, Mrs. Alving?

MRS. ALVING: *(Hoarsely.)* Ghosts. Those two from the greenhouse—are walking again.

PASTOR MANDERS: What are you saying? Regina—is she—?

MRS. ALVING: Yes. Come on. Not a word.

(She grips Manders' arm and goes shakily towards the dining room.)

END OF ACT ONE

ACT TWO

The same room. A mist still lies heavily over the landscape.

(Pastor Manders and Mrs. Alving enter from the dining room.)

MRS. ALVING: *(Still in the doorway.)* You're very welcome, Pastor. *(Calling into the dining room.)* Aren't you joining us, Osvald?

OSVALD: *(Within.)* No thanks. I think I'll go out for a while.

MRS. ALVING: Yes, why don't you do that, now that the rain's let up. *(Closes the dining room door, goes to the hall door and calls.)* Regina!

REGINA: *(Outside.)* Yes, ma'am?

MRS. ALVING: Go down to the laundry and help with the decorations.

REGINA: Yes, ma'am.

(Mrs. Alving makes sure that Regina has gone; then she closes the door.)

PASTOR MANDERS: Are you sure he can't hear anything in there?

MRS. ALVING: Not with the door closed. Besides, he's going out.

PASTOR MANDERS: I'm still in shock. I don't know how I managed to eat a bite of that heavenly meal

MRS. ALVING: *(Controlling her agitation. Pacing up and down.)* I feel the same. But what can we do?

PASTOR MANDERS: Yes, what can we do? Believe me, I don't know—I've got no experience in things like this.

MRS. ALVING: I don't think anything bad has happened yet.

PASTOR MANDERS: No, heaven forbid! But it's a tricky situation all the same.

MRS. ALVING: It's just a whim of Osvald's, you can be sure of that.

PASTOR MANDERS: Well, like I said, I'm not really up on these things, but I definitely think that—

MRS. ALVING: She has to leave the house, without a doubt. Right away. That's as clear as day.

PASTOR MANDERS: Yes, that's understood.

MRS. ALVING: But where should she go? We can't very well—

PASTOR MANDERS: Where? Home to her father, naturally.

MRS. ALVING: To whom did you say?

PASTOR MANDERS: To her—aha—Engstrand's not—of course. But Good Lord, Mrs. Alving, how can this be? You're mistaken, I'm sure.

MRS. ALVING: Unfortunately not—about any of it. Johanna had to come to me and confess everything, and Alving couldn't deny it. The only thing to do was cover up the whole affair.

PASTOR MANDERS: Yes, that's right—that was all you could do.

MRS. ALVING: The girl left right away, with a pretty good sum of money in her pocket to keep quiet. She took care of everything else when she got to town. She revived an old relationship with Engstrand—I'd imagine she let it be known that she had some money—and came up with some story about a foreigner who had docked his yacht here that summer. So she and Engstrand got married in a hurry. Oh, of course—you married them.

PASTOR MANDERS: How am I supposed to make sense of all this—? I distinctly remember when Engstrand came to me to set up his wedding. He was so completely repentant—he did nothing but criticize himself for his own irresponsibility.

MRS. ALVING: Of course he took the blame himself.

PASTOR MANDERS: But the hypocrisy of the man! And against *me!* I would never have believed that of Jakob Engstrand. Well, I'll certainly prepare a rather serious sermon for him—he can look forward to that. And the immorality of that kind of marriage—for money! How much did the girl get?

MRS. ALVING: Three hundred.

PASTOR MANDERS: Think about it—to let yourself get dragged into marrying a fallen woman for a miserable three hundred specie–dollars!

MRS. ALVING: Well, what do you have to say to me—I let myself get dragged into marrying a fallen man.

PASTOR MANDERS: Good God, what are you talking about? A fallen man!

MRS. ALVING: Do you think Alving was any purer when we went to the altar than Johanna was when Engstrand got himself married?

PASTOR MANDERS: But there's all the difference in the world between—

MRS. ALVING: Not so much. In fact—there was, however, a big difference in the price. A miserable three hundred dollars against a whole fortune.

PASTOR MANDERS: How can you compare two completely different things? You were responding to your family's wishes, and your own heart.

MRS. ALVING: *(Not looking at him.)* I thought you knew where what you call my heart was wandering at the time.

PASTOR MANDERS: *(Distantly.)* If I'd known anything like that I certainly wouldn't have been a daily guest in your husband's house.

MRS. ALVING: Still, the fact remains that I really didn't pay any attention to what I wanted.

PASTOR MANDERS: Well, you listened to your nearest relatives anyway— just as you're supposed to—your mother and your two aunts.

MRS. ALVING: Yes, that's very true. The three of them totaled it all up for me. Ah, it's just incredible how neatly they figured out that it would be insane to turn down that offer. If Mother could look down and see the strings that came attached to all that splendor—

PASTOR MANDERS: No one can be held responsible for the way it turned out. None the less, there's one solid fact: your marriage was founded in strict accord with the principles of law and order.

MRS. ALVING: *(By the window.)* Yes—law and order. I often think they cause all the misery in the world.

PASTOR MANDERS: Mrs. Alving, you're heading toward sin—

MRS. ALVING: Well, be that as it may. I just can't stand all these restrictions and obligations any more—I can't stand them! I've got to work my way to freedom.

PASTOR MANDERS: What does that mean?

MRS. ALVING: *(Drumming on the windowpane.)* I should never have covered up the truth about Alving's life. But I didn't dare do otherwise, not at the time. And not just for my own sake, either. I was so cowardly!

PASTOR MANDERS: Cowardly?

MRS. ALVING: If people found out about it they'd just have said something like: "Poor man, no wonder he strays a bit at times— with a wife who runs off and leaves him."

PASTOR MANDERS: And they'd have had some justification.

MRS. ALVING: *(Looking hard at him.)* If I were everything I should be, I would have taken Osvald aside and told him. "Listen, my son, your Father was a fallen man."

PASTOR MANDERS: Merciful God!

MRS. ALVING: And then I would have told him everything I've told you, word for word.

PASTOR MANDERS: Mrs. Alving, you're almost horrifying me.

MRS. ALVING: Yes, I know! I know! I horrify myself when I think about it. *(Walks from the window.)* What a coward I am!

PASTOR MANDERS: What you call cowardice, I call doing your duty, living up to your responsibility! Have you forgotten that a child should love and honor his father and mother?

MRS. ALVING: Let's not talk abstractions. Let's ask: should Osvald love and honor Chamberlain Alving?

PASTOR MANDERS: Doesn't some voice in your mother's heart cry out to you not to shatter your son's ideals?

MRS. ALVING: What about the truth?

PASTOR MANDERS: What about ideals?

MRS. ALVING: Ideals, ideals! If only I weren't such a coward!

PASTOR MANDERS: Don't throw away ideals, Mrs. Alving—that can set a terrible vengeance in motion. Especially in Osvald's case. Osvald's not long on ideals, unfortunately. But as far as I can tell, his father does represent some sort of ideal for him.

MRS. ALVING: You're right about that.

PASTOR MANDERS: You stirred those ideals up yourself, and kept them alive, in your letters to him.

MRS. ALVING: Yes, I was under the spell of duty and convention—so I lied to my boy, year after year. Ah, what a coward—what a coward.

PASTOR MANDERS: You've created a joyful illusion for your son, Mrs. Alving—don't underrate the value of that.

MRS. ALVING: Hmm. I wonder if it's such a good thing after all? But I just won't put up with him fooling around with Regina. He's not going to ruin that poor girl's life.

PASTOR MANDERS: Good God, no. That would be terrible!

MRS. ALVING: If I thought he was serious about—if I thought it could make him happy—

PASTOR MANDERS: Yes, what then?

MRS. ALVING: It still wouldn't work. Regina's not that kind of person.

PASTOR MANDERS: What do you mean?

MRS. ALVING: If I weren't such a coward, I'd say to him. "Go ahead and marry her, or come up with some other arrangement, only do it openly and honestly."

PASTOR MANDERS: May God forgive you—marriage? Of all the terrifying—it's unheard of!

MRS. ALVING: Unheard of? Oh yes! Raise your right hand now—don't you think that you could find plenty of couples just as closely related out here in the country?

PASTOR MANDERS: I absolutely don't understand you.

MRS. ALVING: Oh yes you do.

PASTOR MANDERS: Well—you must be thinking of those instances of—well, yes, unfortunately, family life isn't always as pure as it should be. But in the world you're talking about, you can't really know for certain. In this case, on the other hand—where a Mother would willingly permit her own son to—

MRS. ALVING: I'm not willing. I don't want to let this happen for anything in the world—that's exactly what I was saying.

PASTOR MANDERS: No, because you said you were a coward. But what if you weren't a coward—then, in the Creator's name, what a monstrous union—!

MRS. ALVING: Well, when it comes to that, they say we're all descended from that kind of union. And whose idea was *that*, Pastor Manders?

PASTOR MANDERS: We won't discuss that subject now, Mrs. Alving. You're hardly in the right frame of mind for it. How could you dare to say that it was cowardice on your part—?

MRS. ALVING: Let me tell you what I mean by that. I'm terrified—and it's made me something of a coward—because my mind is haunted by the dead among us, and I'm afraid I can never be completely free from them.

PASTOR MANDERS: What did you call them?

MRS. ALVING: The dead among us—ghosts. When I heard Regina and Osvald in there, I saw ghosts. I almost believe we are ghosts, all of us. It's not just what we inherit from our fathers and mothers that walks again in us—it's all sorts of dead old ideas and dead beliefs and things like that. They don't exactly *live* in us, but there they sit all the same and we can't get rid of them. All I have to do is pick up a newspaper, and I see ghosts lurking between the lines. I think there are ghosts everywhere you turn in this country—as many as there are grains of sand—and then there we all are, so abysmally afraid of the light.

PASTOR MANDERS: Aha! This is your profit after all that reading. Excellent, isn't it? Ach, these detestable, rabble–rousing, free–thinking writings

MRS. ALVING: You're wrong, my dear Pastor. You're the one who egged me on to do my own thinking. You can take all the credit, all the praise for that.

PASTOR MANDERS: I!

MRS. ALVING: Yes—when you forced me to submit to what you called duty and responsibility; when you praised as right and proper what my own mind found hideous and revolting. Then I started to look over your teaching thread by thread. I only wanted to pull apart a knot or two—but when they came loose, the whole thing unraveled. What I thought was a handmade garment turned out to be a mass-produced imitation.

PASTOR MANDERS: *(Softly, moved.)* Is this all I won in my life's hardest battle?

MRS. ALVING: Call it your most pitiful defeat.

PASTOR MANDERS: No, Helene—it was my greatest victory—over myself.

MRS. ALVING: It was a crime against us both.

PASTOR MANDERS: When I commanded you to go home—when I said "Woman, your place is with your lawful husband"—when you came to me crying, pleading, "take me—here I am"—was that a crime?

MRS. ALVING: Yes, I think so.

PASTOR MANDERS: We don't understand each other at all.

MRS. ALVING: At least not any more.

PASTOR MANDERS: Never—not once—not even in my most private thoughts, have I ever thought of you as anything other than another man's wife.

MRS. ALVING: You believe that?

PASTOR MANDERS: Helene—!

MRS. ALVING: Some things are easy to forget, I guess.

PASTOR MANDERS: No, no—I'm the same now as I always was.

MRS. ALVING: *(Changing her tone.)* Well, well, well. Let's not talk about the old days any more. Here you are up to your ears in committee work and boards of trustees, and I'm running around doing battle with ghosts—both inside and out.

PASTOR MANDERS: I can help you with the outer ones at least. After listening to everything you've said today—with growing horror, I'm telling you—I can't in good conscience allow a young, defenseless girl to remain in your house.

MRS. ALVING: Don't you think it would be best to get her settled—I mean married?

PASTOR MANDERS: Absolutely. I think that would be best all around. Regina is at that age right now when—well, I don't really know much about these things—

MRS. ALVING: Regina has matured pretty fast.

PASTOR MANDERS: Yes, she has, hasn't she? I was impressed at how remarkably well developed she was when I was preparing her for her confirmation. Anyway, for the time being she should go home, live with her father—ah—of course—Engstrand's not—and he—*he's* been lying to me this way!

(A knock at the hall door.)

MRS. ALVING: Who can that be? Come in.

ENGSTRAND: *(In the doorway, dressed in Sunday clothes.)* Begging your pardon—

PASTOR MANDERS: Aha! Hmm—

MRS. ALVING: Engstrand—it's you.

ENGSTRAND: There weren't any maids around, so I took the great liberty of knocking, as they say.

MRS. ALVING: All right, come in. You have something to say to me?

ENGSTRAND: *(Entering.)* No, thanks anyway. I really wanted a word with the pastor.

PASTOR MANDERS: *(Pacing up and down.)* Hmm. Really? A word with me? That's what you want?

ENGSTRAND: Yes, I'd be terribly glad—

PASTOR MANDERS: *(Stops in front of him.)* All right, but quickly.

ENGSTRAND: You see, it's like this, Pastor—now that we've gotten paid down there—can't thank you enough, ma'am—now that everything's finished, I was thinking it would be so proper and perfect for all of us who've been working together so beautifully—well, I was thinking we ought to finish up this evening with a little prayer.

PASTOR MANDERS: A prayer? Down at the Memorial?

ENGSTRAND: Yes. But if the pastor thinks it's not proper—

PASTOR MANDERS: Oh, it most certainly is, but—hmm—

ENGSTRAND: I used to hold a little evening prayer service down there myself.

MRS. ALVING: Did you?

ENGSTRAND: Yes, now and then. A little uplift, you might say. But I'm just a simple, ordinary man with no real spiritual gifts, God help me—so I was thinking that since Pastor Manders happened to be out here—

PASTOR MANDERS: I have to ask you a question first. Are you in the right frame of mind for a gathering like this? Do you feel your conscience is free and clear?

ENGSTRAND: God help us, let's not waste our time talking about my conscience, Pastor—

PASTOR MANDERS: That's exactly what we're going to talk about. So, what's your answer?

ENGSTRAND: Oh, that conscience of mine—it can sure be tough sometimes.

PASTOR MANDERS: At least you recognize the fact. Tell me now, and don't try to talk around the question: What is the truth about Regina?

MRS. ALVING: *(Quickly.)* Pastor Manders!

PASTOR MANDERS: *(Reassuringly.)* Just let me—

ENGSTRAND: Regina? Lord, you're scaring me. *(Looks at Mrs. Alving.)* Nothing bad's happened to her, has it?

PASTOR MANDERS: We certainly hope not. I'm talking about you and Regina—what's the truth there? You claim to be her father, don't you? Well?

ENGSTRAND: *(Uncertainly.)* Well—hmm—the Pastor already knows about the business between me and the dearly departed Johanna—

PASTOR MANDERS: No more twisting the truth! Your late wife confided everything to Mrs. Alving before she left the house here.

ENGSTRAND: But it was supposed to be—she did that?

PASTOR MANDERS: So you're exposed, Engstrand.

ENGSTRAND: So she—after taking an oath and swearing to heaven—

PASTOR MANDERS: She swore!

ENGSTRAND: She took an oath, I mean. So sincerely, too.

PASTOR MANDERS: And you've been hiding the truth from me all these years. From *me*, who trusted you completely.

ENGSTRAND: Yes, sorry, but that's what I did.

PASTOR MANDERS: Have I deserved this from you, Engstrand? Haven't I always extended a helping hand to you, in word and deed, if it was in my power to do so? Answer. Haven't I done that?

ENGSTRAND: Things would have looked bad for me plenty of times if it hadn't been for Pastor Manders.

PASTOR MANDERS: And this is how you repay me. Get me to enter false records into the parish register—keep me in the dark, for years, about this information which you owed both to me and the truth. Your conduct is completely unpardonable, Engstrand. From now on I have nothing more to do with you.

ENGSTRAND: *(With a sigh.)* I suppose that's that.

PASTOR MANDERS: Yes. How can you possibly justify yourself now?

ENGSTRAND: But was she supposed to go around here making her shame even worse by talking about it? If the pastor could just imagine himself—for one moment—in poor Johanna's shoes—

PASTOR MANDERS: I?

ENGSTRAND: Oh Lord, I don't mean exactly the same shoes. But if the pastor had something to be ashamed of in the eyes of the world, as they say. We men shouldn't judge a poor woman too severely, Pastor.

PASTOR MANDERS: I'm not doing that. My reproach is for you and you alone.

ENGSTRAND: Do I have permission to ask the Pastor just one little question?

PASTOR MANDERS: Well, ask it.

ENGSTRAND: Isn't it right and proper for a man to raise up the fallen?

PASTOR MANDERS: Yes, of course.

ENGSTRAND: And a man's obliged to keep his word of honor, isn't he?

PASTOR MANDERS: Of course he is, but—

ENGSTRAND: When Johanna fell into her misfortune because of that Englishman—or maybe he was an American or a Russian, whatever they're called—well, that was when she came into town. Poor thing, she'd already turned me down a time or two before—she only had eyes for the handsome gentlemen, and I had this bum leg, you see—well, the pastor remembers how I took it upon myself to go into that dance hall where there was a drunken riot going on—and how when I tried to admonish those seafaring men, as they say, to turn over a new leaf—

MRS. ALVING: *(Over by the window.)* Hmm—

PASTOR MANDERS: I know, Engstrand—they threw you down the stairs. You've told me about that before. You bear your cross honorably.

ENGSTRAND: I don't pride myself on it, Pastor. But here's what I wanted to say: she came to me and confessed everything, crying and groaning and gnashing her teeth. I have to tell you, Pastor, it broke my heart to hear her.

PASTOR MANDERS: Did it really, Engstrand? So. What then?

ENGSTRAND: Well, I said to her. That American, he's off roaming the seven seas. And you, Johanna, I said, have sinned and are a fallen creature. But Jakob Engstrand, I said, he stands on his own two strong legs, and—well, in a manner of speaking, Pastor—

PASTOR MANDERS: I understand. Please go on.

ENGSTRAND: And that's how I raised her up righteously and married her so that no one would ever find out about her wild ways with foreigners.

PASTOR MANDERS: This was all very admirable on your part. But I still can't condone accepting money for—

ENGSTRAND: Money? Me? Not a bit.

PASTOR MANDERS: *(With a glance at Mrs. Alving.)* But—?

ENGSTRAND: Ah, ah, ah—wait a minute—yes, I remember now. Johanna had a little money with her. But I wouldn't have anything to do with it. Fie, Mammon, I said, the wages of sin! We'll throw this dirty gold—or bills, I can't remember what it was—right into that American's face, I said. But by then he was gone off across the wild oceans, Pastor.

PASTOR MANDERS: Was he, my dear Engstrand?

ENGSTRAND: That's right. And so Johanna and I agreed that the money should go for bringing up the child, and it did; I can give you an accurate account of every last penny.

PASTOR MANDERS: This changes things considerably.

ENGSTRAND: That's the way things are, Pastor. I think I can say I've been a good Father to Regina—as good as I could be, since unfortunately I'm a poor weak mortal—

PASTOR MANDERS: There, there, Engstrand—

ENGSTRAND: But I still think I can say I raised the child and built a loving home with my dear Johanna, as it is written. But it would never have occurred to me to go to Pastor Manders, priding myself on this and taking credit for having done a good deed for once in this world, no, no. When something like that happens to Jakob Engstrand, he keeps quiet about it. It's just too bad it doesn't happen very often. When I go to see Pastor Manders, it's all I can do to fit in everything weak and sinful—like I said, this conscience can be awfully tough on me sometimes.

PASTOR MANDERS: Give me your hand, Jakob Engstrand.

ENGSTRAND: Oh for heaven's sake, Pastor.

PASTOR MANDERS: Don't hang back. *(Grasps his hand.)* There now.

ENGSTRAND: And if I could dare the happiness of asking the Pastor's forgiveness—

PASTOR MANDERS: You! No, it's the other way around. I should beg your forgiveness.

ENGSTRAND: Oh, in God's name, no, no.

PASTOR MANDERS: Yes, I insist. With all my heart. Forgive me for misjudging you so completely. If I could only think of some sign of my remorse—something to show you my good will—

ENGSTRAND: Is that what the pastor wants?

PASTOR MANDERS: Yes, absolutely.

ENGSTRAND: Because there's a great opportunity for that right now. With the honest savings from my work out here I'm thinking of setting up some kind of seaman's home in town.

MRS. ALVING: You are!

ENGSTRAND: Yes—it'll be a kind of asylum, you might say. Temptations are legion for the seaman who wanders ashore. But in this house of mine, I was thinking, he could be under a watchful, fatherly eye.

PASTOR MANDERS: What about that, Mrs. Alving?

ENGSTRAND: I don't have a lot to start out with—may the Lord increase and multiply it—but if I could get a friendly helping hand—

PASTOR MANDERS: Yes, yes! Let's consider this idea thoroughly. Your project interests me greatly. Now go ahead and get everything ready—light the candles for the celebration. Then we can have an edifying hour together, Engstrand—now I really believe you're in the proper frame of mind.

ENGSTRAND: I think so too. Good–bye, Mrs. Alving, and thanks. Take extra good care of Regina for me. (*Brushes a tear from his eye.*) Dear Johanna's child—isn't it amazing—she's grown right into my own heart. Yes, she really has. (*He bows and leaves through the hall.*)

PASTOR MANDERS: Well—what do you have to say about the man now, Mrs. Alving? That was a completely different perspective on things, wasn't it?

MRS. ALVING: It certainly was.

PASTOR MANDERS: You see how incredibly careful you have to be when judging your fellow man. But it's such a great joy to discover that you've been in error. So then—what do you say?

MRS. ALVING: I say you are and will always be such a child, Pastor.

PASTOR MANDERS: I?

MRS. ALVING: (*Places both hands on his shoulders.*) And I also say I'd like to wrap you up in a big hug.

PASTOR MANDERS: (*Quickly retreating.*) No, no, God bless you. What an impulse!

MRS. ALVING: (*With a smile.*) Now, you mustn't be afraid of me.

PASTOR MANDERS: (*By the table.*) Sometimes you have the most extravagant means of expressing yourself. I'll just get these documents together and put them in my brief case. (*As he does so.*) There. Now good-bye for the time being. And when Osvald gets back, be on the alert. I'll look in on you later.

(*He takes his hat and goes out through the hall doorway. Mrs. Alving sighs, looks out the window a moment, tidies up a little in the room and starts to go into the dining room, but stops with a stifled cry in the doorway.*)

MRS. ALVING: Osvald—still at the table!

OSVALD: *(From the dining room.)* Just finishing my cigar.

MRS. ALVING: I thought you were taking a little walk up the road.

OSVALD: In this weather?

> *(A glass clinks. Mrs. Alving lets the door stay open and sits with her knitting on the sofa by the window.)*

OSVALD: *(Still inside.)* Wasn't that Pastor Manders?

MRS. ALVING: Yes. He went down to the Memorial.

OSVALD: Hmm.

> *(The glass and decanter clink again.)*

MRS. ALVING: *(With a worried look.)* Osvald dear, be careful with that liqueur. It's very strong.

OSVALD: It works wonders against the dampness.

MRS. ALVING: Don't you want to come in here with me?

OSVALD: But I can't smoke in there.

MRS. ALVING: You know you can smoke a cigar.

OSVALD: All right. I'll come in. Just a splash more. There. *(He enters the room with a cigar and closes the door after him.)* Where's the Pastor gone to?

MRS. ALVING: I told you he went down to the Memorial.

OSVALD: Oh yes. That's right.

MRS. ALVING: You shouldn't sit at the table so long, Osvald.

OSVALD: *(With the cigar behind his back.)* But it's so nice, Mother. *(Patting and fondling her.)* Just imagine what this is for me— coming home, sitting at my mother's own table, in my mother's room, eating my mother's wonderful food.

MRS. ALVING: My dear boy.

OSVALD: *(Somewhat impatiently, pacing and smoking.)* And what else can I do here? I can't get started on anything—

MRS. ALVING: You can't?

OSVALD: In this murk? Not a glimpse of sunlight all day. *(Paces around the room.)* And then this—not being able to work.

MRS. ALVING: Maybe you shouldn't have come home.

OSVALD: No, Mother. I had to.

MRS. ALVING: Because I'd ten times rather give up my happiness at having you here than—

OSVALD: *(Stopping by the table.)* Tell me, Mother—does my being home really make you that happy?

MRS. ALVING: Does it make me happy?!

OSVALD: *(Crumpling a newspaper.)* I'd have thought it was pretty much the same for you here, with me or without me.

MRS. ALVING: You have the heart to say that to your own mother, Osvald?

OSVALD: You got along without me very well before.

MRS. ALVING: Yes, I got along—that's true.

(*Silence. the twilight slowly increases, Osvald paces back and forth. He has set his cigar down.*)

OSVALD: (*Stops by Mrs. Alving.*) Mother, may I sit next to you?

MRS. ALVING: (*Making a place for him.*) Yes, my boy. Please do.

OSVALD: Now, Mother. I have something to tell you.

MRS. ALVING: (*Tense.*) Well?

OSVALD: (*Staring into space.*) I can't carry it around any longer.

MRS. ALVING: Carry what? What is it?

OSVALD: (*As before.*) I couldn't bring myself to write you about it, and since I came home—

MRS. ALVING: (*Gripping his arm.*) Osvald, what is this?

OSVALD: Yesterday and again today I tried to get rid of these thoughts—to break free. But it's no use.

MRS. ALVING: (*Rising.*) Now you've got to tell me, Osvald.

OSVALD: (*Pulls her down to the sofa again.*) Sit down, and I'll try. I've been complaining so much about being tired out by my trip—

MRS. ALVING: Yes? So what?

OSVALD: But that's not what's wrong with me—no ordinary tiredness—

MRS. ALVING: (*Tries to rise.*) You're not sick, Osvald!

OSVALD: (*Pulls her down again.*) Sit still, Mother. Just take it easy. I'm not exactly sick; not what you usually think of as sick, anyway. (*Puts his hand to his head.*) Mother, my mind is sick—broken down—I will never be able to work again. (*With his hands over his face he throws himself down in her lap and bursts into sobbing tears.*)

MRS. ALVING: Osvald! Look at me! No, this isn't true.

OSVALD: (*Looks up with despairing eyes.*) Never work again! Never—never! That's living death! Mother—can you imagine anything so horrible?

MRS. ALVING: My poor boy! How did this terrible thing happen to you?

OSVALD: (*Sitting up again.*) That's exactly what I can't figure out. I haven't lived a wild life. Not in any way. You mustn't think that of me, Mother—I've never done that!

MRS. ALVING: I didn't think so, Osvald.

OSVALD: And this happens to me anyway! This horrible thing.

MRS. ALVING: Everything will turn out right, my blessed boy. It's nothing more than overwork. Please believe me.

OSVALD: *(Heavily.)* That's what I thought at first—but it's not true.

MRS. ALVING: Tell me everything, beginning to end.

OSVALD: It started right after the last time I was home—just after I got back to Paris. I got this piercing pain in my head—mostly toward the back of the head, it seemed. Like an iron band was squeezing tight from the neck up—

MRS. ALVING: And then?

OSVALD: First I thought it was just my usual headaches again—the ones I've had off and on since I was fourteen or so.

MRS. ALVING: Yes, yes—

OSVALD: But that wasn't it. I realized that soon enough. I couldn't work any more. I'd start working on a new painting, a large canvas; but it was as if my powers had left me; my strength was paralyzed; I couldn't concentrate on any particular project; I felt giddy, things would swim in and out of focus. That was a horrible feeling. Finally I saw a doctor, and learned the truth.

MRS. ALVING: What do you mean?

OSVALD: He was one of the foremost doctors in Paris. He made me describe my symptoms; then he started asking me a whole series of questions that I didn't think had anything to do with my case—I couldn't understand what he was getting at.

MRS. ALVING: So—?

OSVALD: Finally he said, "You've been worm–eaten since birth."

MRS. ALVING: *(Tensely.)* What did he mean by that?

OSVALD: I didn't understand either—so I asked him to explain it more clearly. Then the old cynic said . . . *(Clenches his fist.)* Oh . . .

MRS. ALVING: Said what?

OSVALD: He said: "The sins of the fathers are visited on the children."

MRS. ALVING: *(Slowly rises up.)* The sins of the fathers—!

OSVALD: I almost hit him in the face—

MRS. ALVING: *(Walks across the room.)* The sins of the fathers—

OSVALD: *(Smiles sadly.)* Yes, what do you think of that? Of course I told him that was impossible. But he was adamant; only when I showed him your letters, and translated all the passages where you talked about Father—

MRS. ALVING: And then—?

OSVALD: Well, then he had to admit he was on the wrong track and I finally learned the truth. The incredible truth! This beautiful, blissful young life I was leading with my comrades—it was beyond my capacity. I should never have indulged in it. So I actually destroyed myself.

MRS. ALVING: Osvald! No! Don't think that way!

OSVALD: He said that no other explanation made any sense. That's the horrible thing. Wrecked—beyond cure—for the rest of my life—because of my own irresponsibility. Everything I wanted to do in the world—I don't even dare think about it any more—I can't let myself think about it. If I could only live my life over again—undo what I've done.

(He throws himself face down on the sofa. Mrs. Alving wrings her hands and walks in silent inner struggle. After a moment, Osvald looks up, propped up on his elbows.)

OSVALD: If only it was inherited—unavoidable—but this! To throw away health, happiness, everything in the world—the future—life itself!—on trivia!

MRS. ALVING: No, no, my blessed boy. This is impossible. *(Bending over him.)* Things aren't as desperate as you think.

OSVALD: Oh, what do you know? *(Jumps up.)* And on top of it all, Mother, to be causing you all this pain! Lately I've almost been wishing that you didn't care so much about me.

MRS. ALVING: Osvald—my only boy! The only thing I have in the world—the only thing I care about.

OSVALD: *(Holds both her hands and kisses them.)* Yes, yes—now I see. Now that I'm home, I see that you do. And that's one of the hardest things to bear. So—now you know. Now we won't talk about it any more today. I can't stand to think about it for very long. *(Walks around the room.)* Get me something to drink, Mother!

MRS. ALVING: Drink? What do you want to drink now?

OSVALD: Oh, whatever you have. Maybe there's some cold punch?

MRS. ALVING: Yes, but Osvald, my dear—!

OSVALD: Don't deny me this, Mother. Just be kind. I've got to have something to drown all these thoughts that keep nagging at me! *(Goes into the conservatory.)* And it's so dark here!

(Mrs. Alving pulls the bell-rope.)

OSVALD: This rain never stops. It can go on week after week; months at a time. Never a glimpse of sun. All the times I've been home, I can't ever remember seeing the sun shine.

MRS. ALVING: Osvald—you're thinking of leaving me.

OSVALD: Hmm—(*Sighs deeply.*) I'm not thinking of anything. I *can't* think of anything. (*In a low voice.*) I've given up on that.

REGINA: Did you ring, ma'am?

MRS. ALVING: Yes, bring the lamp in here.

REGINA: Right away, ma'am. It's already lit. (*Goes out.*)

MRS. ALVING: (*Goes over to Osvald.*) Osvald, don't hide anything from me!

OSVALD: I'm not, Mother. (*Goes to the table.*) I think I've told you a lot. (*Regina brings the lamp and sets it on the table.*)

MRS. ALVING: Oh, and Regina—you might bring us a half–bottle of champagne.

REGINA: All right, madam. (*Goes out again.*)

OSVALD: (*His arm around Mrs. Alving's neck.*) That's the way it should be. I knew my mother wouldn't let her boy go thirsty.

MRS. ALVING: Poor, dear Osvald—how can I deny you anything now?

OSVALD: (*Eagerly.*) Is that true, Mother? You mean it?

MRS. ALVING: What?

OSVALD: That you can't deny me anything?

MRS. ALVING: But Osvald—

OSVALD: Sssh!

(*Regina brings a tray with a half-bottle of champagne and two glasses, which she sets on the table.*)

REGINA: Should I open—?

OSVALD: No thank you, I'll do it myself.

(*Regina goes out again.*)

MRS. ALVING: (*Sitting at the table.*) What did you mean—about not denying you anything?

OSVALD: (*Busy opening the bottle.*) First a glass—or two. (*The cork pops. He fills one glass and is about to fill the other.*)

MRS. ALVING: Thanks, not for me.

OSVALD: No? More for me then! (*He empties the glass, refills it, empties it again, then sits at the table.*)

MRS. ALVING: (*Expectantly.*) Well?

OSVALD: (*Without looking at her.*) Listen—tell me—I thought you and Pastor Manders were awfully—hmm—quiet at dinner.

MRS. ALVING: You noticed?

OSVALD: Yes. Hmm—(*After a short silence.*) Tell me—what do you think of Regina?

MRS. ALVING: What do I think?

OSVALD: Yes. Isn't she magnificent?

MRS. ALVING: You don't know her as well as I do, Osvald—

OSVALD: So?

MRS. ALVING: Regina lived at home too long. I should have taken her in earlier.

OSVALD: Yes, but she's magnificent to look at, Mother. *(He fills his glass.)*

MRS. ALVING: Regina has problems, Osvald—some serious ones—

OSVALD: Yes? So what? *(Drinks again.)*

MRS. ALVING: But I'm fond of her anyway, and I'm responsible for her. Under no circumstances would I let anything happen to her.

OSVALD: *(Jumps up.)* Mother, Regina is my only hope.

MRS. ALVING: *(Rising.)* What do you mean?

OSVALD: I can't bear this agony all alone any more.

MRS. ALVING: Don't you have your mother to help you with it?

OSVALD: Yes, that's what I thought, that's why I came home. But it's not working. I can see it; it can't work. I can't have a life out here!

MRS. ALVING: Osvald!

OSVALD: I have to live a different way, Mother. That's why I've got to leave you. I don't want you to have to see all this.

MRS. ALVING: My unhappy child! Ah, Osvald, when you're as sick as you— –

OSVALD: If it were just the illness, I'd stay with you. You're the best friend I have in the world.

MRS. ALVING: That's true, Osvald, isn't it?

OSVALD: *(Uneasily paces around.)* But it's the agony, the torment, the remorse—and most of all—the sense of dread. This horrible dread.

MRS. ALVING: *(Following him.)* Dread? What do you mean?

OSVALD: Don't ask me—I don't know. I can't describe it.

(Mrs. Alving walks over and pulls the bell-rope.)

OSVALD: What's going on?

MRS. ALVING: I want my boy to be happy. He's not going to go around brooding. *(To Regina who has appeared at the door-way.)* More champagne—a whole bottle.

OSVALD: Mother!

MRS. ALVING: Don't you think we know how to live out here in the country?

OSVALD: Isn't she great looking? The way she's built—and so incredibly strong and healthy—

MRS. ALVING: *(Sitting by the table.)* Sit down, Osvald. Let's talk calmly together.

OSVALD: *(Sits.)* You probably don't know this—I have something to set straight with Regina. A wrong I did her.

MRS. ALVING: You!

OSVALD: You might just call it an indiscretion. Perfectly innocent, in fact. When I was home the last time—

MRS. ALVING: Yes?

OSVALD: —well, she kept asking me about Paris and I started describing how things are down there. One thing led to another and I remember I happened to say: "Would you like to go there yourself?"

MRS. ALVING: Well?

OSVALD: She turned blood-red and finally she said "Yes—I'd really like to do that.". "All right," I said, "that could probably be arranged."—or words to that effect.

MRS. ALVING: And then?

OSVALD: I'd forgotten the whole thing, of course, but the day before yesterday I asked her in passing if she was glad I would be home so long—

MRS. ALVING: Yes?

OSVALD: —and she looked at me strangely and asked "But what about my trip to Paris?"

MRS. ALVING: Her trip?

OSVALD: And then I got it out of her: she'd taken the whole thing seriously, she'd been up here thinking about me the whole time, started trying to learn French—

MRS. ALVING: So that's why—

OSVALD: Mother, when I saw that magnificent, beautiful, vivacious girl standing in front of me—until that moment I hadn't really noticed her—but now she was right there, arms open wide, ready to take me to her—

MRS. ALVING: Osvald!

OSVALD: —and then it came to me, all of a sudden—she was salvation. I saw the joy of life in her.

MRS. ALVING: The joy of life? There's salvation in that?

REGINA: *(Entering from the dining room with a bottle of champagne.)* I'm sorry it took so long, but I had to go down to the cellar— *(Sets the bottle on the table.)*

OSVALD: And bring another glass.

REGINA: *(Looks at him in surprise.)* Madam's glass is right there, Mr. Alving.

OSVALD: Yes—one for you, Regina.

(Regina starts. Throws a swift, timid glance at Mrs. Alving.)

OSVALD: Well?

REGINA: *(Softly, hesitantly.)* Does Madam—?

MRS. ALVING: Bring the glass, Regina.

(Regina goes into the dining room.)

OSVALD: *(Looking at her.)* Have you noticed the way she walks—so firm and fearless?

MRS. ALVING: This can't happen, Osvald!

OSVALD: It's decided. You must see that. There's no point discussing it.

(Regina enters with an empty glass which she keeps in her hands.)

OSVALD: Please have a seat, Regina.

(Regina looks inquiringly at Mrs. Alving.)

MRS. ALVING: Sit down, Regina.

(Regina sits on a chair near the dining room door, holding the empty glass in her hands.)

MRS. ALVING: Osvald—what were you saying about the joy of life?

OSVALD: Yes, Mother—the joy of life. You don't seem to know much about it. I never feel it here at home.

MRS. ALVING: Not even when you're home with me?

OSVALD: Not when I'm home at all. But you can't understand.

MRS. ALVING: Yes, yes—I think I'm close to understanding—now.

OSVALD: That and the joy of work as well. They're basically the same thing at heart. But none of you knows anything about that.

MRS. ALVING: You're probably right. Osvald, tell me more about it.

OSVALD: What I mean is that people here are taught that work is a curse—a punishment for sin—and that life's one long misery, to be gotten over with as soon as possible.

MRS. ALVING: Yes, a vale of misery. And we work hard at making it that way, with all our honorable and virtuous labors.

OSVALD: But that kind of thinking isn't accepted out there in the world. Nobody believes in that tradition any more. Out there people think it's pure bliss just to be alive. Mother, have you noticed that all my paintings spring from this joy of life? Every one—invariably—about the joy of life. Light and sunshine, and a holiday spirit—people's faces happy and glowing—and that's why I'm afraid to stay here with you at home.

MRS. ALVING: Afraid? What are you afraid of here?

OSVALD: I'm afraid of everything that's best in me degenerating into ugliness.

MRS. ALVING: *(Looks straight at him.)* You think *that* would happen?

OSVALD: I'm certain of it. Live the exact same way here as out there, and it still wouldn't be the same life.

MRS. ALVING: *(Who has been listening intently, rises with big, thoughtful eyes and says.)* Now I see how it all fits!

OSVALD: What do you see?

MRS. ALVING: I see it for the first time. And now I can speak.

OSVALD: *(Rising.)* Mother, I don't understand you.

REGINA: *(Who has also risen.)* Should I go?

MRS. ALVING: No, stay here. Now I can speak. Now, my boy, you're going to know everything. And then you can choose. Osvald! Regina!

OSVALD: Quiet—the pastor.

PASTOR MANDERS: *(Entering through the hall door.)* Ah, ah, ah—we've had a really heart–warming session down there.

OSVALD: So have we.

PASTOR MANDERS: Engstrand must be helped with his seaman's home. Regina will go with him, and give him a helping hand—

REGINA: No, thank you, Pastor.

PASTOR MANDERS: *(Noticing her for the first time.)* What—? Here. And with a glass in your hand?

REGINA: *(Quickly puts down the glass.)* Beg pardon!

OSVALD: Regina is going with me, Pastor.

PASTOR MANDERS: Going! With you!

OSVALD: Yes, as my wife—if she wants that.

PASTOR MANDERS: Good Lord—

REGINA: It's not my doing, Pastor.

OSVALD: Or she'll stay here, if I stay.

REGINA: *(Involuntarily.)* Here!

PASTOR MANDERS: Mrs. Alving, I'm astounded!

MRS. ALVING: None of these things will happen—because now I can speak out freely.

PASTOR MANDERS: You can't do that—! No, no, no!

MRS. ALVING: Yes, I can and will. And even so, not a single ideal will fall.

OSVALD: Mother, what are you hiding from me?

REGINA: *(Listening.)* Madam—listen! People are shouting out there. *(She goes into the garden room.)*

OSVALD: *(Going to the window, left.)* What's going on? Where's that light coming from?

REGINA: *(Crying out.)* Something's burning in the asylum!

PASTOR MANDERS: A fire? Impossible! I was just down there.

OSVALD: Where's my hat? Never mind—! Father's Memor—! *(He runs out through the garden door.)*

MRS. ALVING: My shawl, Regina! It's all in flames!

PASTOR MANDERS: Dreadful! Mrs. Alving, this is a fiery judgment on this wayward house!

MRS. ALVING: Yes, of course. Come on, Regina!

(She and Regina hurry out through the hall.)

PASTOR MANDERS: *(Clasping his hands.)* And no insurance! *(Goes out the same way.)*

END OF ACT TWO

ACT THREE

The room as before. All the doors stand open. The lamp still burns on the table. Dark outside, except for a faint glow of fire in the background left.

(Mrs. Alving, with a large shawl over her head, is standing in the garden room, looking out. Regina, also with a shawl, stands a little behind her.)

MRS. ALVING: Everything burned. Right to the ground.

REGINA: The basement's still burning.

MRS. ALVING: Where's Osvald? There's nothing left to save.

REGINA: Should I take his hat down to him?

MRS. ALVING: He doesn't even have his hat?

REGINA: *(Pointing to the hall.)* No, it's hanging up in there.

MRS. ALVING: Leave it. He's got to come up soon. I'll go look for him. *(She goes out through the garden door.)*

PASTOR MANDERS: *(Enters from the hall.)* Mrs. Alving's not here?

REGINA: She just went down to the garden.

PASTOR MANDERS: This is the most terrible night I've ever lived through.

REGINA: It's an awful piece of luck, isn't it Pastor?

PASTOR MANDERS: Don't talk about it! I can hardly even let myself think about it.

REGINA: How could it happen?

PASTOR MANDERS: Don't ask me, Miss Engstrand! How should I know? Are you also—? Isn't it enough that your Father—?

REGINA: What about him?

PASTOR MANDERS: He's about driven me out of my mind, that's what!

ENGSTRAND: *(Entering through the hall.)* Pastor—!

PASTOR MANDERS: *(Turning in terror.)* You're after me here too?

ENGSTRAND: Yes, God strike me dead, but it's what I have to do. Lord! this is a real mess, Pastor.

PASTOR MANDERS: *(Pacing back and forth.)* Terrible. Terrible.

ENGSTRAND: And all because of that prayer service down there. *(Softly to Regina.)* Now we've got him, girl! *(Aloud.)* And to think that it's my fault that Pastor Manders is to blame for something like this!

PASTOR MANDERS: But, Engstrand, I swear—

ENGSTRAND: Nobody but the pastor was in charge of those candles.

PASTOR MANDERS: *(Stopping.)* Yes. So you claim. But I absolutely cannot remember ever holding a candle in my hands.

ENGSTRAND: And I had such a clear view of how the Pastor took the candle, snuffed the flame with his fingers, and threw the wick down into some shavings.

PASTOR MANDERS: You saw that?

ENGSTRAND: Yes, I saw that for sure.

PASTOR MANDERS: That's what I find impossible to believe. I never snuff candles with my fingers.

ENGSTRAND: Yes, it looked horribly careless. But Pastor—is it really going to be that big a loss?

PASTOR MANDERS: *(Pacing uneasily back and forth.)* Oh, don't ask me!

ENGSTRAND: *(Walking with him.)* Not insured. And then to walk over there and set fire to the whole heap. Lord, oh Lord, what a mess!

PASTOR MANDERS: *(Wiping his brow.)* Yes, Engstrand, you can certainly say that again.

ENGSTRAND: And for something like this to happen to a charitable institution—a place that, so to speak, was to serve the whole community. I don't suppose the papers will handle you too gently.

PASTOR MANDERS: No, that's exactly what I'm thinking. That's almost the worst thing about this whole business. All those attacks and insinuations—it's too awful to think about!

MRS. ALVING: *(Entering from the garden.)* He won't be talked into leaving the ruins.

PASTOR MANDERS: Ah, Mrs. Alving. There you are.

MRS. ALVING: So you didn't have to make your speech, Pastor Manders.

PASTOR MANDERS: Oh, I would have been only too glad—

MRS. ALVING: *(Subdued.)* What's done is done, and for the best. This "Home" would not have turned out a blessing to anyone.

PASTOR MANDERS: You don't think so?

MRS. ALVING: You *do* think so?

PASTOR MANDERS: Still, it was a terrible disaster.

MRS. ALVING: We'll treat it as a business matter, that's all. Engstrand, are you waiting for the pastor?

ENGSTRAND: *(By the hall door.)* Yes, as a matter of fact, I am.

MRS. ALVING: Well, just sit there for the time being.

ENGSTRAND: Thanks, I'd just as soon stand.

MRS. ALVING: *(To Manders.)* You'll be taking the next steamer?

PASTOR MANDERS: Yes—it leaves in an hour.

MRS. ALVING: Would you be good enough to take all the paperwork back with you? I don't want to hear one more word about any of it. I've got other things to think about—

PASTOR MANDERS: Mrs. Alving—

MRS. ALVING: Later I'll send you full authorization to arrange everything as you see fit.

PASTOR MANDERS: I'll gladly see to that, of course. The original terms of the bequest, unfortunately, will have to be modified.

MRS. ALVING: That's understood.

PASTOR MANDERS: Yes. I think that for the moment, I could arrange it so that the Solvik estate can be turned over to the parish. The land certainly can't be written off as worthless, it can always be put to some good use. And as for the interest on the capital in the bank, perhaps I could find some venture to support with it— something that would benefit the town.

MRS. ALVING: Whatever you want. I'm not interested in any of it.

ENGSTRAND: Think about my seamen's home, Pastor!

PASTOR MANDERS: Yes, you may have something there—well, it must all be carefully considered.

ENGSTRAND: Why the devil do you have to consider—aw, Lord.

PASTOR MANDERS: (With a sigh.) And unfortunately, I don't know how long I'll be able to remain in charge. Public opinion might compel me to resign. It all depends on the findings of the official inquiry into the fire.

MRS. ALVING: What?

PASTOR MANDERS: And those findings can't be predicted in any way.

ENGSTRAND: (Edging closer.) Oh yes they can. Because Jakob Engstrand's here.

PASTOR MANDERS: Yes, yes, but—

ENGSTRAND: (In a low voice.) And Jakob Engstrand's not the man to abandon a worthy benefactor in his hour of need, as they say.

PASTOR MANDERS: But—my good—how?

ENGSTRAND: Jakob Engstrand's a ministering angel, Pastor, yes he is!

PASTOR MANDERS: No, no, I couldn't possibly accept that.

ENGSTRAND: Ah, but that's how it'll be, all the same. I know somebody who's taken the blame for somebody else once before, yes I do.

PASTOR MANDERS: Jakob! (Shakes his hand.) You are a rare individual. Well, you'll get your support for your seamen's home; you can count on it.

(Engstrand tries to thank him, but is so choked up with emotion that he can't.)

PASTOR MANDERS: *(Slings his traveling bag over his shoulder.)* So, we're off. We'll travel together.

ENGSTRAND: *(By the dining room door, softly to Regina.)* Follow me, girl! You'll be as cozy as the yolk in an egg.

REGINA: *(Tosses her head.) Merci!*

(She goes out into the hall and fetches the pastor's traveling things.)

PASTOR MANDERS: Good-bye, Mrs. Alving. May the spirit of law and order find an open door into this house.

MRS. ALVING: Good-bye, Manders!

(She goes into the garden room as she sees Osvald enter through the garden door.)

ENGSTRAND: *(While he and Regina help the pastor with his coat.)* Good-bye, my girl. If anything happens to you, you know where to find Jakob Engstrand. *(Quietly.)* Little Harbor Street—! *(To Mrs. Alving and Osvald.)* And my establishment for wayfaring sailors—I'll call it "Captain Alving's Home," that's right. And if I get to run things the way I want, I promise you it'll be a worthy memorial to the sainted Captain.

PASTOR MANDERS: *(In the doorway.)* Hmm—hmm! Come on now, my dear Engstrand. Good-bye, good-bye!

(Pastor Manders and Engstrand go out through the garden door.)

OSVALD: *(Goes over to the table.)* What was this establishment he was talking about?

MRS. ALVING: Some kind of home that he and the pastor want to start.

OSVALD: It'll burn down, just like this one.

MRS. ALVING: What makes you say that?

OSVALD: Everything will burn. Nothing of Father's memory will remain. And here I am, burning up too.

(Regina looks at him in astonishment.)

MRS. ALVING: Osvald! My poor boy, you shouldn't have stayed down there so long.

OSVALD: *(Sits at the table.)* I almost think you're right about that.

MRS. ALVING: Let me dry your face, Osvald. You're still wet.

OSVALD: *(Looking indifferently in front of himself.)* Thank you, Mother.

MRS. ALVING: Are you tired? Do you want to sleep?

OSVALD: *(Fearfully.)* No, no—no sleep! I never sleep. I only pretend to. *(Dully.)* Soon enough, soon enough.

MRS. ALVING: Yes, my dear, dear boy, you're really ill after all.

REGINA: *(Tense.)* Is Mr. Alving ill?

OSVALD: (*Impatiently.*) Now shut the doors! This deathly fear—

MRS. ALVING: Shut them, Regina.

(*Regina shuts the doors and remains standing by the hall door. Mrs. Alving takes off her shawl. Regina does the same.*)

MRS. ALVING: (*Pulls a chair up to Osvald and sits beside him.*) There, now I'm here beside you—

OSVALD: Yes, that's good, and Regina should be here too. Regina will always be near me. You'll give me a helping hand, Regina. You will, won't you?

REGINA: I don't understand—

MRS. ALVING: Helping hand?

OSVALD: When it becomes necessary.

MRS. ALVING: Osvald, isn't your mother right here to give you a helping hand?

OSVALD: You? (*Smiles.*) No, Mother, I don't think you'd ever give me the hand I need. (*Laughs dully.*) You! (*Looks earnestly at her.*) And yet you're certainly the closest one. (*Vehemently.*) Regina, why can't you be easier with me? Why won't you call me Osvald?

REGINA: (*Softly.*) I don't think Mrs. Alving would like it.

MRS. ALVING: You'll have every right to in a little while. So sit here with us—yes, you too.

(*Regina sits modestly and hesitantly at the other side of the table.*)

MRS. ALVING: Now, my poor, suffering boy. Now I'll get rid of this burden on your mind—

OSVALD: You, Mother?

MRS. ALVING: All your self-reproach and remorse and blame—

OSVALD: You think you can?

MRS. ALVING: Yes, Osvald, now I can. You were talking before about the joy of life. Right then it was as if new light began to shine on my whole existence.

OSVALD: (*Shaking his head.*) I don't understand any of this.

MRS. ALVING: You should have known your father when he was just a young lieutenant. You could certainly see the joy of life in him!

OSVALD: That much I know.

MRS. ALVING: Just to look at him was like a sunny day. All that untamed energy, all that vitality!

OSVALD: And so?

MRS. ALVING: And so this child, born out of the joy of life—and he was like a child then—he had to go around here in this perfectly average town—no real joy to offer, only the usual pleasures. He had to try to live without goals, just bogged down in endless paperwork. There was nothing here to challenge his soul, nothing engaged his heart—it was all just routine business. He didn't have a single comrade who had any idea about the joy of life, only loafers and drunks—

OSVALD: Mother!

MRS. ALVING: And so what had to happen, happened.

OSVALD: What had to happen?

MRS. ALVING: You said yourself earlier what would happen to you if you stayed here.

OSVALD: Are you trying to say that Father—

MRS. ALVING: Your poor father could never find any outlet for the overwhelming joy of life in him. And I'm afraid I didn't bring any sunshine into his home either.

OSVALD: No?

MRS. ALVING: No, they'd made me learn all about duty and such, and I went around here believing in those things for the longest time. Everything came down to duty—*my* duties, *his* duties—and, well, I'm afraid I made this house unbearable for your poor father.

OSVALD: Why haven't you ever written me about this?

MRS. ALVING: Until today I've never seen it as something to be discussed with his son.

OSVALD: How did you see it?

MRS. ALVING: *(Slowly.)* I saw only one thing: that your father was a broken man before you were born.

OSVALD: *(In a smothered voice.)* Ah—!*(He gets up and goes to the window.)*

MRS. ALVING: And every day, I had one thought on my mind. That Regina, in all honesty, belonged here in this house—as much as my own son.

OSVALD: *(Turns swiftly.)* Regina!

REGINA: *(Springing up and asking, in a choked voice.)* Me—!

MRS. ALVING: Yes. Now both of you know.

OSVALD: Regina!

REGINA: *(To herself.)* So my mother was—

MRS. ALVING: Your mother was good in many ways, Regina.

REGINA: Yes, but all the same she was like *that*. I've often thought it—well, madam, may I have permission to leave right now?

MRS. ALVING: Do you really want to, Regina?

REGINA: Yes, I certainly do!

MRS. ALVING: Of course, you have to do what you want, but—

OSVALD: *(Goes to Regina.)* You're leaving? But you belong here.

REGINA: *Merci*, Mr. Alving. Oh—I guess I can call you Osvald now. But this certainly isn't the way I planned to.

MRS. ALVING: Regina, I know I haven't been completely open with you—

REGINA: No, you can say that again! If I'd known that Osvald was sick—and anyway now there can't be anything serious between us—no, I really can't stay out here in the country working myself to death for invalids.

OSVALD: Not even someone so close to you?

REGINA: Not if I can help it. A poor girl's got her youth, that's all. If she doesn't make something out of it, she'll find herself out in the cold before she knows what hit her. And *I've* got the joy of life in me, ma'am!

MRS. ALVING: Yes, I'm afraid you do. But don't throw yourself away.

REGINA: Oh, if it happens it happens. Osvald takes after his father, I guess I take after my mother. May I ask madam if Pastor Manders knows anything about this?

MRS. ALVING: Pastor Manders knows everything.

REGINA: Well, I'd better make sure I get on that steamer as fast as I can. The pastor's so easy to get along with—and I really think I've got as much right to some of that money as he does—that filthy carpenter.

MRS. ALVING: You're welcome to it, Regina

REGINA: *(Looking sharply at her.)* You could have brought me up like a gentleman's daughter—that would have been a better fit. *(Tosses her head.)* But what the hell—it's all the same! *(With a bitter glance at the unopened bottle.)* I'll be drinking champagne in the best society, wait and see.

MRS. ALVING: If you ever need a home, Regina, come to me.

REGINA: No thank you ma'am. Pastor Manders will take care of me. And if that doesn't work out, I know a house where I'll always be welcome.

MRS. ALVING: Where's that?

REGINA: Captain Alving's Home.

MRS. ALVING: Regina, I can see it now—you're heading for disaster.

REGINA: Ah—ffft! *Adieu! (She nods and goes out through the hall.)*

OSVALD: *(Standing by the window, looking out.)* Is she gone?

MRS. ALVING: Yes.

OSVALD: *(Muttering to himself.)* It's all insane.

MRS. ALVING: *(Goes over behind him and lays her hands on his shoulders.)* Osvald—my dear boy—all this has given you an awful shock, hasn't it?

OSVALD: *(Turning his face towards her.)* About Father, you mean?

MRS. ALVING: Yes, your unfortunate father. I'm afraid it's been too much for you.

OSVALD: How can you think that? It was a surprise, of course—but finally it can't make much difference to me.

MRS. ALVING: *(Withdrawing her hands.)* No difference—that your father was so incredibly unhappy?

OSVALD: Naturally I'm sympathetic, as I would be for anyone else, but—

MRS. ALVING: And that's all? For your own father.

OSVALD: Oh yes, Father, Father! I never knew anything about my father. All I remember is the time he made me throw up.

MRS. ALVING: That's terrible, to think like that! Shouldn't a child love his father no matter what?

OSVALD: When the child had nothing to thank his father for? Never knew him? You're so enlightened in so many ways—can you really cling to that old superstition?

MRS. ALVING: You say it's only a superstition?

OSVALD: Yes—you see that, Mother, I'm sure. It's just one of those ideas that gets started in the world and then—

MRS. ALVING: *(Shaken.)* Ghosts!

OSVALD: *(Walks across the floor.)* Yes, you certainly could call them ghosts.

MRS. ALVING: *(Crying out.)* Osvald—then you don't love me either!

OSVALD: But at least I know you.

MRS. ALVING: Yes—but that's all?

OSVALD: And I know how much you care for me and I'm very grateful for that. You can be enormously useful to me now that I'm sick.

MRS. ALVING: Yes, I can, Osvald, can't I! I could almost bless this illness that drove you home to me. Because now I can see it: I don't have you yet, I'll have to win you.

OSVALD: *(Impatiently.)* Yes, yes, yes. This is all just talk. Remember I'm a sick man, Mother. I can't worry about others; I have enough to do just thinking about myself.

MRS. ALVING: *(Softly.)* I'll be patient and calm.

OSVALD: And cheerful, Mother!

MRS. ALVING: Yes, my dear, dear boy, you're right. *(Goes over to him.)* Now have I taken away all your remorse? No more reproaching yourself?

OSVALD: Yes, you have. But who will take away the dread?

MRS. ALVING: Dread?

OSVALD: *(Walks across the room.)* Regina would have done it at a word from me.

MRS. ALVING: I don't understand. What's this about dread—and Regina?

OSVALD: Is it late, Mother?

MRS. ALVING: Early morning. *(Looking out through the garden room.)* Up in the mountains the day is beginning to break. And it's going to be a clear day, Osvald! In a little while you'll get to see the sun.

OSVALD: That'll be a joy. Oh, there can be so much to live for—

MRS. ALVING: Yes, I know!

OSVALD: And even if I can't work—

MRS. ALVING: Oh, you'll be able to work again soon. Now that you don't have to brood about these depressing ideas any more.

OSVALD: No, that's true. It's good that you could knock down all those delusions of mine. And when I get rid of this one last thing—*(Sits on the sofa.)* Now, Mother, we've got to have a talk.

MRS. ALVING: All right. *(She pushes an armchair over to the sofa and sits beside him.)*

OSVALD: And then the sun will rise. And then you'll know. And then I'll no longer have this dread.

MRS. ALVING: What will I know? Tell me.

OSVALD: *(Not listening to her.)* Mother, didn't you say that you'd do anything for me, anything in the world, if I asked you?

MRS. ALVING: That's what I said.

OSVALD: Do you stand by that?

MRS. ALVING: You can depend on it, my only boy. You're what I live for now, nothing else.

OSVALD: All right. Now you'll hear it. Mother, you have a strong mind, I know you can take this in—so now you must sit calmly while you hear what it is.

MRS. ALVING: What could be so horrible?

OSVALD: And don't scream. You hear me? Promise me that? We'll sit and talk about it quietly. Promise me that, Mother?

MRS. ALVING: Yes, yes. I promise—just tell me!

OSVALD: Well, all this talk about my being tired—about not being able to think about work—that isn't the illness, only the symptoms.

MRS. ALVING: What is the illness?

OSVALD: The illness I received as my inheritance—*(Points to his forehead.)* It sits right here.

MRS. ALVING: *(Almost speechless.)* Osvald! No, no!

OSVALD: Don't scream. I can't stand it. Yes, Mother, it sits right here, lurking, ready to break out any day, any time.

MRS. ALVING: Horrible!

OSVALD: Just be calm. That's how it is with me.

MRS. ALVING: *(Jumping up.)* It's not true, Osvald! It's impossible! It can't be!

OSVALD: I had one attack down there, it didn't last long. But when I found out what had happened to me, this dread began pursuing me, relentlessly, and so I started back home to you as fast as I could.

MRS. ALVING: And that's the dread—!

OSVALD: Yes, it's revolting beyond words. Don't you see that? Some plain old terminal disease I could—I'm not afraid of dying, even though I'd like to live as long as I can.

MRS. ALVING: Yes, Osvald—you've got to!

OSVALD: But this is beyond disgusting. To be turned into a helpless child again—to have to be fed, to have to be—it's unspeakable!

MRS. ALVING: My child has his mother to take care of him.

OSVALD: *(Leaps up.)* Never, that's exactly what I don't want. I can't stand the idea of lying there for years like that, turning old and gray. And meanwhile you might die before me. *(Sits in Mrs. Alving's chair.)* The doctor said it wouldn't necessarily be fatal right away. He called it a kind of softening of the brain, or something like that. *(Smiles sadly.)* I think that sounds so charming—it always make me think of red velvet curtains—something soft and delicate to stroke.

MRS. ALVING: *(Screaming.)* Osvald!

OSVALD: *(Leaps up again and walks across the room.)* And now you've taken Regina away from me! If only I had her. She'd have given me a helping hand, yes she would.

MRS. ALVING: *(Goes over to him.)* What do you mean, my boy? What help is there in the world that I wouldn't give you?

OSVALD: When I'd recovered from my attack down there, the doctor told me that when it came again—and it will come again—that then it'd be beyond hope.

MRS. ALVING: He was heartless enough to—

OSVALD: I demanded it. I told him I had plans to make—*(Smiles slyly.)*

And so I had. *(Takes a little box from his inside breast pocket.)* See this, Mother?

MRS. ALVING: What is it?

OSVALD: Morphine powder.

MRS. ALVING: *(Looks at him in horror.)* Osvald—my boy!

OSVALD: I've managed to save twelve capsules.

MRS. ALVING: *(Grabbing for it.)* Give me the box, Osvald!

OSVALD: Not yet, Mother! *(He puts it back in his pocket.)*

MRS. ALVING: I can't live through this!

OSVALD: You have to live through it. If Regina were here I'd have told her how things are, and begged her for this last bit of help. And she would have helped me, I'm sure of it.

MRS. ALVING: Never!

OSVALD: When the horrible thing happened, and she saw me lying there like an imbecile, like a child, helpless, lost, beyond hope of rescue—

MRS. ALVING: Regina would never have done that!

OSVALD: Regina would have done it! She was so splendid, so light-hearted, she would have gotten tired pretty fast of looking after an invalid like me.

MRS. ALVING: Well then. Give thanks that Regina's not here!

OSVALD: So—now you have to give me that helping hand, Mother.

MRS. ALVING: *(With a loud scream.)* I!

OSVALD: Who else? Who's closer?

MRS. ALVING: I! Your Mother!

OSVALD: Exactly why.

MRS. ALVING: I, who gave you life!

OSVALD: I didn't ask you for life. And what kind of life have you given me? I don't want it. Take it back!

MRS. ALVING: Help, help! *(She runs into the hall.)*

OSVALD: *(Pursuing her.)* Don't leave me! Where are you going?

MRS. ALVING: *(In the hall.)* To get the doctor, Osvald! Let me go!

OSVALD: *(In the hall.)* You're not leaving. And no one's coming in. *(A key is turned in a lock.)*

MRS. ALVING: *(Coming in again.)* Osvald! Osvald!—my child!

OSVALD: *(Following her.)* Where's your Mother's heart? Can you stand to see me suffer this unspeakable dread?

MRS. ALVING: *(After a moment's silence, says firmly.)* Here's my hand on it.

OSVALD: Will you—?

MRS. ALVING: If necessary. But it won't be necessary. No, never—it's not possible!

OSVALD: Well, let's hope so. And let's live together as long as we can. Thank you, Mother.

(He sits in the armchair that Mrs. Alving had moved over to the sofa. The day is breaking. The lamp is still burning on the table.)

MRS. ALVING: *(Approaching him cautiously.)* Do you feel more at peace now?

OSVALD: Yes.

MRS. ALVING: *(Bends over him.)* You've been carrying a terrible delusion inside, Osvald—but it was all a delusion. Of course you couldn't bear all these agonies. But now you'll get your rest, here at home with your mother, my blessed boy. Anything you want, anything you point out to me, you'll have it! Just like when you were a little child. See, there. The sickness is gone—see how easily it went away! I knew it would. And look, Osvald, what a beautiful day we're going to have. Brilliant sunshine. Now you can really see your home.

(She goes over to the table and puts out the lamp. Sunrise. The glaciers and peaks in the background lie in brilliant morning light.)

OSVALD: *(Sits in the armchair with his back to this view, without stirring. Suddenly he says.)* Mother, give me the sun.

MRS. ALVING: *(By the table, looks at him, startled.)* What did you say?

OSVALD: *(Repeats dully and tonelessly.)* The sun. The sun.

MRS. ALVING: *(Goes over to him.)* Osvald, what's the matter with you?

(Osvald seems to shrink in the chair. All the muscles loosen. His face is expressionless. His eyes stare vacantly.)

MRS. ALVING: *(Shaking in terror.)* What is this? *(Screams loudly.)* Osvald! What's the matter with you! *(Throws herself down on her knees beside him and shakes him.)* Osvald! Osvald! Look at me! Don't you know me!

OSVALD: *(Tonelessly, as before.)* The sun. The sun.

MRS. ALVING: *(Springs up in anguish. Tears at her hair with both hands and screams.)* This is unbearable! *(Whispers as though terrified.)* Unbearable! Never! *(Suddenly.)* Where did he put them? *(Fumbling hastily in his pocket.)* Here! *(Retreats a few steps and screams.)* No, no, no!—Yes! No, no! *(She stands a few steps from him, her hands clutching her hair, staring at him in speechless horror.)*

OSVALD: *(Sits motionless as before, and says.)* The sun. The sun.

END OF PLAY

An Enemy
Of The People

An Enemy of the People was originally produced in the 1989/90 theatrical season at the Center Stage in Baltimore, MD, under the direction of Stan Wojewodski, Jr. The cast was as follows in order of appearance:

Mrs. Stockmann	Kristin Griffith
Billing	Mark Niebuhr
Mayor Stockmann	Derek D. Smith
Hovstad	Armand Schultz
Doctor Stockmann	Kent Broadhurst
Captain Hoster	Mark Wilson
*Eilif Stockmann	Thibault Manekin
	Lance Tinstman
*Morten Stockmann	Justin Durel
	Christopher Montgomery
Petra Stockmann	Katy Selverstone
Morten Kiil	William Hardy
Aslaksen	Wil Love
Townspeople	Keith Allaway
	Linda Cavell
	Brian Chetelat
	Bill Hughes
	Maud Dulany Jones
	Richard Kirstel
	Chris Lamb
	Russell Muth
	Karl Otter
	Bernie Papure
	Matt Ramsey
	Jeff Roberts
	Harry Susser

* alternating performances

An Enemy Of The People

Evening in the doctor's living room which is simply but pleasantly furnished and decorated. In the side wall to the right are two doors, of which the furthest leads out to the hallway and the nearest to the doctor's study. In the opposite wall directly facing the hall door is a door to the family's remaining rooms. In the middle of this wall stands the stove, and nearer to the foreground (downstage) is a sofa with a mirror above it. In front of it is an oval table covered with a cloth on which a shaded lamp is burning. In the back wall, an open door to the dining room. The table is laid for supper. There is a lighted lamp on the table.

(Billing sits at the dining table with a napkin under his chin. Mrs. Stockmann stands by the table and serves him a plate with a large piece of beef. The other places at the table are empty; the settings are in disorder, as if after a meal.)

MRS. STOCKMANN: Well, Mr. Billing, when you're an hour late, you have to expect a cold supper.

BILLING: No, it's perfectly delicious.

MRS. STOCKMANN: You know how particular my husband is about being on time for meals.

BILLING: I don't mind a bit. In fact I almost think it tastes better this way—when I can eat in peace.

MRS. STOCKMANN: Well, if that's the way you like it—(*Listening in the direction of the door.*) That must be Mr. Hovstad now too.

BILLING: Probably.

(Mayor Stockmann enters wearing an overcoat, and with his mayor's hat and stick.)

MAYOR STOCKMANN: My dear Katherine: good evening.

MRS. STOCKMANN: Oh, Peter, it's you! Good evening. It's nice of you to come by.

MAYOR STOCKMANN: I was in the area, so—(*Glancing into the dining room.*) Oh—you have company already.

MRS. STOCKMANN: Oh, no, not really—only by chance. (*Hurriedly.*) Why don't you go in and have a bite?

MAYOR STOCKMANN: Me? Heavens, no! Hot food in the evening—not with my stomach.

MRS. STOCKMANN: Just this once?

MAYOR STOCKMANN: No, no. I stick to my tea, and bread and butter. It's healthier in the long run—and more economical.

MRS. STOCKMANN: (*Smiling.*) Now, don't get the idea that Thomas and I are so extravagant!

MAYOR STOCKMANN: Not you, Katherine. That never entered my mind. (*Points toward the Doctor's study.*) He's not home then?

MRS. STOCKMANN: No, he and the boys went for a little after-dinner walk.

MAYOR STOCKMANN: I wonder—is that healthy for them? (*Listens.*) There he is now.

MRS. STOCKMANN: No, that can't be him. (*A knock on the door.*) Come in! (*Hovstad, the editor, comes in from the hallway.*)

MRS. STOCKMANN: Ah, Mr. Hovstad.

HOVSTAD: Yes, I'm sorry, I got held up at the printer's. Good evening, Mr. Mayor.

MAYOR STOCKMANN: (*Greeting him stiffly.*) Mr. Editor. Here on business, no doubt?

HOVSTAD: Partly. Something we might run in the paper.

MAYOR STOCKMANN: I can imagine. My brother's become quite a fertile contributor to *The People's Herald*—or so I hear, anyway.

HOVSTAD: Yes, he allows himself to write for the *Herald* when he wants to tell the plain truth about something.

MRS. STOCKMANN: (*To Hovstad.*) Won't you—(*Points to the dining room.*)

MAYOR STOCKMANN: And why shouldn't he? I don't blame him for writing for a sympathetic audience. And as far as I'm concerned, I've got no reason to hold anything against your paper, Mr. Hovstad.

HOVSTAD: That's what I think.

MAYOR STOCKMANN: Overall, there's a wonderfully tolerant spirit in our town—a public spirit. And it springs from our having a great common enterprise that unites us all—an enterprise that holds every right-minded citizen to the same high standard.

HOVSTAD: Yes—the baths.

MAYOR STOCKMANN: Precisely. We have a splendid new institution in our town, Mr. Hovstad. Those baths will become our main source of life, no doubt about it.

MRS. STOCKMANN: That's what Thomas always says.

MAYOR STOCKMANN: Just remember what this town was like two years ago! Now people have some money—there's life, there's activity! Property values are going up every day.

HOVSTAD: And unemployment's down.

MAYOR STOCKMANN: Yes, that too. So there's less of a drain on the property owners, thank God—and there'll be even fewer welfare cases if we have a really good summer this year—a real tourist invasion—crowds of invalids to give the baths a reputation.

HOVSTAD: And that's the forecast, I hear.

MAYOR STOCKMANN: All the signs are encouraging. Every day we get a flood of inquiries about reservations and accommodations and so on.

HOVSTAD: That makes the Doctor's article all the more timely.

MAYOR STOCKMANN: Has he written something new?

HOVSTAD: No, this is a piece he wrote during the winter—it's a recommendation for the baths; it tells exactly why our way of life here is so healthful. But I held the article back at the time.

MAYOR STOCKMANN: Ah! Something the matter with it, no doubt.

HOVSTAD: No, not that—I thought it would be better to run it now, in the spring—when people are starting to plan their summer vacations.

MAYOR STOCKMANN: Of course! Absolutely right, Mr. Hovstad.

MRS. STOCKMANN: Yes, Thomas can't do enough where the baths are concerned.

MAYOR STOCKMANN: Well, that's why he's there.

HOVSTAD: And of course he created the project in the first place.

MAYOR STOCKMANN: Really? You know I hear that once in a while in certain circles—but I was under the impression that *I* had a little something to do with it too.

MRS. STOCKMANN: That's what Thomas always says.

HOVSTAD: Who would ever say anything different, Mr. Mayor? Everyone knows you set the whole thing in motion, made it a practical reality—I just meant it was the Doctor's idea.

MAYOR STOCKMANN: Ideas, yes—my brother, unfortunately, has had plenty of those in his day. But when something needs doing, you have to find another sort of man, Mr. Hovstad. And I would have thought that here, in this house at least—

MRS. STOCKMANN: But Peter, dear—

HOVSTAD: Mr. Mayor, how can you—

MRS. STOCKMANN: Go in and have a bite to eat, Mr. Hovstad. My husband will be back any second now.

MAYOR STOCKMANN: (*Somewhat lower.*) Funny thing—these people who come from peasant stock never seem to learn tact.

MRS. STOCKMANN: But why get upset about it? Can't you and Thomas share the honor like brothers?

MAYOR STOCKMANN: Well, I'd have thought so—but it looks like not everyone's happy with his share.

MRS. STOCKMANN: That's nonsense. You and Thomas get along perfectly well on this. (*Listens.*) There he is, I think! (*She goes over and opens the hall door.*)

DOCTOR STOCKMANN: (*Laughing and making a commotion.*) Look, Katherine, you've got another guest. Isn't this great? Here we are, Captain Horster. Hang your coat here. Ah—no coat. Would you believe it, Katherine, I ran into him on the street and almost couldn't get him to come along with me.

(*Captain Horster enters, greets Mrs. Stockmann. Doctor Stockmann appears in the doorway.*)

In you go, boys. Starving again already, darling. All right, Captain Horster, this way—now you'll get a taste of roast beef!

(*Doctor Stockmann propels Horster into the dining room. Eilif and Morten also go in.*)

MRS. STOCKMANN: But Thomas, dear, don't you see—?

DOCTOR STOCKMANN: Oh, Peter! (*Shakes hands.*) Well, this is really a pleasure.

MAYOR STOCKMANN: Unfortunately I have to be going in just a minute.

DOCTOR STOCKMANN: Nonsense. Any second now there'll be liqueurs for everyone. You didn't forget, did you Katherine?

MRS. STOCKMANN: Certainly not.

MAYOR STOCKMANN: Liqueurs, as well?

DOCTOR STOCKMANN: Yes, yes! Now, everyone make yourselves at home.

MAYOR STOCKMANN: Thanks, but I won't indulge.

DOCTOR STOCKMANN: We're not "indulging," Peter.

MAYOR STOCKMANN: Well, it seems to me—(*Glancing toward the dining room.*) It's unbelievable how they manage to eat so much.

DOCTOR STOCKMANN: (*Rubbing his hands.*) Yes—isn't it fantastic to watch young people eat? Always hungry, and that's how it should be. They need their strength. They're the ones who'll shake things up in the years ahead, Peter.

MAYOR STOCKMANN: May I ask what exactly needs "shaking up" here, as you put it?

DOCTOR STOCKMANN: You'll have to ask the younger generation about that—when the time comes. Naturally, we can't see it, a couple of old fossils like us.

MAYOR STOCKMANN: Really! That's a strange way to describe—

DOCTOR STOCKMANN: Don't take me so literally. Oh, I'm so happy and excited, Peter—I feel so indescribably lucky to be right at the center of this extraordinary explosion of life—what an age to be alive in! It's as if a whole new world were being born all around us!

MAYOR STOCKMANN: You see it that way?

DOCTOR STOCKMANN: Of course you can't see it as clearly as I can. You've been right here, in the middle, so you don't notice it any more. But just think of me, stuck up there in the grey north all those years, out of the way of anybody with anything resembling a new idea—for me it's like I've suddenly been dropped into a great world metropolis.

MAYOR STOCKMANN: Metropolis—really!

DOCTOR STOCKMANN: Oh, I know this is small–scale stuff compared to a lot of places—but there's life here, there's promise, there're countless things to work on and fight for—that's the main thing. (*Calls.*) Katherine—did the mailman come?

MRS. STOCKMANN: (*In the dining room.*) No, not yet.

DOCTOR STOCKMANN: And finally to have some money, Peter—you learn to value that after you've lived on starvation wages for a while.

MAYOR STOCKMANN: Now—

DOCTOR STOCKMANN: Yes, yes, it's true. We had it pretty bad up there. But now, to be able to live like a real citizen! Like today, for example—roast beef for lunch, and again for supper! Don't you want a piece? At least come look at it—here, let me show you—

MAYOR STOCKMANN: No, no thank you. Definitely not.

DOCTOR STOCKMANN: No? Here then. See? We got a new tablecloth.

MAYOR STOCKMANN: I noticed.

DOCTOR STOCKMANN: And a new lampshade. Look. Katherine saved up for all of this. It makes the room so warm, doesn't it? Stand here—no, no, no, not there . . . that's right! With the light falling that way it's really sort of elegant, don't you think?

MAYOR STOCKMANN: Well, yes, if you can afford all this—

DOCTOR STOCKMANN: Now I really can. Katherine says I'm earning almost as much as we spend.

MAYOR STOCKMANN: Almost as much!

DOCTOR STOCKMANN: But then a man of science ought to have a little style. I'm sure the average district judge spends more than I do—

MAYOR STOCKMANN: Yes, I should think so—a judge—

DOCTOR STOCKMANN: Well, or an average businessman, then. They spend many times what—

MAYOR STOCKMANN: That depends on the businessman.

DOCTOR STOCKMANN: Anyway I don't throw money away on useless things, Peter. I just can't deny myself the pleasure of having people in my home. You see, I need that. After being cut off from things for so long, it's like life-blood to me to have these young, brave, cheerful people around—freethinking people, eager to change things. And there they are—sitting at that table, eating their fill. I wish you knew Hovstad a little better.

MAYOR STOCKMANN: Oh yes, Hovstad. He tells me he's about to print another article of yours.

DOCTOR STOCKMANN: Of mine?

MAYOR STOCKMANN: Yes—about the baths. You wrote it this winter.

DOCTOR STOCKMANN: Oh, that one! No, I don't want him to run that just now.

MAYOR STOCKMANN: You don't? I think this is precisely the right moment for it.

DOCTOR STOCKMANN: True—at least under the usual circumstances.

MAYOR STOCKMANN: (*Watching him.*) And is there something unusual about the circumstances?

DOCTOR STOCKMANN: (*Stops.*) Peter, right now I can't tell you. Not tonight, anyway. But they might be very unusual—or not at all. It might just be my imagination.

MAYOR STOCKMANN: Well, this is mysterious. Is there anything wrong? Something I'm not being told? I assume that as chairman of the Board of Directors, I'd—

DOCTOR STOCKMANN: And I also assume that I—no, let's not get after each other like this.

MAYOR STOCKMANN: Heaven forbid—it's not my habit to "get after" people—but I most emphatically insist that everything be handled in the appropriate manner and by the proper authorities. I can't allow anything devious or covert.

DOCTOR STOCKMANN: Have I ever been devious or covert?

MAYOR STOCKMANN: At the very least, you have a pretty strong tendency to go your own way, and in a well-ordered society, that's almost as bad. The individual's true role is always to subordinate himself to the whole community—more precisely, to those in authority, who look after the community's good.

DOCTOR STOCKMANN: Maybe so. But what the hell does that have to do with me?

MAYOR STOCKMANN: That is just what you're never been able to understand. But watch out. Someday you'll have to pay for it. Sooner or later. There—I've told you. Goodnight.

DOCTOR STOCKMANN: Are you crazy? You're completely on the wrong track here—

MAYOR STOCKMANN: That's hardly a habit of mine. Now, if you don't mind, I have to excuse myself. (*Calling toward the dining room.*) Goodnight, Katherine. Goodnight, gentlemen. (*He exits.*)

MRS. STOCKMANN: Is he gone?

DOCTOR STOCKMANN: Yes—in a foul mood.

MRS. STOCKMANN: Oh no, what have you done to him this time?

DOCTOR STOCKMANN: Nothing. He can't expect me just to come out with a full report—not until the right moment.

MRS. STOCKMANN: What are you supposed to report to him about?

DOCTOR STOCKMANN: Uh—I'll deal with that, Katherine. Isn't the mailman usually here by now?

(*Hovstad, Billing, and Horster have risen from the table and come into the dining room. Eilif and Morten follow a little later.*)

BILLING: (*Stretches his arms.*) Oh, a meal like that makes you feel like a new man.

HOVSTAD: The mayor wasn't exactly in a great mood tonight.

DOCTOR STOCKMANN: Blame it on his digestion—he's got a bad stomach.

HOVSTAD: It's really us over at the *People's Herald* he can't stomach.

MRS. STOCKMANN: I thought you were all getting along.

HOVSTAD: Only a cease-fire.

BILLING: That's it! That's exactly the word for it!

DOCTOR STOCKMANN: We should remember that poor Peter's a lonely man. Nowhere to call home—his whole life's just business, business. And that horrible weak tea he keeps pouring down. Ah, come on—pull your chairs up to the table, boys. Katherine, doesn't anybody get anything to drink?

MRS. STOCKMANN: (*Going to the dining room.*) Coming.

DOCTOR STOCKMANN: And you, Captain Horster, sit here by me. A rare guest like you—please, everyone, sit down.

(*The men seat themselves around the table. Mrs. Stockmann brings a tray with glasses, decanters, etc.*)

MRS. STOCKMANN: Here we go!—help yourselves.

DOCTOR STOCKMANN: (*Takes a glass.*) That's exactly what we'll do. Cigars, Eilif—you know where I keep the box. And you, Morten, can bring me my pipe.

(*The boys go into the room right.*)

I suspect Eilif sneaks a cigar now and then, but I play innocent. (*Calls.*) Katherine, can you tell him where I left it?—no—he found it.

(*The boys bring in the various items.*)

Help yourselves, my friend. I'll stick with my pipe—we've been through an awful lot of foul weather together up North. (*A clink of glasses.*) Skoal! Yes, this is much better—all of us sitting here, snug and warm.

MRS. STOCKMANN: (*Knitting.*) Are you sailing soon, Captain Horster?

HORSTER: Next week, I think.

MRS. STOCKMANN: And you're bound for America?

HORSTER: That's the idea.

BILLING: So you'll miss the election!

HORSTER: There's an election?

BILLING: Didn't you know that?

HORSTER: No—I don't get mixed up in all that.

BILLING: But you do take an interest in political affairs—

HORSTER: No—I can't follow them.

BILLING: Even so, you should get involved.

HORSTER: Without understanding what's going on?

BILLING: Understanding? What do you mean? See—society's like a ship. Everyone should help steer the course.

HORSTER: That may be true on shore; on board ship it wouldn't work so well.

HOVSTAD: Funny how sea people don't care what happens on land.

BILLING: Amazing!

DOCTOR STOCKMANN: Sea people are like birds of passage—they're at home both north and south. That's why the rest of us have to be even more active, Mr. Hovstad. Anything of public interest in tomorrow's *Herald?*

HOVSTAD: Nothing about town business. But the day after tomorrow, I think I'll run your piece.

DOCTOR STOCKMANN: Oh, for Christ's sake—that article! Listen—that'll have to wait.

HOVSTAD: Really? We have a good spot for it, and I thought the timing was perfect.

DOCTOR STOCKMANN: Yes, yes, you might be right, but you'll just have to wait.

(*Petra, wearing a hat and coat, comes in from the hall, carrying a stack of workbooks.*)

PETRA: Hello.

DOCTOR STOCKMANN: Petra—good evening!

(*General greetings. Petra puts her hat and coat and books on a chair by the door.*)

PETRA: So—here you're all enjoying yourselves while I'm out slaving away.

DOCTOR STOCKMANN: Well, now it's your turn.

BILLING: Can I get you a drink?

PETRA: Thanks—I'll get it. You always make it too strong. Oh—Father, I've got a letter for you. (*Goes to her things.*)

DOCTOR STOCKMANN: A letter? From whom?

PETRA: (*Searching her coat pocket.*) I got it from the mailman as I was leaving.

DOCTOR STOCKMANN: (*Gets up.*) And you didn't bring it till now!

PETRA: I didn't have time.

DOCTOR STOCKMANN: (*Grabbing the letter.*) Let me see, let me see. Yes—this is it.

MRS. STOCKMANN: The one you've been waiting for, Thomas?

DOCTOR STOCKMANN: Yes, yes. Now I need to go where I can read— Katherine, I suppose there's no light in my study, as usual.

MRS. STOCKMANN: The lamp's on your desk, already lit.

DOCTOR STOCKMANN: Oh, good. Excuse me for a moment. (*Goes into study, right.*)

PETRA: I wonder what that's about?

MRS. STOCKMANN: I don't know. The last few days he's constantly been asking about the mailman.

BILLING: Some out-of-town patient, probably.

PETRA: Poor father—he works too hard. (*Mixes drink.*) Ah—this'll be good.

HOVSTAD: Did you teach Night School again today?

PETRA: (*Sips.*) Two hours.

BILLING: And four hours this morning at the Academy.

PETRA: Five.

MRS. STOCKMANN: And papers to grade tonight, I see.

PETRA: Quite a stack of them, yes.

HORSTER: It looks like you also work too hard.

PETRA: But I like it. I feel so wonderfully tired afterwards.

BILLING: You like that?

PETRA: Yes—you sleep so well then.

MORTEN: You must be an awful sinner, Petra.

PETRA: Sinner?

MORTEN: If you have to work so hard. Mr. Rørlund says that work is the punishment for our sins.

EILIF: (Snorts.) Uch—what an idiot! You believe that stuff?

MRS. STOCKMANN: Now, now Eilif!

BILLING: (Laughing.) No, this is great!

HOVSTAD: You'd rather not work so hard, Morten?

MORTEN: No, not me.

HOVSTAD: Well, then, what do you want to be in life?

MORTEN: What I really want to be is a Viking.

EILIF: Then you'd have to be a pagan.

MORTEN: So I'll be a pagan.

BILLING: I'm with you there, Morten. That's just what I say.

MRS. STOCKMANN: (Signaling.) No, you don't really mean that, Mr. Billing.

BILLING: May God strike me dead, I'm a pagan and proud of it. You'll see—pretty soon we'll all be pagans.

MORTEN: And then we can do whatever we want?

BILLING: Well, Morten, you see—

MRS. STOCKMANN: All right, boys, in you go: you've got homework for tomorrow.

EILIF: I can stay a little.

MRS. STOCKMANN: No, you too—off you go!

(The boys say goodnight and go into room left.)

HOVSTAD: You don't think it's bad for the boys to talk about these things, do you?

MRS. STOCKMANN: Oh, I don't know. I just don't like it.

PETRA: Mother, I think you're wrong about that.

MRS. STOCKMANN: Maybe so. But I don't like it—not here at home.

PETRA: There's so much hypocrisy everywhere—at home and in school. At home we don't dare say anything, and at school we have to stand in front of the children and lie to them.

HORSTER: You have to lie?

PETRA: Yes—we have to teach them all kinds of things we don't believe in ourselves.

BILLING: Only too true.

PETRA: If I had the means to do it, I'd start a school of my own— where things would be done very differently.

BILLING: Oh yes—the means!

HORSTER: Well, Miss Stockmann, if that's what you have in mind, you're more than welcome to use my place. My father's old house is practically empty. There's a huge dining room you could use for—

PETRA: (*Laughing.*) Oh, thank you, that's very good of you; but it'll never happen.

HOVSTAD: That's right. I think Petra's headed for a career in journalism. By the way—have you had a chance to look at that English article you promised to translate for us?

PETRA: Not yet. But you'll get it in plenty of time.

(*Doctor Stockmann comes in from his study with the opened letter in his hand.*)

DOCTOR STOCKMANN: (*Waving the letter.*) Now here's some news for the town!

BILLING: News?

MRS. STOCKMANN: What kinds of news?

DOCTOR STOCKMANN: A great discovery, Katherine!

HOVSTAD: Really?

MRS. STOCKMANN: Did you make it?

DOCTOR STOCKMANN: Yes, I made it. (*Walks up and down.*) Just let them try to pass this off as one of my "fantasies," one of my "delusions." No, this time they'll have to watch out—oh ho— they'll really have to watch out!

PETRA: But father, tell us what it's all about!

DOCTOR STOCKMANN: Yes, yes, give me a minute, and you'll hear all about it. If only I had Peter here right now. This just shows you how we human beings go around making our decisions, when really we're as blind as moles.

HOVSTAD: What do you mean, Doctor?

DOCTOR STOCKMANN: (*Standing by the table.*) It's generally agreed, is it not, that our town's a healthful place?

HOVSTAD: Yes—that's well known.

DOCTOR STOCKMANN: An exceedingly healthful place, in fact—a place that deserves the highest recommendation, for both the sick and the healthy—

MRS. STOCKMANN: But, Thomas—

DOCTOR STOCKMANN: And we certainly have praised it to the skies, haven't we? I've touted it over and over, in *The People's Herald,* in pamphlets, brochures—

HOVSTAD: Well, and so?

DOCTOR STOCKMANN: This institution, the baths—this establishment we celebrate as "the town's main artery" and "nerve center" and— what the hell *haven't* we called it—

BILLING: "The beating heart of our community," as I once wrote when I was feeling particularly festive.

DOCTOR STOCKMANN: Yes, that too. But—do you know what they really are, these great, splendid, celebrated baths, constructed at such enormous expense? Do you know what they are?

HOVSTAD: No, what are they?

DOCTOR STOCKMANN: The whole thing's a sewer!

PETRA: The baths, Father?

MRS. STOCKMANN: Our baths?

HOVSTAD: But, Doctor!

BILLING: Incredible!

DOCTOR STOCKMANN: The whole establishment's a whited sepulcher— it's poisoned! It's actually a menace to health! All that pollution up there at Milldale—which is the source of the foul-smelling stuff we're getting down here—it's all seeping into the supply for the pump room. And it's this same damned poisonous ooze that's been washing up on the beaches as well.

HORSTER: At the public swimming area?

DOCTOR STOCKMANN: Exactly.

HOVSTAD: Can you prove this, Doctor?

DOCTOR STOCKMANN: I've run as rigorous an investigation as I can. See, I've suspected something like this for quite a while. Last year there were a number of cases of odd illnesses among the visitors—both typhoid and gastritis.

MRS. STOCKMANN: That's true, there were!

DOCTOR STOCKMANN: At the time, of course, we thought they brought their infections with them. But then during the winter I started to have some other ideas—so I began analyzing the water as scientifically as I could.

MRS. STOCKMANN: So that's what kept you so preoccupied!

DOCTOR STOCKMANN: You might well say I've been preoccupied, Katherine. But I didn't have the right equipment here, so I sent samples of both the drinking water and the seawater off to the University, to get a precise chemical analysis.

HOVSTAD: And now you're got it?

DOCTOR STOCKMANN: (*Showing the letter.*) Right here! Proven. Decayed organic matter in the water—millions of bacteria. This water is absolutely hazardous to health, whether it's used internally or externally.

MRS. STOCKMANN: Thank God you found it in time!

DOCTOR STOCKMANN: Yes, you might say that.

HOVSTAD: So what'll you do, Doctor?

DOCTOR STOCKMANN: Of course, I'll see to it that the right action is taken.

HOVSTAD: Can it be done?

DOCTOR STOCKMANN: It'll have to be done. Otherwise the whole thing is useless—ruined. But it won't come to that. I know exactly what we need to do.

MRS. STOCKMANN: But Thomas, why did you keep this such a secret?

DOCTOR STOCKMANN: Oh yes—I should have run through town, shooting off my mouth, before I had the proof. No thanks—I'm not that naive.

PETRA: But here at home—

DOCTOR STOCKMANN: No, not a living soul. In the morning you can run over and tell the Badger.

MRS. STOCKMANN: Thomas, please.

DOCTOR STOCKMANN: All right—your grandfather. Now the old man will really have something to cackle about. He's always thought I was a little crazy. And I'll bet he's not alone in that opinion. But now these good people are going to see something—(*Walks around rubbing his hands.*) This is going to wake this town up, Katherine—you can hardly imagine how much. The entire water system has to be rebuilt.

HOVSTAD: The whole system?

DOCTOR STOCKMANN: That's right, you heard it. The intake is situated too low—we'll have to move it much higher up.

PETRA: So you were right all along.

DOCTOR STOCKMANN: You remember that, Petra? I wrote all about it during the planning process. But no one would listen to me then. Well, you can bet they're going to get an earful now. I've written a full report for the Board of Directors—I've had it finished for a week, just waiting for this to come. And now I can send it. (*Goes into the study, returns with a sheaf of papers.*) Look at this! Four pages, single-spaced. And a cover letter. Katherine! Get me a newspaper, something to wrap it in. Good. Now give it to—to— (*Stamps his foot.*) What the hell's her name? Give it to the girl and tell her it goes straight to the Mayor.

(*Mrs. Stockmann goes out through the dining room with the packet.*)

PETRA: What do you think Uncle Peter will say, Father?

DOCTOR STOCKMANN: What can he say? He'll be thrilled that something this important has been caught in time!

HOVSTAD: Can I run a little story on your discovery in the *Herald?*

DOCTOR STOCKMANN: I'd be delighted.

HOVSTAD: The public's got to know the truth about this—and the sooner the better.

DOCTOR STOCKMANN: Absolutely.

MRS. STOCKMANN: She's on the way.

BILLING: God damn it, Doctor, you're the number one man in this town.

DOCTOR STOCKMANN: (*Walking happily up and down.*) No, really. When you come right down to it, I've only done my duty. I'm just a lucky treasure-hunter, that's all. Still—

BILLING: Hovstad, don't you think the town should put together a parade in honor of the Doctor?

HOVSTAD: I vote yes.

BILLING: I'll talk to Aslaksen about it.

DOCTOR STOCKMANN: My dear friends, you can drop this crazy idea right now. No ceremonies, no parades. And if the Board starts making noises about raising my salary, tell them I won't take it. Katherine, I'm telling you—I won't take it.

MRS. STOCKMANN: Good for you.

PETRA: (*Lifts her glass.*) Skoal, father!

HOVSTAD and BILLING: Skoal, skoal, Doctor!

HORSTER: (*Clinking glasses with the Doctor.*) May this bring you nothing but joy.

DOCTOR STOCKMANN: Thank you, thanks, my friends. I'm so incredibly happy. What a blessing to know that you've done something for your hometown and your fellow citizens. Katherine!

(*He puts both arms around her neck and whirls her around the room. Mrs. Stockmann screams and struggles. Laughter, applause, and cheers for the Doctor. The boys poke their heads through the doorway.*)

END OF ACT ONE

ACT TWO

The Doctor's living room; the door to the dining room is closed. It is morning.

(Mrs. Stockmann, with a sealed letter in hand, comes from the dining room, crosses to the first door on the right, and looks in.)

MRS. STOCKMANN: Thomas, are you home?

DOCTOR STOCKMANN: (*Within.*) Just got back. (*Comes in.*) Any mail?

MRS. STOCKMANN: A letter from your brother. (*Gives it to him.*)

DOCTOR STOCKMANN: Let's see. (*Opens envelope, reads in a low murmur.*) "Your manuscript is herewith returned." Hmmm.

MRS. STOCKMANN: What does he say?

DOCTOR STOCKMANN: (*Puts the paper in his pocket.*) Nothing much. He'll be coming over around noon.

MRS. STOCKMANN: So you have to remember to be here.

DOCTOR STOCKMANN: I can do that. I've made all my morning calls.

MRS. STOCKMANN: I can't wait to see how he takes it.

DOCTOR STOCKMANN: He'll be unhappy that I made the discovery instead of him.

MRS. STOCKMANN: Yes—doesn't that worry you?

DOCTOR STOCKMANN: No. In the end he'll be glad of it. Peter is so incredibly afraid that someone else might do something good for this town.

MRS. STOCKMANN: Then you should be really nice and share the credit with him. Couldn't you hint that *he* first put you on the track—?

DOCTOR STOCKMANN: I wouldn't mind that, as long as I can get the truth out.

(Old Morten Kiil sticks his head through the hall doorway, looks around inquisitively, laughing to himself.)

MORTEN KIIL: (*Slyly.*) Is it—is it true?

MRS. STOCKMANN: (*Greeting him.*) Father—you're here?

DOCTOR STOCKMANN: Well, well, good morning, Father–in–law, good morning.

MRS. STOCKMANN: Come in, for heaven's sake.

MORTEN KIIL: Only if it's true. Otherwise I'm leaving.

DOCTOR STOCKMANN: If what's true?

MORTEN KIIL: This nonsense about the waterworks. Is it really true?

DOCTOR STOCKMANN: Of course it's true. But how did you find out about it?

MORTEN KIIL: (*Enters.*) Petra stopped by on her way to school—

DOCTOR STOCKMANN: Did she?

MORTEN KIIL: Yes, and she told me. I thought she was just making a fool of me—but that's not like Petra.

DOCTOR STOCKMANN: No, how could you think that?

MORTEN KIIL: You should never trust anybody. They can make a fool out of you before you know it. So—it's really true then?

DOCTOR STOCKMANN: Yes—it's definitely true. Have a seat. (*Directs him to the sofa.*) Isn't this a stroke of luck for the town?

MORTEN KIIL: (*Fighting back laughter.*) Luck for the town?

DOCTOR STOCKMANN: Yes—that I caught it in time.

MORTEN KIIL: (*As before.*) Yes, yes, yes. But I never thought you'd play these kind of monkeyshines on your own brother.

DOCTOR STOCKMANN: Monkeyshines?

MRS. STOCKMANN: Really, father.

MORTEN KIIL: (*Resting his hands and chin on his cane and winking slyly at the Doctor.*) Now then, what's your story again? Some little animals have gotten into the water pipes?

DOCTOR STOCKMANN: Yes—bacteria.

MORTEN KIIL: Now, Petra says that a whole lot of these little animals have gotten in there. Mobs of them.

DOCTOR STOCKMANN: Yes, well—there could be millions of them.

MORTEN KIIL: But no one can see them—isn't that right?

DOCTOR STOCKMANN: That's right—no one can see them.

MORTEN KIIL: (*Quietly chuckling.*) Damn me if this isn't the best one I've heard from you yet!

DOCTOR STOCKMANN: What do you mean?

MORTEN KIIL: But you'll never get the Mayor to believe it.

DOCTOR STOCKMANN: We'll see.

MORTEN KIIL: You're hoping he'll be that stupid?

DOCTOR STOCKMANN: I'm counting on the whole town being that stupid.

MORTEN KIIL: The whole town! Yes, you're probably right. Well, they've got it coming to them. They like to think of themselves as so much smarter than us old folks. They hounded me off the town council—yes, I'm telling you—voted me right off, chased me off like an animal—but now they'll be paid back. So go ahead: keep up your monkeyshines, Stockmann.

DOCTOR STOCKMANN: But I'm not—

MORTEN KIIL: Just keep up your monkeyshines, I'm telling you. If you can fix it so that the mayor and his friends end up running around with their tails between their legs, I'll give a hundred kroner to the poor the very next minute.

DOCTOR STOCKMANN: Well, that's very nice of you.

MORTEN KIIL: Yes, it is—although I don't have that much to throw around, as you can imagine. But you do what you say, and I'll remember the poor with fifty kroner next Christmas.

(*Hovstad comes in from the hall.*)

HOVSTAD: Good morning!—oh, I'm sorry—

DOCTOR STOCKMANN: No, come in, come in.

MORTEN KIIL: (*Chuckling again.*) Him! Is he in on this too?

HOVSTAD: What do you mean?

DOCTOR STOCKMANN: Of course he's in on it.

MORTEN KIIL: I should have known it. This way it'll get in the paper. Well, you really are a sly one. Now I'll get going and leave you two alone together.

DOCTOR STOCKMANN: Why don't you stay for a bit—

MORTEN KIIL: No, I've really got to do. Just keep up your monkeyshines—you'll find it won't be for nothing.

(*Morten Kiil goes out, accompanied by Mrs. Stockmann.*)

DOCTOR STOCKMANN: (*Laughs.*) What do you think of that—the old Badger doesn't believe a word about the water system.

HOVSTAD: Oh—so that was—

DOCTOR STOCKMANN: Yes, that was what we were talking about. I suppose that's why you're here, too?

HOVSTAD: Exactly. Do you have a minute, Doctor?

DOCTOR STOCKMANN: My dear Hovstad, as long as you like.

HOVSTAD: Have you heard anything from the Mayor?

DOCTOR STOCKMANN: Not yet—he'll be here later.

HOVSTAD: I've been thinking a lot about this business since last night.

DOCTOR STOCKMANN: Oh yes?

HOVSTAD: For you, as a doctor and a scientist, the issue of the water system stands alone—I mean, for you it's not tied up with a lot of other things.

DOCTOR STOCKMANN: No, that's right—but how do you mean that? Let's sit down. No, there on the sofa.

(*Hovstad sits on the sofa, the Doctor on the other side of the table in an armchair.*)

Now, you were saying?

HOVSTAD: You said yesterday that the water pollution comes from contamination in the soil.

DOCTOR STOCKMANN: Yes—there's no question that it comes from that poisonous swamp up at Milldale.

HOVSTAD: Excuse me, Doctor, but I think it comes from another swamp altogether.

DOCTOR STOCKMANN: And which swamp is that?

HOVSTAD: The swamp in which our whole community lies rotting.

DOCTOR STOCKMANN: Now what the hell is *that* supposed to mean?

HOVSTAD: Little by little, all the affairs of this town have slipped into the hands of a small group of politicians.

DOCTOR STOCKMANN: Now, they're not all politicians.

HOVSTAD: No, but the rest are all cronies of the politicians, or their followers. All the established names, all the well-to-do families. And they're the ones who control life for the rest of us.

DOCTOR STOCKMANN: Yes, but those people have real ability and insight.

HOVSTAD: Did they demonstrate their ability and insight when they laid the water pipes where they did?

DOCTOR STOCKMANN: No, of course not—that was a colossal piece of stupidity. But we can fix all that.

HOVSTAD: You think it will be that easy?

DOCTOR STOCKMANN: Easy or not—it's going to happen, no matter what.

HOVSTAD: Yes it will—as long as the press has a hand in it.

DOCTOR STOCKMANN: I guarantee you that won't be necessary. I'm confident that my brother—

HOVSTAD: Excuse me, Doctor, but I have to tell you that I intend to take this matter up.

DOCTOR STOCKMANN: In the paper?

HOVSTAD: Yes. When I took over the *Herald,* my idea was to break up this circle of obstinate, obsolete reactionaries who've gotten a hold of all the power.

DOCTOR STOCKMANN: And you told me yourself what the result was— you almost killed the paper.

HOVSTAD: Yes—we had to pull in our horns for a while, that's true. The baths might never have been built if those old men had fallen. But now the baths are in place, and these fine gentlemen can be dispensed with.

DOCTOR STOCKMANN: Maybe. But we still owe them our thanks.

HOVSTAD: The fact will be scrupulously acknowledged. But a journalist in my position—a radical—can't pass up an opportunity like this. The fiction of the infallibility of the authorities must be destroyed—uprooted, just like every other superstition.

DOCTOR STOCKMANN: I agree with you there, Hovstad, wholeheartedly. If it's a superstition, then get rid of it.

HOVSTAD: I'm not eager to tangle with your brother the Mayor—but I'm sure you agree that the truth comes before anything else.

DOCTOR STOCKMANN: That's self-evident. (*Vehemently.*) Yes, but—but—

HOVSTAD: Don't think badly of me—I'm no more ambitious than most people.

DOCTOR STOCKMANN: But I never said you were.

HOVSTAD: You know I come from poor people. I've had more than enough chances to see what the working classes really need. What they need, Doctor, is some say in their own political destiny. *That's* what leads to power, knowledge, and self-respect.

DOCTOR STOCKMANN: Absolutely, I understand.

HOVSTAD: Yes. So I think a journalist bears a heavy burden if he ignores any opportunity that might lead to the liberation of the masses—of the poor and neglected. Oh, I know perfectly well that our town fathers will call this agitation and so on—but so be it. As long as I keep my conscience clear—

DOCTOR STOCKMANN: Exactly, Mr. Hovstad—exactly! All the same—damn it—(*A knock at the door.*) Come in!

(*Aslaksen the printer appears at the hall door. He is poorly but decently dressed in black with a white, somewhat crumpled necktie, gloves, and a silk hat in his hands.*)

ASLAKSEN: (*Bowing.*) Pardon me, Doctor, for presuming to—

DOCTOR STOCKMANN: Well, well—it's Mr. Aslaksen!

ASLAKSEN: That's right, Doctor.

HOVSTAD: (*Stands.*) Are you looking for me, Aslaksen?

ASLAKSEN: No, I didn't know you'd be here. No, actually I was looking for the Doctor—

DOCTOR STOCKMANN: Well, what can I do for you?

ASLAKSEN: Is it true, as I heard from Mr. Billing, that the Doctor is thinking of getting us a better water system?

DOCTOR STOCKMANN: For the baths, yes.

ASLAKSEN: Yes, I understand. Then I've come to say that I'll support you with everything I've got.

HOVSTAD: (*To the Doctor.*) You see!

DOCTOR STOCKMANN: I'm very grateful, but—

ASLAKSEN: Because it might be necessary to have the backing of us small businessmen—we more or less make up a solid majority in town, when we really want to. And you know, Doctor, it's always good to have the majority behind you.

DOCTOR STOCKMANN: That's certainly true. But I really don't believe anything like that will be necessary here. The situation's so clear, so obvious—

ASLAKSEN: Oh, it might still be a good idea. You see, I know these local authorities too well—the ones in charge never appreciate ideas from outsiders. So I was thinking that it might not be a bad thing if we staged a little demonstration.

HOVSTAD: Yes, exactly!

DOCTOR STOCKMANN: A demonstration? How would you demonstrate?

ASLAKSEN: With great moderation, naturally. I'm always striving to be moderate, Doctor. Because moderation is a citizen's chief virtue—as I see it.

DOCTOR STOCKMANN: And you're certainly noted for it, Mr. Aslaksen.

ASLAKSEN: Yes, I think I can say that. And this issue of the water system is highly important to us small businessmen. The baths show every sign of turning into a little gold mine for this town. We'll all be living off of them, especially the homeowners. So of course we'll support the institution all we can. And now that I'm chairman of the Homeowner's Association—

DOCTOR STOCKMANN: Yes?

ASLAKSEN: And also a representative of the Temperance Union—you're aware that I'm active in Temperance affairs?

DOCTOR STOCKMANN: Yes, I know.

ASLAKSEN: Well—then you know that I get to meet a great many people. And since I'm known for being a sober and law-abiding citizen as you yourself have noted, Doctor—I have a certain influence in town—a little power-base, if I do say so myself.

DOCTOR STOCKMANN: I know that very well, Mr. Aslaksen.

ASLAKSEN: Indeed. And so it wouldn't take much for me to prepare a tribute, should that become necessary.

DOCTOR STOCKMANN: A tribute?

ASLAKSEN: Yes—a sort of an outpouring of gratitude from the people for the way you've acted in the public interest. Of course it would have to be phrased with proper moderation, so as not to offend the authorities—or anyone in a position of power. As long as we take care of that, I don't think anyone can fault us, do you?

HOVSTAD: Well, and what if they don't like it?

ASLAKSEN: No, no, no. Nothing that could give offense, Mr. Hovstad. Nothing to antagonize our local officials. I've had enough of that in my time, and it never works. But the truthful and prudent opinions of a citizen can't possibly offend anyone.

DOCTOR STOCKMANN: (*Shakes his hand.*) I just can't tell you, Mr. Aslaksen, how moved I am to discover all this support in our community. Listen—what about a little glass of sherry?

ASLAKSEN: No!—thank you. I never indulge.

DOCTOR STOCKMANN: Well, then, a glass of beer. How about that?

ASLAKSEN: Thank you, no. I really can't so early in the day. Now I'm going to talk to a number of homeowners—begin to prepare public opinion.

DOCTOR STOCKMANN: Well that's extremely kind of you, Mr. Aslaksen, but I just can't get it into my head that any of these arrangements will be necessary. I think it'll really take care of itself.

ASLAKSEN: Well, Doctor, the authorities sometimes tend to drag their feet a bit—though I'm not criticizing, you understand!

HOVSTAD: Tomorrow, Aslaksen, we'll force them to act—in print!

ASLAKSEN: But without violence, Mr. Hovstad! Proceed in moderation, otherwise you won't gain an inch. Take my word for it as a graduate of the School of Life. Well then—I'll say goodbye, Doctor. Now you know that the middle classes stand behind you like a wall. You've got the solid majority at your side, Doctor.

DOCTOR STOCKMANN: Thank you for that, Mr. Aslaksen. (*Offers his hand.*) Good-bye, good-bye!

ASLAKSEN: Coming with me to the pressroom, Mr. Hovstad?

HOVSTAD: I'll be by later—I've still got a couple of things to do.

ASLAKSEN: Fine.

(*Aslaksen bows and leaves. Doctor Stockmann follows him into the hall.*)

HOVSTAD: (*As the Doctor returns.*) Well, how about that, Doctor? Don't you think it's time to clear this place out? Get rid of all the spinelessness, the halfheartedness, the cowardice?

DOCTOR STOCKMANN: Are you talking about Aslaksen?

HOVSTAD: Yes. He's right there in the swamp with the rest of them—even though he's a decent enough man in many ways. Most of them are like that here—they swing from one side to the other—so full of doubts and scruples that they're afraid to take a stand.

DOCTOR STOCKMANN: But I really thought Aslaksen seemed well-meaning.

HOVSTAD: There's one thing I value more: backbone. Standing up for yourself, a confident and self-sufficient man.

DOCTOR STOCKMANN: You're absolutely right about that, I agree with you.

HOVSTAD: So that's why I want to seize this moment to get all the well-meaning people to act like men for once. We have to root out the cult of authority from this town. Every eligible voter has to be made aware of this grotesque mistake with the water system.

DOCTOR STOCKMANN: All right. If you think it's in the public interest, go ahead. But please wait till I've talked with my brother.

HOVSTAD: Meanwhile, I'll prepare an editorial—and if the Mayor won't pursue the matter—

DOCTOR STOCKMANN: How can you even think that—

HOVSTAD: Oh, I'd say it's thinkable. And *then*—

DOCTOR STOCKMANN: Well, in that case, I promise you—listen—you can print my report—put it all in, word for word.

HOVSTAD: Can I? That's a promise?

DOCTOR STOCKMANN: (*Giving him the manuscript.*) Here it is. Take it with you—read it through, no harm in that—and you can give it back to me later.

HOVSTAD: Good, good. I'll do that, definitely. And so—goodbye, Doctor!

DOCTOR STOCKMANN: Goodbye, goodbye. But you'll see—this'll be smooth sailing—nothing but smooth sailing.

HOVSTAD: We'll see. (*Bows and goes out by the hall door.*)

DOCTOR STOCKMANN: (*Looks into the dining room.*) Katherine—Petra, you're home!

PETRA: (*Enters.*) Yes, I just got back from school.

MRS. STOCKMANN: He hasn't come yet?

DOCTOR STOCKMANN: Peter? No, but I've had a long talk with Hovstad. He's extremely excited about my discovery. See, it has a much broader impact than I thought at first. So he's put his paper at my disposal, if we need it.

MRS. STOCKMANN: Will we need it?

DOCTOR STOCKMANN: No, probably not—but anyway it's very gratifying to feel that you have the liberal, independent press on your side. And guess what? The chairman of the Homeowners' Association came by.

MRS. STOCKMANN: Yes? What did he want?

DOCTOR STOCKMANN: Same thing—to support me. They're all going to support me—every one of them—if worse comes to worst. Katherine—do you know what I've got behind me?

MRS. STOCKMANN: Behind you? No, I can't imagine what you've got behind you.

DOCTOR STOCKMANN: The solid majority.

MRS. STOCKMANN: I see. Is that good for you, Thomas?

DOCTOR STOCKMANN: Damn right it's good. (*Rubs his hands and walks back and forth.*) Lord! It's wonderful to stand like this, in brotherhood with your fellow citizens.

PETRA: And to be doing something good and useful, father!

DOCTOR STOCKMANN: Yes—and on top of that, for my hometown, too!

MRS. STOCKMANN: There's the bell.

DOCTOR STOCKMANN: That must be him. (*A knock.*) Come in.

MAYOR STOCKMANN: (*Enters from the hall.*) Good morning.

DOCTOR STOCKMANN: Welcome, Peter! It's good to see you.

MRS. STOCKMANN: Good morning, Peter. How are you today?

MAYOR STOCKMANN: So-so, thank you. (*To the Doctor.*) I received yesterday—after office hours—your report concerning the condition of the water at the baths.

DOCTOR STOCKMANN: Yes. Have you read it?

MAYOR STOCKMANN: Yes. I have.

DOCTOR STOCKMANN: And what do you say?

MAYOR STOCKMANN: (*Glancing around.*) Well—

MRS. STOCKMANN: Petra, let's—

(*Mrs. Stockmann and Petra go into the room on the left.*)

MAYOR STOCKMANN: (*After a pause.*) Was it necessary to undertake all these investigations behind my back?

DOCTOR STOCKMANN: Yes—as long as I didn't have absolute proof, then—

MAYOR STOCKMANN: And you mean to imply you have that now?

DOCTOR STOCKMANN: Yes. You must have convinced yourself of that.

MAYOR STOCKMANN: Is that your intention, to submit this report to the Board of Directors as some sort of official document?

DOCTOR STOCKMANN: Of course. Something's got to be done about this. And fast.

MAYOR STOCKMANN: You use, in your customary way, some rather hyperbolic terms in your report. You say, among other things, that what we're offering our visitors is "permanent toxic contamination."

DOCTOR STOCKMANN: But, Peter, what else can you call it? Think about it! The water's poison, whether you drink it or just bathe in it!

And we feed this stuff to poor, sick people who pay us huge fees to get their health back!

MAYOR STOCKMANN: And then your deductions lead you to the conclusion that we must build a sewer to drain off this alleged contamination from Milldale, and that the water mains have to be relaid.

DOCTOR STOCKMANN: Yes. Can you think of another way out? I certainly can't.

MAYOR STOCKMANN: I made up some pretext to pay a little visit to the town engineer this morning. Then I floated this proposal—almost as a joke—as something we might want to consider some time in the future.

DOCTOR STOCKMANN: In the future!

MAYOR STOCKMANN: Of course he smiled at what he took to be my extravagance. Have you bothered to consider what these changes would cost? According to my information, the most reasonable estimate runs into several hundred thousand kroner.

DOCTOR STOCKMANN: That much?

MAYOR STOCKMANN: Yes—and that's not the worst part. The work would take at least two years.

DOCTOR STOCKMANN: Two years? Two whole years?

MAYOR STOCKMANN: At least. And what should we do with the baths in the meantime? Close them? We'd have to! Do you think a single soul would come here if the rumor got out that the water was a health hazard?

DOCTOR STOCKMANN: But, Peter, that's exactly what it is!

MAYOR STOCKMANN: And the timing—just when the baths were beginning to establish themselves! Other towns around here have the same resources to develop as health resorts Don't you see? They'll immediately start to divert the flow of visitors to themselves, no question. That's where we stand. We'll probably have to abandon the whole costly enterprise. And you'll have ruined your own hometown.

DOCTOR STOCKMANN: I—ruined—?

MAYOR STOCKMANN: The only real future for this town lies in those baths—you know that as well as I do.

DOCTOR STOCKMANN: So what do you think should be done?

MAYOR STOCKMANN: I find nothing in your report to persuade me that the condition of the water in the baths is as serious as you contend.

DOCTOR STOCKMANN: More likely it's a lot more! Or it will be by summer, with the warm weather.

MAYOR STOCKMANN: As I said before, I think you exaggerate considerably. A competent doctor should know the right precautions to take—he ought to be able to prevent the worst effects, and treat any noticeable symptoms that might appear.

DOCTOR STOCKMANN: And then—? What else—?

MAYOR STOCKMANN: The existing water system is simply a fact; consequently it must be accepted as such. However—in a reasonable period of time, the Directors might not be disinclined to consider whether, within our fiscal constraints, some certain improvements might not feasibly be undertaken.

DOCTOR STOCKMANN: And you think I'll go along with this kind of duplicity?

MAYOR STOCKMANN: Duplicity?

DOCTOR STOCKMANN: All right—fraud, lies, an out-and-out crime against the people, against the whole of society.

MAYOR STOCKMANN: I haven't, as I mentioned earlier, been able to bring myself to believe that there is any really imminent danger here.

DOCTOR STOCKMANN: Yes you have! There's no other possibility. My report is conclusively true and correct. I know that! And so do you, Peter, but you won't admit it. You're the one responsible for the water system being laid out this way—and it's *this*—it's this hideous error that you won't admit!

MAYOR STOCKMANN: What if that were true? If I feel the need to take some care of my reputation, it's only for the good of the town. Without moral authority I couldn't steer events in the direction I consider best for the welfare of the whole. Therefore—and for several other reasons—I think it's imperative that your report not be presented to the Board. It should be kept quiet, in the public interest. Then, later, I'll raise the issue, and we'll do the best we can in silence. But absolutely nothing—not one word—can be allowed to reach the public about this disastrous situation.

DOCTOR STOCKMANN: Ah—but you can't prevent that, my dear Peter.

MAYOR STOCKMANN: It can and must be prevented.

DOCTOR STOCKMANN: It's no use. Too many people know about it already.

MAYOR STOCKMANN: Know about it? Who? Not those people at the *Herald?*

DOCTOR STOCKMANN: Oh yes. They too. Our free and independent press will see that you do your duty.

MAYOR STOCKMANN: (*After a short pause.*) You are an exceedingly thoughtless man, Thomas. Haven't you considered the consequences to yourself?

DOCTOR STOCKMANN: Consequences? To me?

MAYOR STOCKMANN: To you and your family.

DOCTOR STOCKMANN: What the hell does that mean?

MAYOR STOCKMANN: I believe, over the years, that I've proven myself to be a helpful and obliging brother.

DOCTOR STOCKMANN: Yes you have. And I thank you for it.

MAYOR STOCKMANN: I don't want your thanks. In large part, what I did was necessary, in my own interest. I've always hoped that I could somehow hold you in check if I helped improve your financial situation.

DOCTOR STOCKMANN: What? It was in your own interest?

MAYOR STOCKMANN: I said in part. It's painful for a public figure when his closest relative goes around compromising himself again and again.

DOCTOR STOCKMANN: And you think I do that?

MAYOR STOCKMANN: Yes, unfortunately, that's exactly what you do, without even realizing it. You have an unruly, aggressive, rebellious nature. And then you have this compulsion to publish essays on every subject, no matter how farfetched. No sooner do you get an idea than you're instantly writing newspaper articles on it, or whole pamphlets.

DOCTOR STOCKMANN: Isn't it a citizen's duty to inform the public when he gets a new idea?

MAYOR STOCKMANN: Oh, the public doesn't need new ideas. The public is best served by the good, old, accepted ideas it already has.

DOCTOR STOCKMANN: That's putting it bluntly!

MAYOR STOCKMANN: Yes—for once I have to speak bluntly to you. Up till now I've tried to avoid that, because I know how easy it is to set you off. But now I have to tell you the truth, Thomas. You haven't the slightest suspicion of how much you're hurting yourself with your recklessness. You complain about the authorities—yes, even the government, you're always tearing it down—claiming you've been ignored, persecuted—but what can you expect, someone who's as much trouble as you are?

DOCTOR STOCKMANN: What? So I'm "trouble" now?

MAYOR STOCKMANN: Yes, Thomas, you're a great deal of trouble to work with. It's cost me a lot to learn that. You place yourself above all the usual considerations. You seem to forget that you have me to thank for your job as medical supervisor at the baths.

DOCTOR STOCKMANN: I was the obvious choice—who else could there be? I was the first one who saw that this town could turn itself into a popular health resort. And, at the time, I was the only one who could see it. I stood alone and fought for that idea for many years, writing and writing—

MAYOR STOCKMANN: No question. But the time wasn't right—and up there you were too isolated from civilization to understand that. But when the opportune moment arrived, I—and some others— took action.

DOCTOR STOCKMANN: Yes, and made a complete mess of my whole magnificent plan. Oh, it's becoming quite clear now what a brilliant group you were.

MAYOR STOCKMANN: What's becoming clear to me is that once again you're looking for someone higher up to pick a fight with. It's an old habit—you can't stand anyone having authority over you. You resent anyone who's your superior—you regard him as your personal enemy, and you'll use whatever weapons you've got to attack him. But now I've made you aware of what vital interests are at stake for the town—and, consequently, for me as well. So I'm warning you, Thomas, the demand I'm about to make is not negotiable.

DOCTOR STOCKMANN: And what demand is that?

MAYOR STOCKMANN: Because of your indiscretion—talking freely about this sensitive issue when it should have been treated as strictly confidential to the Board of Directors—obviously we can't just hush it up. All kinds of rumors will start spreading, and the more malicious tongues in town will no doubt add their own embellishments to these rumors. So—every rumor will have to be publicly denied by you.

DOCTOR STOCKMANN: Me? How can—? I don't get you.

MAYOR STOCKMANN: After conducting further studies, it is expected that you will come to the conclusion that the situation is neither so urgent nor so dangerous as you first imagined.

DOCTOR STOCKMANN: Aha! That's what you expect?

MAYOR STOCKMANN: Furthermore, you will be expected to make a public declaration of your confidence in the Board's ability to take whatever thorough and conscientious steps are found necessary to remedy any possible defects.

DOCTOR STOCKMANN: But you'll never fix it—not in a million years—if you go after it with wallpaper and patchwork. I'm telling you, Peter—and this is my absolute and heartfelt conviction—

MAYOR STOCKMANN: As an employee, you have no right to any independent convictions.

DOCTOR STOCKMANN: (*Startled.*) No right—

MAYOR STOCKMANN: As an employee, I said. As a private person, God knows, that's something else. But as a subordinate staff member of the baths, you have no right to express any conviction that conflicts with your superiors.

DOCTOR STOCKMANN: That's going too far! As a doctor, as a scientist, I don't have the right to—?

MAYOR STOCKMANN: This issue is not a purely scientific one—the issue is complex; there are both technical and economic issues involved—

DOCTOR STOCKMANN: It can be whatever the hell it likes as far as I'm concerned. I insist on my freedom to speak out on any issue in the whole world.

MAYOR STOCKMANN: Absolutely—only not on the baths. That, we forbid you.

DOCTOR STOCKMANN: (*Shouting.*) You forbid! You! Men like—

MAYOR STOCKMANN: *I* forbid it—*I*, your immediate superior. And when I forbid it, you have to obey.

DOCTOR STOCKMANN: (*Controlling himself.*) Peter—truly—if you weren't my brother—

PETRA: (*Flings the door open.*) Father, you don't have to stand for this!

MRS. STOCKMANN: (*Following her.*) Petra, Petra!

MAYOR STOCKMANN: So little ears at the door!

MRS. STOCKMANN: You're so loud, we couldn't help but—

PETRA: No, I was listening.

MAYOR STOCKMANN: Actually, I'm glad you—

DOCTOR STOCKMANN: (*Going closer.*) You were talking about forbidding and obeying—

MAYOR STOCKMANN: You forced me to speak in that tone.

DOCTOR STOCKMANN: And I'm supposed to make a statement in public, taking back my own words?

MAYOR STOCKMANN: We think it's absolutely essential that you offer a public explanation along the lines I laid out.

DOCTOR STOCKMANN: And if I don't—obey?

MAYOR STOCKMANN: Then we'll issue an explanation ourselves.

DOCTOR STOCKMANN: All right. But I'll attack you in print. I'll stand my ground. I'll prove that I'm in the right and you're in the wrong.

MAYOR STOCKMANN: In that case I won't be able to prevent your removal.

DOCTOR STOCKMANN: What?

PETRA: Father—removal?

MRS. STOCKMANN: Removal.

MAYOR STOCKMANN: Removal! You'll be removed as medical supervisor. I will feel myself compelled to see that you are given immediate notice, and that you sever any connection between yourself and the baths.

DOCTOR STOCKMANN: You wouldn't dare.

MAYOR STOCKMANN: You're the one who's daring something here.

PETRA: Uncle—this is a shocking way to treat a man like Father.

MRS. STOCKMANN: Petra—be quiet.

MAYOR STOCKMANN: Ah—we've already begun to express our opinions. Yes, naturally. Katherine, you're probably the most sensible person in this house. Exercise whatever influence you might have over your husband. Make him see what he'll bring down on himself—on his family and—

DOCTOR STOCKMANN: My family's got nothing to do with anyone but me.

MAYOR STOCKMANN: As I was saying, on his family and on the town he lives in.

DOCTOR STOCKMANN: I'm the one who's truly looking out for the town. I want to throw some light on all the hidden flaws—because they'll be exposed sooner or later anyway. Yes—and then people will see clearly how I love my hometown.

MAYOR STOCKMANN: You—who would blindly charge ahead and dry up the major source of the town's prosperity.

DOCTOR STOCKMANN: That source is poisoned! Are you mad? We live by peddling corruption and disease! The whole, thriving town sucks up its nourishment from a pool of lies.

MAYOR STOCKMANN: Sheer fantasies—or something even worse. The man who can sling such wild and reckless slanders at his own hometown can't be anything other than an enemy of society.

DOCTOR STOCKMANN: (*Going for him.*) You dare—

MRS. STOCKMANN: (*Throwing herself between them.*) Thomas!

PETRA: (*Grasping her father's arm.*) Easy, father!

MAYOR STOCKMANN: I will not expose myself to violence. Now you've been warned. Consider what you owe yourself and your family. Goodbye. (*Goes.*)

DOCTOR STOCKMANN: (*Walking up and down.*) And I have to put up with this? In my own house, Katherine? What do you say to all this?

MRS. STOCKMANN: It's shameful and humiliating, there's no question.

PETRA: If I could only tell him what I think of him.

DOCTOR STOCKMANN: It's my own fault. I should have fought it out with them long ago—shown my teeth—bitten back! And to call me an enemy of society! Me! Even if my life depended on it, I will not stand for that!

MRS. STOCKMANN: Your brother has an awful lot of power, Thomas.

DOCTOR STOCKMANN: But I have the *right!*

MRS. STOCKMANN: Oh, the right, the right—what good does the right do you if you don't have the power?

PETRA: Mother—how can you say that?

DOCTOR STOCKMANN: So having the right on your side's not worth anything in a free society? Katherine, that's ridiculous. Besides, don't I also have the free and liberal press out in front with me? And the solid majority behind me? I'd say that's power enough.

MRS. STOCKMANN: But, good Lord, Thomas—surely you're not thinking of—

DOCTOR STOCKMANN: What am I surely not thinking of—

MRS. STOCKMANN: Of taking on your brother, I mean.

DOCTOR STOCKMANN: What the hell do you want me to do? Give up standing for the truth and the right?

PETRA: That's my question too.

MRS. STOCKMANN: But it won't do you any good—people won't do what they don't want to do.

DOCTOR STOCKMANN: Katherine, just give me time! You'll see, I'll fight this fight to the bitter end.

MRS. STOCKMANN: Yes—and you'll end up fighting yourself right out of a job—that's what you'll do.

DOCTOR STOCKMANN: As long as I've done my duty to the people—to society. I mean it—even though they call me its enemy.

MRS. STOCKMANN: And your family, Thomas? Doesn't your duty apply to us at home, too?

PETRA: Mother, don't always think of us first.

MRS. STOCKMANN: Yes, it's easy for you to talk. If need be, you can stand alone. But remember the boys, Thomas, and think of yourself a little—and of me—

DOCTOR STOCKMANN: I really think you've gone completely crazy, Katherine! If I fell fearfully at their feet—Peter's and the rest of his damn gang's—I'd never have a moment's happiness the rest of my life.

MRS. STOCKMANN: Well, I don't know—but God preserve us from the kind of happiness we'll have if you go on making trouble. There you'll be again, with no livelihood, no secure income. Haven't we had enough of that? Remember, Thomas, and think about what could happen.

DOCTOR STOCKMANN: (*Twisting in anguish, wringing his hands.*) So this is how these bureaucrats crush a free and honest man. Isn't it horrible, Katherine?

MRS. STOCKMANN: Yes, you're been treated badly, that's plain to see. But, good Lord—there are so many injustices we have to put up with in this world. And the boys, Thomas! What'll become of them? You couldn't have the heart to—

(*Meanwhile, Eilif and Morten enter, carrying schoolbooks.*)

DOCTOR STOCKMANN: The boys—! (*Suddenly stops with a determined look.*) No! Even if the whole world comes crashing down around me, I will not bow my neck under the yoke! (*He walks into his study.*)

MRS. STOCKMANN: Thomas, what are you talking about?

DOCTOR STOCKMANN: (*At the door.*) I want the right to look my boys straight in the eye when they've grown up into free men. (*He goes in.*)

MRS. STOCKMANN: (*Bursts into tears.*) Oh God, help and comfort us all!

PETRA: Father—he's magnificent! He's not giving in.

(*The boys wonderingly ask what is going on; Petra signals to them to be quiet.*)

END OF ACT TWO

ACT THREE

Editorial office of The People's Herald. *To the left, on the back wall, is an entrance door; to the right, on the same wall is a glazed door through which one can see the pressroom. On the wall to the right, a third door. At the center of the room is a large table covered with papers, newspapers and books. Downstage, left, is a window near which is a writing desk with a high stool. A couple of armchairs by the table and other chairs along the walls. The room is dismal and uncomfortable; the furniture is old, the armchairs dirty and torn. Within the pressroom a couple of typesetters can be seen working. Further back a handpress is being worked.*

(Hovstad sits at the desk, writing. A little after, Billing enters from the right with Dr. Stockmann's manuscript in his hand.)

BILLING: Well—I have to say—

HOVSTAD: (*Writing.*) Did you finish it?

BILLING: (*Puts the manuscript on the desk.*) I sure did.

HOVSTAD: Doesn't the Doctor have a nice edge to his style?

BILLING: Edge? He's Goddamn devastating! Every word crashes down like—how can I put it—like a blow from a sledgehammer!

HOVSTAD: Yes—but that crowd won't be knocked out by a single blow.

BILLING: True. So we'll just keep smashing them—blow after blow—until their whole world collapses. I sat there reading this and I could already see the revolution breaking like the dawn.

HOVSTAD: (*Turning.*) Shh! Don't let Aslaksen hear that.

BILLING: (*Lowers his voice.*) Aslaksen's a lily-livered little coward—no heart in him at all. But this time you're going to get your way, right? The Doctor's article is going in?

HOVSTAD: Yes—unless the Mayor does the right thing.

BILLING: That would be boring.

HOVSTAD: Fortunately, however, we get something out of it no matter what happens. If the Mayor rejects the Doctor's proposal, he'll bring all the small businessmen down on him—the whole Homeowners Association, and so on. And if he adopts it, he goes against all the big stockholders in the baths—and they've been his strongest supporters up to now.

BILLING: Yes, that's right. They'll have to lay out a huge pile of cash.

HOVSTAD: You can bet on it. And then the circle is broken, see? And every day, here in the paper, we'll be enlightening the people on the Mayor's incompetence in one thing after another, and how every elective office—the whole administration—ought to be handed over to the liberals.

BILLING: That's the plain and simple truth, God damn it! I can see it—I can see it—we're standing on the brink of a revolution!

(*A knock at the door.*)

HOVSTAD: Shhh. (*Calls.*) Come in!

(*Doctor Stockmann enters through the door at the back, left.*)

HOVSTAD: Oh—you're here, Doctor.

DOCTOR STOCKMANN: Roll the presses, Mr. Hovstad!

HOVSTAD: Then it's come to that!

BILLING: Bravo!

DOCTOR STOCKMANN: Roll the presses, I said. Yes, it's come to that. They'll get what they deserve now, Mr. Billing—now it's war in this town!

BILLING: Our knives at their throats!

DOCTOR STOCKMANN: This article's just the beginning. My head's already swimming with outlines for another four to five pieces. Where's Aslaksen gone?

BILLING: (*Calling.*) Aslaksen, come here a minute.

HOVSTAD: Four or five more pieces? On the same subject?

DOCTOR STOCKMANN: Oh, no—far from it, my friend. No, they'll be about other issues. But they all flow from the water system and the sewers. One thing leads to another, you see? It's like when you start to tear down an old building—exactly like that!

BILLING: My God, that's true. You can't stop until the whole thing's torn down.

ASLAKSEN: (*From the pressroom.*) Torn down! Surely you're not thinking of tearing down the baths, are you, Doctor?

HOVSTAD: No, of course not—don't be afraid.

Doctor Stockmann; No, that was something else altogether. So—what do you think of my article?

HOVSTAD: I think it's an absolute masterpiece.

DOCTOR STOCKMANN: Isn't it? Well, I'm very pleased, very pleased.

HOVSTAD: It's so straightforward and clear—you don't have to be a specialist to follow the argument at all. I'm sure you'll have every enlightened man in town on your side.

ASLAKSEN: And every moderate man as well?

BILLING: Moderate, immoderate—both! I mean, practically the whole town!

ASLAKSEN: Then I think we might dare print it.

DOCTOR STOCKMANN: I should think so!

HOVSTAD: It'll go in first thing tomorrow.

DOCTOR STOCKMANN: Yes—by God, we can't afford to waste a single day. Listen—Mr. Aslaksen—there's a favor I'd like to ask you. Would you give the manuscript your personal attention?

ASLAKSEN: I certainly will.

DOCTOR STOCKMANN: Treat it like gold. No misprints; every word is important. I'll be back later to look over the proofs. Oh, I can't tell you how anxious I am to see this thing in print, hurled out to the people—

BILLING: Hurled—yes! Like a thunderbolt!

DOCTOR STOCKMANN: So that every informed citizen can make up his own mind. Ah, you wouldn't believe what I've been subjected to today. They made one threat after another—they even wanted to take away my most basic human rights—rights that are as clear as day.

BILLING: What? Your human rights?

DOCTOR STOCKMANN: They wanted to make a coward of me—humiliate me—they tried to make me put personal interest ahead of my deepest and holiest convictions.

BILLING: Now that is just too God damn disgusting.

HOVSTAD: Well—that crowd will stop at nothing.

DOCTOR STOCKMANN: But they'll meet their match in me: they'll have it all spelled out in black and white. From now on, I'll be lying at anchor, bombarding them with one explosive article after another—

ASLAKSEN: Yes, but listen a moment—

BILLING: All right! It's war! It's war!

DOCTOR STOCKMANN: I'll smash them to the ground, crush them, lay waste to their defenses in the eyes of every right-thinking man. That's what I'll do!

ASLAKSEN: But in moderation, Doctor—crush them temperately—

BILLING: No—no—don't spare the dynamite.

DOCTOR STOCKMANN: (*Continues serenely.*) You see, it's no longer just the water system and the sewers that need to be cleaned and disinfected—it's the whole society.

BILLING: (*Fervently.*) Words to save us!

DOCTOR STOCKMANN: All these doddering incompetents must be swept away, wherever we find them. Such endless vistas have opened up for me today. It's not completely clear to me yet; but soon I'll be able to put words to it. There are strong, young standard-bearers out there, and we've got to go and seek them out, my friends. We need new commanders at all our outposts.

BILLING: Bravo!

DOCTOR STOCKMANN: And if we stand by one another, it will all be such clear sailing, such clear sailing. The whole revolution will be launched as smoothly as a ship. Don't you think so?

HOVSTAD: I think we have every chance of placing control of the community in the proper hands.

ASLAKSEN: And as long as we proceed in moderation, this shouldn't be dangerous.

DOCTOR STOCKMANN: What the hell does it matter if it's dangerous? What I'm doing, I'm doing in the name of truth—and for the sake of my conscience.

HOVSTAD: And you deserve our support, Doctor.

ASLAKSEN: Yes—it's clear that the Doctor is the town's true friend—a real friend of society is what he is!

BILLING: God damn it, Aslaksen, Doctor Stockmann is a Friend of the People!

ASLAKSEN: I think that's a slogan that the Homeowners Association can use.

DOCTOR STOCKMANN: (*Moved, pressing their hands.*) Thank you, thank you, my loyal friends: this is all so refreshing to hear, after what my own brother called me. Well, he's going to get it back with interest soon. Now I've got to go and look in on a poor bastard of a patient, but I'll be back as promised. Take very good care of my article, Mr. Aslaksen—and whatever you do, don't cut any exclamation points. If anything, add a couple! Well—good-bye for now—good-bye, good-bye—

(*Good-byes all around as he is escorted to the door and leaves.*)

HOVSTAD: He can be unbelievably useful to us.

ASLAKSEN: Yes, as long as he sticks to the issue. If he starts branching out, it might not be prudent to be associated with him.

HOVSTAD: Well—that all depends—

BILLING: You're always so damned scared, Aslaksen.

ASLAKSEN: Scared? Yes—when it has to do with the local authorities, I do get scared: it's a lesson I learned in the School of Life. But put me up against national politics—even against the government itself—and see if that scares me.

BILLING: That's true, it doesn't. That's what makes you so inconsistent.

ASLAKSEN: The thing is, I'm a man with a conscience. If you attack the national government, you don't do any harm to society—because the men up there don't take any notice—they'll stay in power no matter what. But the local authorities can actually be thrown out, and then you get stuck with a bunch of incompetents in power, with disastrous consequences for homeowners, and others.

HOVSTAD: But what about a citizen's right to improve himself through self-government? Don't you care about that?

ASLAKSEN: Well, Mr. Hovstad, when a man acquires property and possessions to care for, he doesn't have time to think about everything.

HOVSTAD: Then God grant me no property and possessions to care for.

BILLING: Hear, hear!

ASLAKSEN: (*Smiles.*) Hmf. (*Points to the desk.*) Councilman Stensgaard used to sit in that editor's chair.

BILLING: (*Spits.*) Uch! That traitor!

HOVSTAD: I don't play on both sides, and I never will.

ASLAKSEN: A politician, Mr. Hovstad, should never rule out anything in this world. And you, Mr. Billing, should pull in your sails a bit these days, I'd say—now that you're after the Council Secretary's position.

BILLING: I—?

HOVSTAD: Are you, Billing?

BILLING: Well, yes—but you can be damned sure I'm only doing it to irritate our so-called leaders.

ASLAKSEN: That's none of my concern. But when I'm accused of being cowardly and inconsistent, just let me make one thing clear: the political views of Aslaksen the printer are all on the public record for anyone to inspect. I haven't changed in any way—except that I've become more moderate. I tell you my heart is still with the people—but I won't deny my reason inclines a bit toward the authorities—I mean the local ones. (*He goes into the pressroom.*)

BILLING: Couldn't we get along without him, Hovstad?

HOVSTAD: Do you know anyone else who'll do our printing on credit?

BILLING: It's a damn shame we don't have the capital.

HOVSTAD: (*Sits at the desk.*) Yes—if we only had *that*—

BILLING: What about approaching the Doctor?

HOVSTAD: What good's that? He hasn't got anything.

BILLING: No, but he's got a good man behind him—the Badger—old Morten Kiil.

HOVSTAD: (*Writing.*) Are you so sure he's got anything?

BILLING: Yes, God damn it, he must have! And some of it is bound to go to the Stockmanns. At the least he'll leave something for—for the children.

HOVSTAD: (*Half turning.*) Are you counting on that?

BILLING: Counting on it? I'm not counting on anything.

HOVSTAD: That's smart. And that job on the Council—I wouldn't count on that either. Because I promise you, you won't get it.

BILLING: You think I don't know that? That's what I'm looking forward to— not getting it. A slap in the face like that fires up your fighting spirit—and you really need that in a little backwater like this, where nothing exciting ever happens.

HOVSTAD: (*Writing.*) Yes, yes.

BILLING: Well, they'll hear from me soon enough! Now I'm going to write that pitch to the Homeowners' Association. (*He goes into the room, right.*)

HOVSTAD: Hmm. So that's how it is. (*A knock.*) Come in! (*Petra enters from the door back left.*)

PETRA: Excuse me—

HOVSTAD: (*Pulls an armchair forward.*) Won't you sit down?

PETRA: No thank you—I'm leaving right away.

HOVSTAD: Is it something from your Father, perhaps—?

PETRA: No, it's something from me. (*She takes a book from her coat pocket.*) Here's that English story.

HOVSTAD: Why are you returning it?

PETRA: Because I don't want to translate it.

HOVSTAD: But you gave me such a firm commitment.

PETRA: Yes—because I hadn't read it yet. And you certainly haven't read it, have you?

HOVSTAD: You know I don't read English—but—

PETRA: All right. That's why I wanted to tell you to find something else. (*Lays the book on the table.*) You could never use this in *The People's Herald.*

HOVSTAD: Why not?

PETRA: Because it goes against everything you believe in.

HOVSTAD: Well—whatever harm that might—

PETRA: You don't quite understand. It's all about how a supernatural power watches over the so-called good people here on earth, and arranges everything in their lives for the best—and how all the so-called wicked people get punished.

HOVSTAD: But that's fine—it's exactly what people like to read.

PETRA: Do you really want to be the kind of person who feeds the public that stuff? You don't believe a word of it yourself—you know perfectly well that's not the way the world works in reality.

HOVSTAD: You're absolutely right. But an editor can't always do what he wants. We have to bow to the public in a lot of little ways. See, politics is the main thing in life—at least for a newspaper. And if I'm going to win people over to the side of freedom and progress I can't afford to scare them away. When people find a story with a comfortable moral in the back pages, they go along more easily with what we print up front. They feel more secure.

PETRA: Uch! You wouldn't be so deceitful, would you? Trapping your readers like a spider?

HOVSTAD: (*Smiling.*) Thanks for thinking so well of me. No, actually it was Billing's idea, not mine.

PETRA: Billing's!

HOVSTAD: Yes: he was talking about it just the other day. Billing was very eager to get that story in—I don't know the book at all.

PETRA: But how could Billing, with his progressive ideas—?

HOVSTAD: Oh, there are many sides to our Mr. Billing. Now he's after the Council Secretary's position.

PETRA: I don't believe that, Mr. Hovstad. How could he possibly bring himself to do that?

HOVSTAD: You'll have to ask him yourself.

PETRA: I would never have thought that of Billing.

HOVSTAD: (*Looks intently at her.*) Never? It is really so unthinkable?

PETRA: Yes. Or maybe not, after all. Oh, I don't know.

HOVSTAD: We journalists aren't all that noble, Miss Stockmann.

PETRA: Do you really mean that

HOVSTAD: I think so, now and then.

PETRA: I can understand that about your everyday squabbles—but when you're part of a great cause—

HOVSTAD: You mean all this with your father?

PETRA: Yes, exactly. I imagine that now you feel just a little more noble than most men.

HOVSTAD: Yes, I do feel a bit like that today.

PETRA: Yes, it's true—you do, don't you. Oh, it's a wonderful profession you've chosen. To be able—like now—to clear the way for misunderstood truths and bold new ways of thinking—or even just to stand up without fear for a man who's been wronged.

HOVSTAD: Even moreso, when that man who's been wronged—hm—I don't quite know how to say this—

PETRA: When he's so decent and honest, you mean?

HOVSTAD: (*Softly.*) Even more so, when that man is your father, I mean.

PETRA: (*Suddenly startled.*) Is that it?

HOVSTAD: Yes, Petra—Miss Petra.

PETRA: Is *that* what you're interested in? Not the issue itself? Not the truth? Not my father's concern for his fellow men?

HOVSTAD: Well, yes, of course, all that as well.

PETRA: No thank you. You've given yourself away, Mr. Hovstad. And now I can never believe you again—about anything.

HOVSTAD: Can you really blame me, when it was mainly for your sake—

PETRA: The thing that makes me so furious with you is that you didn't play straight with my father. You talked as if all your thoughts were for the truth and the good of society. But you made fools of us both. You're not the man you represent yourself to be. And for that I'll never forgive you—never!

HOVSTAD: You shouldn't be quite so critical of me—at least, not right now.

PETRA: Why now, especially?

HOVSTAD: Because your father won't survive without my help.

PETRA: (*Looking down at him.*) You'd do that too?

HOVSTAD: No, no. That just came over me without warning. I'm not like that, you've got to believe me.

PETRA: I know what to believe. Good-bye.

ASLAKSEN: (*From the pressroom, urgently and secretively.*) Damn it to hell, Hovstad—(*sees Petra*) Oops.

PETRA: There's the book—give it to someone else. (*She goes to the entrance door.*)

HOVSTAD: (*Calling after.*) Petra—!

PETRA: Good-bye. (*She goes.*)

ASLAKSEN: Mr. Hovstad, listen!

HOVSTAD: All right, what is it?

ASLAKSEN: The mayor's in the pressroom.

HOVSTAD: The mayor?

ASLAKSEN: Yes, and he wants to talk to you. He came in the back way—doesn't want to be seen, I guess.

HOVSTAD: Find out what it's about—no, wait, I'll go myself. (*He goes to*

the pressroom door, opens it, and invites Mayor Stockmann in.)
Keep a lookout, Aslaksen, so that nobody—

ASLAKSEN: I understand. (*Goes into the pressroom.*)

MAYOR STOCKMANN: Mr. Hovstad, I imagine you never expected to see me here, did you?

HOVSTAD: No, as a matter of fact I didn't.

MAYOR STOCKMANN: (*Looking around.*) You've set yourself up quite nicely here—very comfortable.

HOVSTAD: Oh—

MAYOR STOCKMANN: And now here I come, uninvited, and monopolize your time.

HOVSTAD: Please, Mr. Mayor—I'm at your service. Let me take these for you. (*Puts the Mayor's hat and stick on a chair.*) And won't you sit down?

MAYOR STOCKMANN: (*Sits at the table.*) Thank you.
(*Hovstad also sits at the table.*)

MAYOR STOCKMANN: I've been through—really a most disagreeable experience today, Mr. Hovstad.

HOVSTAD: Yes? But then, of course, with all the problems the Mayor must have—

MAYOR STOCKMANN: This one, today, involves the Medical Supervisor at the baths.

HOVSTAD: Really? The Doctor?

MAYOR STOCKMANN: He's authored some kind of report to the Board of Directors concerning a number of alleged flaws—

HOVSTAD: He did that?

MAYOR STOCKMANN: Yes, hasn't he told you? I thought he said—

HOVSTAD: Ah, yes, that's right. He did drop a hint—

ASLAKSEN: (*From the pressroom.*) I'd better get that manuscript.

HOVSTAD: (*Vexed.*) Uh there it is, on the desk.

ASLAKSEN: (*Finds it.*) Good!

MAYOR STOCKMANN: But look, that's it, isn't it?

ASLAKSEN: Yes, that's the Doctor's article, Mr. Mayor.

HOVSTAD: What? Is *that* what you were talking about?

MAYOR STOCKMANN: That's it, precisely. What do you think of it?

HOVSTAD: Well, I'm no expert, and I've only skimmed through it.

MAYOR STOCKMANN: And yet you're printing it?

HOVSTAD: I could hardly refuse such a prominent figure—

ASLAKSEN: Mr. Mayor, I have no say in what goes into this paper.

MAYOR STOCKMANN: That's understood.

ASLAKSEN: I just print what's put in my hands.

MAYOR STOCKMANN: Of course.

ASLAKSEN: And so, if I may—?

MAYOR STOCKMANN: No, just a moment, Mr. Aslaksen. With your permission, Mr. Hovstad.

HOVSTAD: Please, Mr. Mayor, go ahead.

MAYOR STOCKMANN: You're a thoughtful man, Mr. Aslaksen—a sensible man.

ASLAKSEN: I'm glad the Mayor should think so.

MAYOR STOCKMANN: A man whose influence is felt in many circles.

ASLAKSEN: Mostly among the working classes.

MAYOR STOCKMANN: The small taxpayers make up the great majority, here as elsewhere.

ASLAKSEN: That's very true.

MAYOR STOCKMANN: And I have no doubt that you understand their sentiments, by and large.

ASLAKSEN: Yes. I think I dare say that, Mr. Mayor.

MAYOR STOCKMANN: Yes, well—the fact that our town's less affluent citizens should have such a laudable spirit of self-sacrifice is truly—

ASLAKSEN: What's that?

HOVSTAD: Self-sacrifice?

MAYOR STOCKMANN:—is truly a beautiful sign of community spirit—an exceedingly beautiful sign. I almost said I wouldn't have expected it—but you understand the people's feelings much more deeply than I do.

ASLAKSEN: Yes, but—Mr. Mayor—

MAYOR STOCKMANN: And to tell you the truth, it's no small sacrifice the town will be making.

HOVSTAD: The town.

ASLAKSEN: But I don't understand—it's the baths that will—

MAYOR STOCKMANN: The initial estimate indicates that the modifications deemed desirable by the Medical Supervisor will cost up to a couple of hundred thousand kroner.

ASLAKSEN: That's a lot of money, but—

MAYOR STOCKMANN: Obviously it will be necessary to take out a municipal loan.

HOVSTAD: (*Rising.*) You can't really mean that the town—

ASLAKSEN: Out of property taxes! Out of the empty pockets of the working people!

MAYOR STOCKMANN: But, my excellent Mr. Aslaksen, where else would the capital come from?

ASLAKSEN: That's a problem for the Board of Directors to work out.

MAYOR STOCKMANN: The Directors see themselves in no position to stretch their resources further than they already have.

ASLAKSEN: Is that absolutely certain, Mr. Mayor?

MAYOR STOCKMANN: I have assured myself of it. If all these expensive modifications are really desired, then the town itself will have to pay for them.

ASLAKSEN: But damn it to hell—please excuse me—but this is a completely different situation, Mr. Hovstad.

HOVSTAD: Yes, it certainly is.

MAYOR STOCKMANN: The deadliest part of it is that we'll be forced to shut down the baths for a two-year period.

HOVSTAD: Shut them down? Completely?

ASLAKSEN: For two years!

MAYOR STOCKMANN: Yes—the work will take at least that long.

ASLAKSEN: Yes, but damn it all, we'll never survive that, Mr. Mayor! What'll we homeowners live on in the meantime?

MAYOR STOCKMANN: That is, unfortunately, an extremely difficult question to answer, Mr. Aslaksen. But what should we do? Do you think we'll get a single summer visitor here as long as someone is running around fantasizing that the water is poisoned, that we're living in a sewer, that the whole town—

ASLAKSEN: And you're certain it's only fantasy?

MAYOR STOCKMANN: With the best will in the world, I haven't been able to persuade myself otherwise.

ASLAKSEN: Yes, but then it's utterly reprehensible for Doctor Stockmann to—I beg your pardon, Mr. Mayor, but—

MAYOR STOCKMANN: Regrettably, what you say is true, Mr. Aslaksen. My brother, unfortunately, has always been intemperate.

ASLAKSEN: And you still support him, Mr. Hovstad?

HOVSTAD: But who could have thought—?

MAYOR STOCKMANN: I have drafted a brief account of the actual situation, seen from a sober point of view; in it, I suggest how any anticipated inconveniences could be fixed with a moderate outlay of the baths' resources.

HOVSTAD: Do you have this document with you, Mr. Mayor?

MAYOR STOCKMANN: (*Fumbling in his pocket.*) I brought it with me just in case—

ASLAKSEN: Damn it to hell, there he is!

MAYOR STOCKMANN: Who—my brother?

HOVSTAD: Where, where?

ASLAKSEN: Coming through the pressroom.

MAYOR STOCKMANN: How unfortunate! I really don't want to run into him here, but I have more to say to you—

HOVSTAD: (*Pointing to the door, right.*) Step in there for a minute.

MAYOR STOCKMANN: But—?

HOVSTAD: Only Billing.

ASLAKSEN: Hurry, hurry, Mr. Mayor, here he comes!

MAYOR STOCKMANN: Yes, yes, all right: but get him out of here quickly. (*He goes out through the door on the right as Aslaksen opens and closes it for him.*)

HOVSTAD: Act busy, Aslaksen.

(*Hovstad sits down and starts writing. Aslaksen rummages through a pile of papers on a chair, right.*)

DOCTOR STOCKMANN: (*Coming in from the pressroom.*) Here I am again! (*Puts down his hat and stick.*)

HOVSTAD: (*Writing.*) Here already, Doctor? Aslaksen, hurry up with what we were talking about. Time's really in short supply today.

DOCTOR STOCKMANN: (*To Aslaksen.*) No proofs yet, I hear.

ASLAKSEN: (*Without turning.*) No. How could you expect that, Doctor?

DOCTOR STOCKMANN: No, of course not, I'm just impatient, as I'm sure you can imagine. I can't rest or relax until I see it in print.

ASLAKSEN: Hmmm. It'll be a good while yet. Wouldn't you say so, Hovstad?

HOVSTAD: Yes, I'm afraid so.

DOCTOR STOCKMANN: Well, well, my friends, I'll come back. I'd gladly come back twice if need be. With such a major issue at stake— the whole town's welfare—it's no time for me to be holding things up. (*He is about to go, but stops and comes back.*) Oh listen—there's one more thing I want to talk to you about.

HOVSTAD: I'm sorry, but couldn't it wait?

DOCTOR STOCKMANN: It'll take a second. It's just that—when people read my article in the paper, and then find out that all through the winter I've been silently working for the good of the town—

HOVSTAD: Yes, but Doctor—

DOCTOR STOCKMANN: Oh, I know what you're going to say—it was nothing more than my damn duty, my simple civic duty, and I agree with you. But my fellow citizens, bless them, have such a high opinion of me—

ASLAKSEN: Yes, the people have had the greatest regard for you up till now, Doctor.

DOCTOR STOCKMANN: And just because of that I'm afraid—what I want to say is—when something like this comes along, the people—especially the underprivileged classes—look on it as a challenge to take the town's future into their own hands—

HOVSTAD: (*Getting up.*) Hmm. Doctor, I don't want to conceal from you that—

DOCTOR STOCKMANN: Aha! I guessed there was something in the works! But I won't allow it. If anyone is trying to arrange something like that—

HOVSTAD: Like what?

DOCTOR STOCKMANN: Well, any kind of thing—a parade, or a banquet, or donations for a testimonial award—whatever it is—then promise me, swear you'll put a stop to it. That goes for you too, Mr. Aslaksen—do you hear?

HOVSTAD: Forgive me, Doctor—but we'd better tell you the real truth of the matter—the whole truth.

(*Mrs. Stockmann, in hat and coat, enters through back door left.*)

MRS. STOCKMANN: (*Seeing the Doctor.*) Just as I thought!

HOVSTAD: (*Goes over to her.*) You're here too, Mrs. Stockmann?

DOCTOR STOCKMANN: What the hell are you doing here, Katherine?

MRS. STOCKMANN: You can very well imagine what I'm doing.

HOVSTAD: Won't you at least sit down—or perhaps—

MRS. STOCKMANN: Thanks, but don't bother. And please don't be offended that I've come here to fetch Stockmann—I'm the mother of three children, you know.

DOCTOR STOCKMANN: Katherine, for God's—we all know that.

MRS. STOCKMANN: Well it doesn't look as if you're thinking much about your wife and children these days, or you wouldn't be acting like this and throwing our lives away.

DOCTOR STOCKMANN: Are you completely mad, Katherine? Does a man who happens to have a wife and children have no right to speak the truth?—no right to be active as a citizen?—no right to serve the town he lives in?

MRS. STOCKMANN: But everything in moderation, Thomas!

ASLAKSEN: Exactly what I say. Moderation in all things.

MRS. STOCKMANN: And so you harm each one of us, Mr. Hovstad, when you lure my husband away from house and home and fool him into taking part in all of this.

HOVSTAD: I'm certainly not trying to fool anyone—

DOCTOR STOCKMANN: Fool me! Do you think I let anyone fool me?

MRS. STOCKMANN: Yes, you do. Oh, I know you're the smartest man in town, Thomas, but you're so easy to fool. (*To Hovstad.*) Just keep in mind that he'll lose his job if you print that article he wrote.

ASLAKSEN: What's that!

HOVSTAD: Well, Doctor, you know what—?

DOCTOR STOCKMANN: (*Laughing.*) Just let them try! Oh, no, they'd better watch out—because, you see, I have a solid majority behind me.

MRS. STOCKMANN: That's the whole trouble—having a horrid thing like that behind you.

DOCTOR STOCKMANN: Garbage, Katherine! Go home and take care of your house and let me take care of society. How can you be so afraid when I'm so ecstatic and confident? (*Rubbing his hands and walking up and down.*) Truth and the people will win this battle, you can take an oath on that. Ah, I see every freethinking citizen coming together as a victorious army—! (*Stops by a chair.*) What the hell is *that* doing here?

ASLAKSEN: Oops.

HOVSTAD: Hmm.

DOCTOR STOCKMANN: Here lies the pinnacle of authority. (*He picks up the Mayor's hat carefully by the tips of his fingers and holds it aloft.*)

MRS. STOCKMANN: The Mayor's hat!

DOCTOR STOCKMANN: And here, the scepter of command! How in the name of the Devil—?

HOVSTAD: Uh—well—it's—

DOCTOR STOCKMANN: Ah! I see! He's been here to try to win you over—(*Laughs.*) He came to the right people, didn't he? And then he caught a glimpse of me in the pressroom. (*Bursts into laughter.*) So he ran away, Mr. Aslaksen?

ASLAKSEN: (*quickly*) That's right, Doctor, he ran away.

DOCTOR STOCKMANN: Ran away from his stick and—oh, nonsense, Peter never runs away from anything. But where the hell have you put him? Ah—of course. Now, Katherine, watch this!

MRS. STOCKMANN: Thomas—I beg you!

(*The Doctor puts on the Mayor's hat, takes his stick, walks over, throws open the door, and stands there, saluting. Mayor Stockmann enters, red with anger. Behind him comes Billing.*)

MAYOR STOCKMANN: What's the meaning of this display?

DOCTOR STOCKMANN: Show some respect, my worthy Peter. I'm the authority now. (*He struts up and down.*)

MRS. STOCKMANN: (*Almost in tears.*) Please, Thomas, no!

MAYOR STOCKMANN: (*Following him.*) Give me those!

DOCTOR STOCKMANN: (*As before.*) You may be the police chief, but I'm the Mayor! See? I'm in charge of the whole town.

MAYOR STOCKMANN: Take off that hat, I tell you. Remember, it's an official symbol of office.

DOCTOR STOCKMANN: Ffft! Do you think you can scare the waking lion of the people with a hat? Yes, because you'd better understand that we're having a revolution in town tomorrow. You threatened to remove me, but now I'm removing you—removing you from all your official positions. You think I can't do it? But I can. I have the swelling voice of the people on my side. Hovstad and Billing will thunder in the *Herald* and Aslaksen will take to the field with the whole Homeowners' Association.

ASLAKSEN: I won't do it, Doctor.

DOCTOR STOCKMANN: Of course you will.

MAYOR STOCKMANN: Ah. But perhaps Mr. Hovstad has chosen to ally himself with this agitation.

HOVSTAD: No, Mr. Mayor.

ASLAKSEN: No, Mr. Hovstad's not so crazy as to go and ruin himself and his paper for the sake of a fantasy.

DOCTOR STOCKMANN: (*Looking around.*) What does all this mean?

HOVSTAD: You've misrepresented your case, Doctor. I can't support it.

BILLING: No, after what the mayor was kind enough to tell me in there—

DOCTOR STOCKMANN: Misrepresented? Let me be the judge of that. Just print my article. I'll be man enough to answer for it.

HOVSTAD: I'm not printing it. I can't, and I won't, and I don't dare print it.

DOCTOR STOCKMANN: You don't dare? What kind of talk is that? You're the editor, and the editor controls the paper, I should hope!

ASLAKSEN: Ah, no, Doctor, it's the subscribers.

MAYOR STOCKMANN: Yes, fortunately.

ASLAKSEN: Public opinion, enlightened citizens, homeowners and the rest: they're the ones that control the paper.

DOCTOR STOCKMANN: (*Calmly.*) And all these forces are against me?

ASLAKSEN: Yes they are. If your article were published, it would mean total ruin for the town.

DOCTOR STOCKMANN: I see.

MAYOR STOCKMANN: My hat and stick!

(*Doctor Stockmann takes off the hat and sets it on the table with the stick.*)

Your first term as mayor has come to an abrupt end.

DOCTOR STOCKMANN: It's not the end, yet. (*To Hovstad.*) No chance, then, of running my article in *The People's Herald?*

HOVSTAD: No chance. Also out of consideration for your family.

MRS. STOCKMANN: Don't trouble yourself about his family, Mr. Hovstad.

MAYOR STOCKMANN: (*Takes a paper from his pocket.*) For the public's information, this will be sufficient. It's an authorized statement. If you please.

HOVSTAD: (*Takes paper.*) Good. I'll make sure it goes in.

DOCTOR STOCKMANN: And not mine! You think you can keep me quiet and kill the truth. But it won't be as easy as you imagine. Mr. Aslaksen, take my manuscript and print it as a pamphlet—right away—at my own expense, on my own authority. I'll need four hundred—no, I'll take five—six hundred copies.

ASLAKSEN: Not if you paid me in gold. I don't dare let my press do something like that, for the sake of public opinion. You won't get that printed anywhere in town.

DOCTOR STOCKMANN: Then give it back to me.

HOVSTAD: (*Hands him the manuscript.*) Here it is.

DOCTOR STOCKMANN: (*Picks up his hat and stick.*) It will appear, all the same. I'll read it out at a mass meeting! All my fellow citizens will hear the voice of the truth!

MAYOR STOCKMANN: You won't find an organization in town to give you a hall.

ASLAKSEN: Not a single one. I'm certain of it.

BILLING: No, God damn it, they won't.

MRS. STOCKMANN: But that would be utterly shameful! Why are they all turning against you like this, these men?

DOCTOR STOCKMANN: (*Angrily.*) I'll tell you why. It's because in this town all these men are really old biddies—like you. They can only think about their families, not about the community.

MRS. STOCKMANN: (*Taking his arm.*) Then I'll show them what—what an old biddy can do. I'm standing beside you, Thomas.

DOCTOR STOCKMANN: Well said, Katherine. This will come out if it's the last thing I do! If I can't rent a hall, I'll hire a drummer to walk through town with me, and I'll proclaim the truth on every corner!

MAYOR STOCKMANN: You're just crazy enough to do that!

DOCTOR STOCKMANN: Yes I am!

ASLAKSEN: You won't get a single man in the whole town to go with you.

BILLING: No, God damn it, you won't.

MRS. STOCKMANN: Don't give up now, Thomas. I'll ask the boys to go with you.

DOCTOR STOCKMANN: That's a magnificent idea!

MRS. STOCKMANN: Morten would love to do it, and Eilif—well, he'll go along.

DOCTOR STOCKMANN: Yes, and Petra. And you too, Katherine!

MRS. STOCKMANN: No, no, not me. But I'll stand at the door and watch you—that I'll do.

DOCTOR STOCKMANN: (*Takes her in his arms and kisses her.*) Thanks for that! And now we're ready for battle, gentlemen! Let's see if your shabby tactics can muzzle the mouth of a patriot bent on cleansing the community!

(*Doctor and Mrs. Stockmann go out through the door, back left.*)

MAYOR STOCKMANN: (*Thoughtfully shaking his head.*) Now he's driven her mad, too!

END OF ACT THREE

Act Four

A large, old-fashioned room in Captain Horster's house. Double doors in the back of the room open onto an anteroom. On the wall, left, are three windows. Against the opposite wall is a platform, and on that a little table with no candles, a water carafe, a glass and a bell. The room is mainly illuminated by wall lamps between the windows. Downstage, left, stands a table with candles and a chair. Downstage right is a door and beside it two chairs.

(There is a great crowd of citizens of all classes. A few women and one or two schoolboys can be seen among them. More and more people keep coming in through the back door until the room fills up.)

A CITIZEN: *(To another whom he bumps into.)* So you're here tonight too, Lamstad?

2ND MAN: I always go to public meetings.

3RD MAN: Then I suppose you brought your whistle?

2ND MAN: You bet I did. How about you?

3RD MAN: Oh yes. And Skipper Evensen's bringing one hell of a big horn, he told me.

2ND MAN: Evensen—what a guy!

(Laughter in the group.)

4TH MAN: *(Joining them.)* Hey, what brings you all here tonight?

2ND MAN: It's Dr. Stockmann—he's holding a public meeting to speak against the Mayor.

A NEWCOMER: But the Mayor's his brother.

1ST MAN: Doesn't matter—the Doctor's not afraid.

3RD MAN: But he's got it all wrong. It says so in *The People's Herald*.

2ND MAN: Yes, he must be wrong this time. No one would let him have a meeting hall—not the Homeowners' Association, not the civic club—

1ST MAN: He couldn't even get the hall at the baths.

2ND MAN: Well, you can understand why.

A MAN: *(In another group.)* Whose side are we on in this?

ANOTHER MAN: *(In the same group.)* Just keep watching Aslaksen, and do what he does.

BILLING: *(With a briefcase under his arm, pushing his way through the crowd.)* Excuse me, gentlemen! Can I just squeeze through? I'm covering this for *The People's Herald*. Many thanks! *(He sits at table, left.)*

A Workman: Who was that?

Another Workman: Don't you know him? That's that Billing who writes for Aslaksen's paper.

(*Captain Horster leads Mrs. Stockmann and Petra through the door right front. Eilif and Morten follow them.*)

Horster: I thought the family should sit right here. You can easily slip out if anything happens.

Mrs. Stockmann: Do you think there'll be any trouble?

Horster: You never know—with so many people—but just keep calm.

Mrs. Stockmann: (*Sits.*) You were very kind to offer my husband this room.

Horster: Well, nobody else would, so—

Petra: (*Who has also taken a seat.*) And it was brave, too, Captain Horster.

Horster: Oh, there's nothing particularly brave about it, as far as I can see.

(*Hovstad and Aslaksen arrive at the same time but make their way through the crowd separately.*)

Aslaksen: (*Walks over to Horster.*) Isn't the Doctor here yet?

Horster: He's waiting in there.

(*Movement around the door in back.*)

Hovstad: (*To Billing.*) Here comes the Mayor. Look!

Billing: Well, God damn it if he didn't show up after all.

(*Mayor Stockmann proceeds calmly through the crowd, politely greeting people and positioning himself by the wall to the left. Soon after, Doctor Stockmann comes in through the door right front. He wears a black frock coat with a white cravat. Some people applaud tentatively and are met by subdued hissing. Then there is silence.*)

Doctor Stockmann: (*In an undertone.*) How do you feel, Katherine?

Mrs. Stockmann: Oh, I'm all right. (*Lowering her voice.*) Try not to lose your temper, Thomas.

Doctor Stockmann: I can control myself, don't worry. (*Looks at his watch, steps up on the platform, and bows.*) It's a quarter after— I'd like to begin now. (*Takes out his manuscript.*)

Aslaksen: First we should elect a chairman.

Doctor Stockmann: No, that really won't be necessary.

Voices: Yes, yes!

MAYOR STOCKMANN: I agree that a moderator should be chosen.

DOCTOR STOCKMANN: But I've called this meeting to read a lecture, Peter!

MAYOR STOCKMANN: The doctor's lecture is likely to elicit many conflicting expressions of opinion.

MANY VOICES: A chairman! A moderator!

HOVSTAD: The general will of the people seems to demand a moderator.

DOCTOR STOCKMANN: (*Self-restrained.*) All right, fine. Let the will of the people have its way.

ASLAKSEN: Would the Mayor consent to assume that office?

THREE MEN: (*Applauding.*) Bravo! Bravo!

MAYOR STOCKMANN: For a number of self-evident reasons, I must decline. Happily, however, we have among us a man who is, I believe, acceptable to everybody. I refer, of course, to the chairman of the Homeowners' Association, the publisher Mr. Aslaksen.

MANY VOICES: Yes, yes! Three cheers for Aslaksen! Hurray for Aslaksen!

(*Doctor Stockmann takes his manuscript and steps down from the platform.*)

ASLAKSEN: As my fellow citizens have demonstrated their trust in me, I cannot decline—

(*Applause and shouts of approval as Aslaksen mounts the platform.*)

BILLING: (*Writing.*) And so—"the publisher Aslaksen chosen by acclamation."

ASLAKSEN: From the vantage point of my new position I ask permission to say a few concise words. I am a tranquil and peace-loving man who believes in prudent moderation—and in moderate prudence as well. That is acknowledged by everyone who knows me.

MANY VOICES: Yes, yes! That's right, Aslaksen!

ASLAKSEN: In the Schools of Life and Experience, I've learned that moderation is the chief virtue of a citizen—

MAYOR STOCKMANN: Hear, hear!

ASLAKSEN: And that moderation and discretion are the qualities that serve society best. And so I would appeal to the honorable gentleman who called this meeting that he strive to conduct himself within the bounds of temperance.

A Man: Skoal to the Temperance Union!

A Voice: Shut the hell up!

Many Voices: Shh! Shh!

Aslaksen: No interruptions, gentlemen, please! Does anyone wish the floor?

Mayor Stockmann: Mr. Chairman!

Aslaksen: The Mayor has the floor.

Mayor Stockmann: Considering my close relationship to the present Medical Supervisor of the baths, I would really have preferred not to voice my views tonight. But my position with the baths and my concern for the vital interests of the town compel me to put forward a motion. I believe it's safe to assume that not a single citizen present here tonight would approve of irresponsible and exaggerated accounts of the sanitary conditions of both the baths and the town being spread around in the wider world.

Voices: No, no, no! Not that! We protest!

Mayor Stockmann: I therefore move that at this meeting the Medical Supervisor not be allowed to read or otherwise present his version of the situation.

Doctor Stockmann: (*Flaring up.*) Not allowed! What is this?

Mrs. Stockmann: (*Coughing.*) Ahem! Ahem!

Doctor Stockmann: (*Calming himself.*) So! Not allowed.

Mayor Stockmann: In my statement to *The People's Herald* I acquainted the public with the basic facts, so that every well-meaning citizen might easily make his own judgment. As you can see, the Doctor's proposals—besides constituting a vote of no confidence in the town's leading citizens—would in fact be a prescription for burdening our taxpayers with a needless expenditure of—at the least—several hundred thousand kroner. (*Cries and whistles.*)

Aslaksen: Order, gentlemen! Allow me to speak in support of the Mayor's motion. And what's more, I suspect that there is an ulterior motive for the Doctor's agitation. He talks about the baths, but he's really driving at a revolution. He wants to put the power of government into other hands. Nobody doubts the integrity of the Doctor's intentions—Lord knows, no one can be of two minds about that. I'm all in favor of the power of the people as long as it doesn't cost the taxpayers too much. But that would be just the situation here. And that's why I'll be damned— please excuse me—if I'll go along with Doctor Stockmann this time. You can pay too much, even for gold—that's my opinion.

HOVSTAD: I also think I ought to state my position. Doctor Stockmann's agitation seemed to be gaining enormous popularity in the beginning, and I supported it as impartially as I could. But then we began to get wind that we had been misled by a false representation—

DOCTOR STOCKMANN: False!

HOVSTAD: A less accurate representation, then. The Mayor's statement has demonstrated that. I trust that nobody here at this meeting questions my liberal credentials—the policy of *The People's Herald* on all the major political issues is well known to everyone. But I have learned—from experienced and thoughtful men—that in matters which are strictly local, a paper should proceed with a certain caution.

ASLAKSEN: I agree completely with the speaker.

HOVSTAD: And, regarding the matter at hand, it's now beyond argument that public opinion has turned against Doctor Stockmann. Now, gentlemen, what is an editor's first and foremost duty? Isn't it to work in concert with his readers? Doesn't he have a tacit mandate to work tirelessly, advancing the causes of those whose convictions he shares? Or maybe I'm mistaken about that?

MANY VOICES: No, no, no! Hovstad is right.

HOVSTAD: It's been a difficult struggle to break with a man in whose house I have been a frequent guest until now—a man who, until today, could bask in the unmitigated goodwill of his fellow citizens—a man whose only—or at least, whose characteristic failing is that he follows his heart instead of his head.

SCATTERED VOICES: That's true! Hurray for Doctor Stockmann.

HOVSTAD: But my civic duty demanded that I break with him. There's still another consideration that compels me to oppose him and, if I can, stop him from going any farther down the fateful path he's chosen: and that's my concern for his family—

DOCTOR STOCKMANN: Stick to the water mains and sewers!

HOVSTAD: My concern for his life's partner and his unfortunate children.

MORTEN: Is that us, Mother?

MRS. STOCKMANN: Shh!

ASLAKSEN: I will now put the Mayor's motion to a vote.

DOCTOR STOCKMANN: Forget it. Tonight I won't bother to speak about all the filth down at the baths. No, you're going to hear about something quite different.

MAYOR STOCKMANN: (*In an undertone.*) Now what are we in for?

A DRUNK: (*By the entrance door.*) I'm a taxpayer, and I've got my rights to an opinion too! And I want a plastered—a platform for my incomprehensible opinion that—

MANY VOICES: Be quiet over there!

OTHERS: He's drunk! Throw him out!

(*The Drunk is ejected.*)

DOCTOR STOCKMANN: Do I have the floor?

ASLAKSEN: (*Ringing the bell.*) Doctor Stockmann has the floor.

DOCTOR STOCKMANN: If anyone had dared—only a few days ago—to try to silence me as they have tonight, I would have leapt like a lion to the defense of my sacred human rights. But now I hardly care at all—because now I have much bigger things to talk about. (*The crowd presses closer around him. Morten Kiil can be seen in the crowd.*)

DOCTOR STOCKMANN: (*Continuing.*) I've been thinking and pondering a great deal these last few days—pondering so much that finally my thoughts became quite confused—

MAYOR STOCKMANN: (*Coughs.*) Hm—!

DOCTOR STOCKMANN: But then things began to come clear: I began to see so clearly how everything fits together. That's why I'm standing here this evening. I have a great revelation to announce, my fellow citizens! I'm about to proclaim a discovery of a far greater dimension than this little matter that our water system is poisoned, that our health spa is built on polluted ground.

MANY VOICES: (*Shouting.*) Don't talk about the baths! We won't listen! None of that!

DOCTOR STOCKMANN: I've said I'll speak of my great discovery of the last few days—the discovery that all the sources of our spiritual life are poisoned, that our entire community is built on polluted ground.

STARTLED VOICES: (*In undertones.*) What's he saying?

MAYOR STOCKMANN: What kind of insinuation is this—

ASLAKSEN: (*His hand on the bell.*) The speaker is urged to moderate himself.

DOCTOR STOCKMANN: I have loved my birthplace as much as any man possibly can. I was still young when I left here—and distance, longing, and memory cast the town and its people in a beautiful light in my mind.

(*Some applause and cheers.*)

And then, I sat up there for so many years, in that miserable hole up north. When I'd come across some of the people who lived scattered through that desert of rocks, it struck me more than once that what those poor, half-alive creatures needed, more than someone like me, was a veterinarian.

(*Murmuring in the room.*)

BILLING: (*Laying down his pen.*) I'll be God damned if I've ever heard such—

HOVSTAD: That's an insult to the common man.

DOCTOR STOCKMANN: Wait a minute. I don't think anyone could say that I forgot my hometown up there. Like an old hen, I brooded on my egg and what I hatched—was the plan for the baths here.

(*Applause and protests.*)

DOCTOR STOCKMANN: And then, finally, when fate relented and smiled on me, bringing me home again—my friends, it seemed to me then that I couldn't possibly want anything else in the world. But I had one desire left over: an ardent, inexhaustible, burning desire to work for my home and its people.

MAYOR STOCKMANN: (*Gazing into space.*) You've chosen a rather strange method of—Hmm—

DOCTOR STOCKMANN: And so I went around town blinded by my joy, dazzled by my good fortune. But yesterday morning—no, actually it was the evening before that—the eyes of my spirit were opened wide, and the first thing I saw with my new vision was the colossal stupidity of our authorities.

(*Noises, shouts, and laughter. Mrs. Stockmann coughs urgently.*)

MAYOR STOCKMANN: Mr. Chairman!

ASLAKSEN: (*Ringing the bell.*) By the authority vested in me—

DOCTOR STOCKMANN: Don't let yourself get hung up on a word, Mr. Aslaksen. I only mean that then I began to get wind of the immeasurable extent to which our leaders had been guilty of fouling up the baths. For the life of me, what I can't take are leaders. I've seen enough of them in my time: they're like goats in a plantation of saplings—they wreak havoc everywhere—they block the path of every free man wherever he turns. And I don't see why we can't exterminate them just like any other vermin.

(*Uproar in the room.*)

MAYOR STOCKMANN: Mr. Chairman, will such statements be allowed?

ASLAKSEN: (*Hand on the bell.*) Dr. Stockmann—!

DOCTOR STOCKMANN: I just can't imagine why it's taken me till now to wake up to the nature of these gentlemen, when every day I've had a prime example right here before my eyes—my brother, Peter, set in his ways and slow of wit—

(*Laughter, noise, and whistles. Mrs. Stockmann coughs. Aslaksen rings the bell violently.*)

THE DRUNK: (*Who has reappeared.*) Are you referring to me? All right, my name's Petersen, but I'll be damned if—

ANGRY VOICES: Get that drunk out of here! Out the door!

(*The Drunk is ejected again.*)

MAYOR STOCKMANN: Who was that person?

A BYSTANDER: Don't know him, Mr. Mayor.

2ND MAN: He's not from here.

3RD MAN: Must be some lumberman—(*The rest is inaudible.*)

ASLAKSEN: The man was obviously dead drunk. Go on, Doctor Stockmann, but please try to be more moderate.

DOCTOR STOCKMANN: Very well then, my fellow citizens, enough about our leaders. If anyone imagines that I'm out for anyone's blood this evening, then he's wrong, absolutely wrong. Because I nourish the benign conviction that these relics, these fossils from a world of dying ideas, are all working feverishly on the project of their own extinction—they don't need a doctor to push them into the pit. And anyhow, men like these aren't really the greatest menace to society—they're not the ones who are most actively engaged in poisoning our spirits and polluting the ground beneath us. These men are not the deadliest enemies of truth and freedom in our society.

SHOUTS FROM ALL SIDES: Who, then? Who are they? Name them!

DOCTOR STOCKMANN: You can bet I'll name them! Because that's precisely the great discovery I made yesterday. (*Raises his voice.*) The deadliest enemies of truth and freedom among us are the solid majority—yes, the damned, solid, liberal majority! That's it! Now you know!

(*Unrestrained commotion in the room. Most are shouting, stamping, whistling. Some elderly men exchange stealthy glances and seem to be amused. Mrs. Stockmann anxiously rises to her feet. Eilif and Morten move threateningly towards some schoolboys who are making a disturbance. Hovstad and Billing are both speaking, but can't be heard. At last there is silence.*)

ASLAKSEN: As Chairman, I urge the speaker to take back his irresponsible remarks.

DOCTOR STOCKMANN: Not for all the world, Mr. Aslaksen. It's the great majority in our society that robs me of my freedom, and forbids me from speaking the truth.

HOVSTAD: The majority always has the right on its side!

BILLING: And it always has the truth, too, God damn it!

DOCTOR STOCKMANN: I say that the majority is never right! That's just one of those shibboleths that any free man capable of thinking must rebel against. Take any country—who makes up this majority? The intelligent people or the stupid ones? I think we can all agree that the stupid people are a terrifying, overwhelming majority anywhere in the world. But damn it, it can't be right that the stupid should hold power over the intelligent.

(*Noises and shouts.*)

Yes, yes, you can shout me down, but you can't refute me. The majority has the power, unfortunately—but it doesn't possess the right. The right is with me and a few others, the lonely few. The minority is always in the right.

(*Huge noise again.*)

HOVSTAD: Ha, ha! Doctor Stockmann's become an aristocrat these last few days.

DOCTOR STOCKMANN: I've already said that I'm not going to waste my breath on that scrawny, short-winded pack of old has-beens. The beating pulse of life has already passed them by. No, I'm thinking about the few, the rare individuals, who've seen all the new truths springing up around us. These men stand at the outposts—so far in the vanguard that the solid majority hasn't even caught sight of them yet—and out there, they're fighting for truths too newly born into the world's consciousness for the majority to support.

HOVSTAD: And now, it seems, the Doctor's a revolutionary.

DOCTOR STOCKMANN: You're damn right I am, Mr. Hovstad. I'm making a revolution against this lie that the majority has the truth on its side. What are these truths the majority rallies around? These truths are so decrepit with age that they're nearly senile. But, gentlemen, when a truth has grown so ancient, it's well on its way to becoming a lie.

(*Laughter and jeering.*)

Oh, yes, believe what you like—but truths aren't the hardy Methuselahs people take them for. An ordinary established truth lives—let's say—as a rule, maybe seventeen, eighteen, at the most twenty years—rarely longer. But such venerable truths always get worn horribly thin. Even so, it's only then that the majority takes them up and recommends them to society as wholesome spiritual food. But let me tell you, there's not a lot of nourishment in that kind of diet. And I'm a doctor, so I know. All these majority-truths are like salt meat that's been kept too long— like moldy, stinking pork. And that's the source of all the moral scurvy that's rampant among us.

ASLAKSEN: It appears to me that the honorable speaker is straying rather far from his text.

MAYOR STOCKMANN: I agree with the chairman most emphatically.

DOCTOR STOCKMANN: I think you must be out of your mind, Peter. I'm sticking to the text as closely as I can! This is precisely what I'm trying to say: that the masses, the body politic, this damned solid majority—this, I say, is what's poisoning our sources of spiritual life and contaminating the ground beneath us.

HOVSTAD: And the great, liberal majority is doing this because they're sensible enough to acknowledge only the established and well-recognized truths?

DOCTOR STOCKMANN: Ah, my dear Mr. Hovstad, don't talk about established truths! The truths the masses recognize now are the truths that were established by the frontier guard in the days of our grandfathers. Those of us in the front lines today, we don't recognize them any longer. I believe in only one established truth: that no society can live a healthy life on the dry, sucked-out bones of these ancient truths.

HOVSTAD: Well, instead of standing here spouting to the sky about nothing in particular, why don't you name some of these dried-out truths we're living on?

DOCTOR STOCKMANN: Oh, I could write a whole catalogue of these horrors: but, to begin with, I'll stick to one recognized truth which, in actuality, is a vicious lie—but which, all the same, both Mr. Hovstad and *The People's Herald* and all the *Herald's* followers live by.

HOVSTAD: And what's that?

DOCTOR STOCKMANN: It's a doctrine that you've inherited from your forefathers, which you mindlessly proclaim throughout the land— the doctrine that the multitude, the common people, the masses are the core of society—in fact, are the people itself! That the common man, crass and uncultivated, has just as much right to condemn and approve, to govern and advise as the solitary few, the intellectually distinguished.

BILLING: Well, I'll be Goddamned.

HOVSTAD: (*At the same time, shouting.*) Citizens, mark this in your memories!

ANGRY VOICES: Oh, so we're not the people? Only the elite will rule?

A WORKMAN: To hell with the man who can stand there and talk like that!

OTHERS: Throw him out! Show him the door!

A CITIZEN: Blast that horn, Evensen!

(*Deep blasts on a horn can be heard; whistles and uproar in the room.*)

DOCTOR STOCKMANN: (*When the uproar has died down somewhat.*) Just be reasonable! Can't you stand hearing the voice of truth for once? I didn't for a moment expect that all of you'd agree with me right away. But I really thought that Mr. Hovstad would admit I'm right, after he'd calmed down a bit. Mr. Hovstad claims to be a freethinker.

STARTLED VOICES: (*In undertones.*) Freethinker, did he say? What? Hovstad's a freethinker?

HOVSTAD: (*Shouting.*) Prove it, Doctor Stockmann! When have I said that in print?

DOCTOR STOCKMANN: (*Reflecting.*) No, damn it, you're right—you've never had the courage. Well, I don't want to put you in the stocks, Mr. Hovstad. Let's say I'm the freethinker, then. Because I want to prove to all of you, scientifically, that *The People's Herald* is leading you by the nose when it says that you, the common folk, the multitude and the masses, are the true core of the people. You see, that's just a journalistic lie! The masses are nothing more than the raw material for the making of a nation! (*Murmurs, laughter, general disturbance.*) Well, isn't that how it goes in the rest of the living world? What's the difference between a well-bred and a carelessly bred animal? Just look at common barnyard fowl. How much meat do you get from these scrawny skeletons of chickens? Not much! What kind of eggs do they lay? Any tolerably competent crow could do as well. But take a purebred Spanish or Japanese hen, or a fine pheasant or turkey—there'll you'll see the difference! And now let's turn our attention to the world of dogs, to which we humans are so closely related. Consider first the simple mongrel—I refer to the nasty plebeian cur whose only pleasure in life is running the streets and staining the walls of houses. Now set that mongrel beside a pedigreed dog whose bloodlines can be traced back many generations to a distinguished house where he was fed fine food and raised to the sounds of harmonious voices and music. Don't you think the brain of that dog is of a totally different order from the mongrel's brain? You can bet on it. A cultivated dog like that can be taught to perform the most incredible feats. A common farm mongrel couldn't learn those things if you stood it on its head.

(*General noise and derision.*)

A CITIZEN: Are you making dogs of us, now?

ANOTHER MAN: We're not animals, Doctor.

DOCTOR STOCKMANN: But in the name of God, we are, my friend! And as animals, we're generally about as good as we could want to be. But as for really distinguished animals, I'm afraid there are very few among us. Oh, there's a great gulf between well-bred men and mongrel-men. And the final absurdity is that Mr. Hovstad totally agrees with me as long as we're talking about four-legged animals—

HOVSTAD: Yes, because I take them for what they are.

DOCTOR STOCKMANN: All right. But as soon as I extend the law to the two-legged, Mr. Hovstad stops cold. He doesn't dare believe his own beliefs any more, or think his own thoughts through to the end. So he turns the whole doctrine upside down and proclaims in *The People's Herald* that barnyard fowl and street mongrels— that these are the really fine specimens in the menagerie. But that's how it always is when mediocrity clogs your system—when you haven't worked your way free to intellectual distinction.

HOVSTAD: I make no claims to such distinction. My parents were simple peasants; and I'm proud to have roots deep down among those common people who've been so degraded here tonight.

MANY WORKERS: Hurray for Hovstad! Hurray, hurray!

DOCTOR STOCKMANN: The kind of mediocrity I'm talking about isn't only found down in the lower depths—it teems and swarms all around us, even up to the highest echelons of society. Just consider your own fine and fancy Mayor! My brother Peter is as common a man as anything that goes on two legs—

(*Laughter and hisses.*)

MAYOR STOCKMANN: I must protest against such personal allusions!

DOCTOR STOCKMANN: (*Imperturbably.*) And not because he's descended, just like I am, from a rotten old pirate from Pomerania or somewhere around there—because we are—

MAYOR STOCKMANN: An absurd fiction. I deny it!

DOCTOR STOCKMANN:—but because he thinks only what his superiors are thinking, and believes only what his superiors believe. People who do that are common in spirit. This is why my magnificent brother Peter is so utterly lacking in natural distinction—and, consequently, why he has so little independence of mind.

MAYOR STOCKMANN: Mr. Chairman—!

HOVSTAD: So it's the elite who are the freethinkers in our country. That's a very original insight.

(*Laughter in the room.*)

DOCTOR STOCKMANN: Yes, that's part of my new discovery. And along with that goes the fact that freethinking is almost exactly the same thing as morality. So I say that it is thoroughly irresponsible of *The People's Herald* to preach, day in and day out, the heresy that the masses and the multitudes, the solid majority, are the true guardians of free thought and morality—and that vice and corruption and everything foul and degenerate are things that seep down from the high culture just like the pollution that seeps down to the baths from the tanneries up at Milldale—

(*Uproar and interruptions: Doctor Stockmann continues, unperturbed, smiling in his enthusiasm.*)

And yet this same *Herald* can preach that the masses and the multitudes should be raised up to higher and higher standards of living. But, by all that's holy, if what the *Herald* preaches is true, it would mean that raising up the masses would be just the same thing as whipping them headlong into hell! Fortunately, the idea that good culture makes bad morality is just an old, inherited superstition. No—stupidity, poverty, and ugliness do the devil's work in our lives. In a house that isn't aired out and swept every day—my wife Katherine insists that the floors should be scrubbed as well, but you could no doubt argue that point—however, in such a house, I say, within two or three years the people lose their power of thinking and acting morally. The shortage of oxygen starves the conscience. And it would seem that there's a critical shortage of oxygen in many, many houses in this town, since the whole solid majority is so lacking in conscience that they want to build the town's prosperity on a quagmire of lies and deceit.

(*Noise and protestation.*)

ASLAKSEN: Such a gross accusation against a whole community cannot be tolerated.

A MAN: I move the Chairman rule the speaker out of order.

ANGRY VOICES: Yes, yes! That's right! Out of order!

DOCTOR STOCKMANN: (*Flaring up.*) Then I'll shout the truth from every street corner. I'll write it in out-of-town newspapers! The whole country will learn what's going on here.

HOVSTAD: It almost seems that the Doctor is determined to destroy the town.

DOCTOR STOCKMANN: Yes. I love my hometown so much that I would rather destroy it than see it growing fat on a diet of lies.

ASLAKSEN: Those are strong words.

(*Noises and whistles. Mrs. Stockmann coughs in vain; the Doctor no longer hears her.*)

HOVSTAD: (*Shouting above the din.*) The man who could want to destroy a whole community must be a public enemy!

DOCTOR STOCKMANN: (*With mounting indignation.*) What does it matter if a lie-infested community gets destroyed? It should be burned to the ground, I say! Eradicate everyone who lives by lies—just like vermin! You'll contaminate the entire country in the end—you'll see to it that the whole land deserves to be destroyed. And if it ever comes to that, then I'd say with all my heart—let it be done! Let the people be wiped out!

A MAN: (*In the crowd.*) That's talking like a real enemy of the people.

BILLING: Now there, God damn it, is the people's voice speaking!

THE WHOLE CROWD: (*Shrieking.*) Yes, yes, yes! He is the enemy of the people! He hates his country! He hates the people!

ASLAKSEN: As both a citizen and a human being, I am deeply shocked by what I have had to listen to here. Doctor Stockmann has revealed himself in a manner I never could have dreamt of. I regret to say that I must ally myself with the verdict just now expressed by my worthy fellow citizens; and I move that we pronounce this verdict in the form of a resolution. I propose the following: "This meeting declares that it considers the Medical Supervisor of the baths, Dr. Stockmann, to be an enemy of the people."

(*Storm of applause and cheers. Many crowd around Doctor Stockmann, whistling at him. Mrs. Stockmann and Petra have risen. Morten and Eilif fight with the other schoolboys who have also been whistling. Several adults separate them.*)

DOCTOR STOCKMANN: (*To the hecklers.*) Oh, you fools—for so you are—I'm telling you that—

ASLAKSEN: (*Ringing the bell.*) The Doctor no longer has the floor. A formal vote must be taken; but to protect personal feelings, it should be a secret ballot. Do you have any blank paper, Mr. Billing?

BILLING: Here's both blue and white.

ASLAKSEN: (*Coming down from platform.*) That's fine. This way it'll be quicker. Tear it into slips—there we are, now. (*To the meeting.*) Blue means no, white means yes. I myself will go around and collect the votes.

(*Mayor Stockmann leaves the room. Aslaksen and a couple of other citizens go around the crowd collecting pieces of paper in their hats.*)

A MAN: (*To Hovstad.*) What's happening with the Doctor? What are we supposed to think?

HOVSTAD: Well, you know how hot-headed he is.

2ND MAN: (*To Billing.*) Listen—you're over there a lot. Have you noticed if he drinks?

BILLING: I don't know what to say, God damn it—liquor's always on the table when anyone calls.

3RD MAN: No—I think he just goes crazy sometimes.

1ST MAN: Is there insanity in his family?

BILLING: That's a possibility, yes.

4TH MAN: It's nothing more than spite, that's all. It's revenge for something or other.

BILLING: He was saying something the other day about a raise—but he never got it.

ALL THE GENTLEMEN: (*With one voice.*) Aha! Then it's easy to understand!

THE DRUNK: I'll take a blue one! And I'll take a white one too!

VOICES: It's that drunk again! Throw him out!

MORTEN KIIL: (*Approaches the Doctor.*) Well, Stockmann, do you see now where your monkeyshines have landed you?

DOCTOR STOCKMANN: I've done my duty.

MORTEN KIIL: What was that you said about the tanneries up at Milldale?

DOCTOR STOCKMANN: You heard me. I said they were the source of all the filth.

MORTEN KIIL: My tannery too?

DOCTOR STOCKMANN: I'm afraid your tannery is the worst of all.

MORTEN KIIL: And you're going to print that in the papers?

DOCTOR STOCKMANN: I'm not sweeping anything under the rug.

MORTEN KIIL: That could cost you, Stockmann. (*Kiil goes out.*)

A FAT MAN: (*Goes up to Horster without greeting the ladies.*) So, Captain, you lend your house out to enemies of the people.

HORSTER: I think I can use my property as I see fit.

THE MAN: So you won't object if I do the same with mine.

HORSTER: What do you mean?

THE MAN: You'll hear from me in the morning. (*He turns and goes.*)

PETRA: Wasn't that the man who owns your ship, Captain Horster?

HORSTER: Yes, that was Mr. Vik, the merchant.

ASLAKSEN: (*With ballots in hand, ascends the platform.*) Gentlemen, here are the results of the balloting. By a unanimous vote, except for one—

A YOUNG MAN: And that was the drunk!

ASLAKSEN: By a unanimous vote, except for that of an intoxicated man, this citizens' meeting has resolved that the Medical Supervisor of the baths, Doctor Thomas Stockmann, is an enemy of the people. (*Shouts and applause.*) Long live our ancient and honorable community! Long live our able and effective Mayor, whose public spirit transcended the ties of blood! (*Cheers.*) This meeting is adjourned. (*He steps down from the platform.*)

BILLING: Long live the chairman!

THE WHOLE GATHERING: Hurray for Aslaksen!

DOCTOR STOCKMANN: My hat and coat, Petra! Captain, do you have room for passengers to the New World?

HORSTER: For you and yours, we'll make room, Doctor.

DOCTOR STOCKMANN: (*While Petra helps him into his coat.*) Good. Come, Katherine! Come, boys! (*He takes his wife by the arm.*)

MRS. STOCKMANN: (*Softly.*) Thomas, dear, let's go out the back way.

DOCTOR STOCKMANN: No back ways, Katherine. (*With raised voice.*) You shall hear again from the enemy of the people before he shakes the dust from his feet! I'm not as sweet-natured as a certain person; I'm not saying "I forgive you; for you know not what you do."

ASLAKSEN: (*Cries out.*) That is a blasphemous comparison, Doctor Stockmann!

BILLING: Now that, God damn—er—that's too much for a respectable man to take!

A COARSE VOICE: And then he threatened us, too!

EXCITED VOICES: Let's smash his windows! Throw him in the fjord!

A MAN: Blast that horn, Evensen! Toot, toot!

(*Horn sounds, whistles, wild shouts. The Doctor moves with his family toward the exit. Horster clears the way for them.*)

THE WHOLE CROWD: (*Howling after them.*) Enemy of the people! Enemy of the people! Enemy! Enemy! Enemy!

BILLING: (*While cleaning up his papers.*) I'll be Goddamned if I'd be caught drinking at the Stockmanns' tonight!

(*The crowd makes for the exit; the noise continues outside; from the street the cry can be heard: "Enemy of the People! Enemy! Enemy! Enemy! Enemy!"*)

END OF ACT FOUR

ACT FIVE

Doctor Stockmann's study. Bookshelves and cabinets with various medicines along the walls. In the background is the door to the hall; in the foreground to the left the door to the living room. On the right wall are two windows, where all the panes are broken. In the middle of the room is the Doctor's desk covered with books and papers. The room is in disorder. It is morning.

(Doctor Stockmann in dressing gown, slippers and smoking cap, is bent down and raking under one of the cupboards with an umbrella. At last he manages to rake out a stone.)

DOCTOR STOCKMANN: *(Calling through the open living room door.)* Katherine! I found another one!

MRS. STOCKMANN: Oh, I'm sure you'll find a lot more yet.

DOCTOR STOCKMANN: *(Placing the stone on a pile of others.)* I'm going to save these stones as sacred relics. Eilif and Morten will look at them every day, and when they're grown up, they'll receive them as a legacy from me. *(Raking under a bookcase.)* Hasn't—what the hell's her name—her, that wench—hasn't she gone to see about the glass yet?

MRS. STOCKMANN: *(Coming in.)* Yes, but the man said he didn't know if he could come today.

DOCTOR STOCKMANN: More likely he doesn't dare—you'll see.

MRS. STOCKMANN: Yes, Randine also thought he wouldn't dare— because of the neighbors. *(Calling into living room.)* What do you want, Randine? All right. *(Goes in and returns immediately.)* Here's a letter for you, Thomas.

DOCTOR STOCKMANN: Let me see. *(Opens the letter.)* Ah, yes!

MRS. STOCKMANN: Who's it from?

DOCTOR STOCKMANN: The landlord. He's giving us notice.

MRS. STOCKMANN: Can that be true? He's such a decent man—

DOCTOR STOCKMANN: *(Scanning the letter.)* He doesn't dare do otherwise, he says. He's very sorry to be doing it, but . . . doesn't dare do otherwise . . . out of concern for his fellow citizens . . . consideration for public opinion . . . dependent on others . . . mustn't offend those at the top—

MRS. STOCKMANN: There, you see, Thomas.

DOCTOR STOCKMANN: Oh, yes, yes, I see well enough. They're cowards, all of them here in town. Not one of them dares to do anything, out of consideration for all the others. (*Throws letter on the table.*) But now that's nothing to us, Katherine. We're leaving for the New World—and so—

MRS. STOCKMANN: Yes, but Thomas—have you really thought this through?

DOCTOR STOCKMANN: Maybe I should stay here, where they've put me in the stocks as an enemy of the people, branded me, smashed my windows to pieces! And would you look at this, Katherine— they've ripped a hole in my black trousers as well.

MRS. STOCKMANN: Oh, no—and they're the best you have!

DOCTOR STOCKMANN: You should never have your best trousers on when you go out fighting for truth and freedom. Oh, I'm not so worried about the trousers, you understand; you can always sew them back up for me. But it's *this*—the mob going after me as if they were my equals—that's what I can't stand, damn it!

MRS. STOCKMANN: Yes, they've been horrible to you in this town, Thomas, but does that mean we have to leave the country completely?

DOCTOR STOCKMANN: Don't you think the masses are just as insolent in other towns? Oh, yes, they're just like peas in a pod. Oh, shit—let the mongrels snarl! That's not the worst—the worst is that all over this country everyone has to speak the official truth. But that's not the reason either—it's probably no better in the "free" west. There they have epidemics of solid majorities and liberal blocs of opinion and all the other devilments as well. But everything there is on a grand scale, you see—they may kill you, but they don't go in for slow torture; they don't clamp a free soul in a vise as they do here at home. And if need be, you can get away from it all. (*Walks up and down.*) If I only knew where there was a primeval forest or a little South Sea island I could get cheap—

MRS. STOCKMANN: Yes, but what about the boys, Thomas?

DOCTOR STOCKMANN: (*Stops.*) Katherine, you're amazing! Would you rather have the boys grow up in a society like ours? You saw yourself last night that half the population is certifiably insane— and if the other half hasn't lost their minds it's only because they're just sheepdogs who don't have minds to lose in the first place.

MRS. STOCKMANN: Yes, but Thomas, my dear—you're so reckless in what you say.

DOCTOR STOCKMANN: Well—isn't what I'm saying true? Don't they turn every idea upside down? Don't they stir right and wrong together in the same pot? Don't they call a lie everything I know to be the truth? But the greatest delusion of all is that here you find grown-up liberals running around in packs imagining that they and the others are independent thinkers! Have you ever seen anything like it, Katherine?

MRS. STOCKMANN: Yes, yes, it's all quite ridiculous, but—

(*Petra enters from the living room.*)

MRS. STOCKMANN: Back from school so early?

PETRA: Yes. I got my notice.

MRS. STOCKMANN: Your notice!

DOCTOR STOCKMANN: You too!

PETRA: Mrs. Bush gave me notice, so I thought it was better to leave right away.

DOCTOR STOCKMANN: You were right to do it.

MRS. STOCKMANN: Who would have thought that Mrs. Bush was like that!

PETRA: Oh, Mother, she isn't really—I could see how miserable it made her. But she said she didn't dare do anything else. And so I was fired.

DOCTOR STOCKMANN: (*Laughing and rubbing his hands.*) She didn't dare do anything else! She too. Oh, this is beautiful!

MRS. STOCKMANN: But, of course, after that horrible scene last night—

PETRA: It wasn't only that. Just listen to this, Father.

DOCTOR STOCKMANN: What is it?

PETRA: Mrs. Bush showed me three letters she'd received this morning.

DOCTOR STOCKMANN: Unsigned, of course.

PETRA: Yes.

DOCTOR STOCKMANN: Yes, because they don't dare give their names, Katherine!

PETRA: And in two of them it said that a gentleman who often visits here announced in the club last night that I had some extremely advanced ideas about a lot of things.

DOCTOR STOCKMANN: And you didn't deny that—

PETRA: No, you know that perfectly well. Mrs. Bush has some pretty advanced ideas herself—when there's nobody else around—but with all this about me coming out now, she doesn't dare keep me on.

MRS. STOCKMANN: And just think—a regular visitor here! You see where your hospitality gets you, Thomas.

DOCTOR STOCKMANN: We won't live amid this kind of squalor any longer. Start packing as fast as you can, Katherine—let's get away from here, the quicker the better.

MRS. STOCKMANN: Shh! I think there's someone in the hall. Go and see, Petra.

PETRA: Oh, it's you, Captain Horster. Please come in.

CAPTAIN HORSTER: (*From the hall.*) Good morning. I thought I should look in and see how things are with you.

DOCTOR STOCKMANN: (*Shaking his hand.*) Thanks. That's very kind of you.

MRS. STOCKMANN: And thanks for helping us through it all last night, Captain Horster.

PETRA: How did you get back home?

CAPTAIN HORSTER: Oh, I managed. I can be pretty tough—and with these people it's mostly just talk.

DOCTOR STOCKMANN: Yes, isn't that extraordinary—this revolting cowardice! Here, let me show you something! See, here are all the stones they pelted us with. But look at them! I swear, not more than two decent fighting rocks in the whole heap—the others are just pebbles—bits of gravel! And yet they stood out there howling and swearing they were going to batter me into oblivion. But action—action—no, you don't see much of that in this town.

CAPTAIN HORSTER: Just as well for you this time, Doctor.

DOCTOR STOCKMANN: That's true. But it's still frustrating—because if the time comes for a serious fight—say, to defend the country—you'll see, Captain Horster, how public opinion will take to its heels; you'll witness the solid majority rushing into the woods like a flock of sheep. That's what so painful to think about, that's what hurts so much. No, what the hell—this is all so stupid. They've called me an enemy of the people, and an enemy of the people I'll be.

MRS. STOCKMANN: Thomas, you could never be that.

DOCTOR STOCKMANN: Don't count on that, Katherine. An ugly word can work like a pin-prick in the lung. And that damn word, I can't get rid of it—it's lodged itself here below my heart, and it lies there and stings and burns like acid. And nothing will cure it!

PETRA: Ffft! Just laugh at them, Father.

CAPTAIN HORSTER: Sooner or later they'll change their way of thinking, Doctor.

MRS. STOCKMANN: Yes, Thomas, as sure as you're standing here.

DOCTOR STOCKMANN: Yes, perhaps they will—when it's too late. Well, they'll get what they wanted! So let them continue here in their piggishness: they'll come to regret that they've driven a patriot into exile. When do you sail, Captain Horster?

CAPTAIN HORSTER: Well—as a matter of fact, that was what I came to talk to you about.

DOCTOR STOCKMANN: Oh, is there a problem with the ship?

CAPTAIN HORSTER: No. But it seems I won't be sailing with her.

PETRA: Don't tell me you've been fired?

CAPTAIN HORSTER: (*Smiling.*) Yes, exactly.

PETRA: You, too.

MRS. STOCKMANN: There you are—you see, Thomas?

DOCTOR STOCKMANN: And all for the sake of the truth! If I had thought for one minute that—

CAPTAIN HORSTER: Don't give it a second thought. I'll find a new berth soon enough with some out-of-town ship owner.

DOCTOR STOCKMANN: And that's our Mr. Vik—a wealthy man, completely independent—Uch, he can go to hell.

CAPTAIN HORSTER: He's a good enough man otherwise. For his part, he'd gladly have kept me on if he'd only dared—

DOCTOR STOCKMANN: But he didn't dare? No, of course not!

CAPTAIN HORSTER: He told me it's not so easy when you belong to a party—

DOCTOR STOCKMANN: There's a true word from that heroic gentleman. A party! That's like a meat grinder—everybody's head gets ground up into a mash, and then out come mushheads and meatheads, all in a pile.

MRS. STOCKMANN: Really, Thomas!

PETRA: (*To Captain Horster.*) If only you hadn't seen us home, maybe it wouldn't have turned out this way.

CAPTAIN HORSTER: I don't regret a thing!

PETRA: Thanks for that.

CAPTAIN HORSTER: (*To the Doctor.*) So, what I wanted to say was, since you're set on leaving, I've thought of another plan—

DOCTOR STOCKMANN: That's great! As long as we can get out quickly—

MRS. STOCKMANN: Shh! Wasn't that a knock?

PETRA: It must be Uncle.

DOCTOR STOCKMANN: Aha! (*Calls.*) Come in!

MRS. STOCKMANN: Thomas, promise me that at least—

(*Mayor Stockmann enters from the hall.*)

MAYOR STOCKMANN: (*In the doorway.*) Ah, you're busy. I'd better—

DOCTOR STOCKMANN: No, no; come right in.

MAYOR STOCKMANN: But I wanted to speak to you alone.

MRS. STOCKMANN: We'll just go into the living room for a while.

CAPTAIN HORSTER: And I'll be back later.

DOCTOR STOCKMANN: No, Captain Horster, go in with them—I need to hear more about—

CAPTAIN HORSTER: All right. I'll wait then.

(*Captain Horster follows Mrs. Stockmann and Petra into the living room.*)

MAYOR STOCKMANN: (*Says nothing, but glances at the windows.*)

DOCTOR STOCKMANN: You might find it a bit drafty here today—better put your hat on.

MAYOR STOCKMANN: Thanks, if I may. (*He does so.*) I think I caught a cold yesterday. I stood there freezing.

DOCTOR STOCKMANN: Really? It seemed plenty warm to me.

MAYOR STOCKMANN: I regret that it was not in my power to prevent last night's excesses.

DOCTOR STOCKMANN: Do you have anything else to tell me besides that?

MAYOR STOCKMANN: (*Takes out a large envelope.*) I have this document for you from the Directors of the baths.

DOCTOR STOCKMANN: My notice?

MAYOR STOCKMANN: Yes, effective today. (*Lays the envelope on the table.*) It pains us deeply; but, to speak frankly, we didn't dare do otherwise, because of public opinion.

DOCTOR STOCKMANN: (*Smiling.*) You didn't dare? It's not the first time I've heard that today.

MAYOR STOCKMANN: I hope you'll see your situation clearly. From now on you can't count on any sort of practice here in town.

DOCTOR STOCKMANN: My practice can go to hell. But what makes you so sure?

MAYOR STOCKMANN: The Homeowners' Association is circulating a list from house to house. Every respectable citizen is being urged to boycott you; and I'll venture that not a single householder will refuse to sign. Quite simply, they wouldn't dare.

DOCTOR STOCKMANN: Yes, yes, I don't doubt that. Still—so what?

MAYOR STOCKMANN: If I might offer you some advice, it would be to leave this place for a while—

DOCTOR STOCKMANN: Yes, I've been thinking a little about leaving this place—

MAYOR STOCKMANN: Good. And when you've had somewhere around six months to think it over, and if, after mature consideration, you find yourself moved to write a few words of apology, admitting your misguided—

DOCTOR STOCKMANN: Then, maybe, I could get my job back, you mean?

MAYOR STOCKMANN: Perhaps. It's not entirely out of the question.

DOCTOR STOCKMANN: Yes, but what about public opinion? You wouldn't dare fly in the face of public opinion.

MAYOR STOCKMANN: Opinion is an extremely variable commodity. And, to speak frankly, we consider it very important to get some such admission from you.

DOCTOR STOCKMANN: Yes, wouldn't you just lap that up. But I'm sure you remember what the hell I told you about that kind of duplicity.

MAYOR STOCKMANN: Your position was more favorable then—you dared to believe that you had the whole town at your side.

DOCTOR STOCKMANN: Yes, and now I feel like they're at my throat—(*flaring up*)—But no—not if the devil and his grandmother were at my throat—Never—never, do you hear!

MAYOR STOCKMANN: A man with a family to provide for doesn't dare behave the way you do, Thomas.

DOCTOR STOCKMANN: Doesn't dare! There's only one thing in the world that a free man dares not do—do you know what that is?

MAYOR STOCKMANN: No.

DOCTOR STOCKMANN: Of course not. But I'll tell you. A free man doesn't dare wallow in filth like a savage—he doesn't dare drag himself down to where he wants to spit in his own face.

MAYOR STOCKMANN: That sounds quite reasonable—if there weren't already another explanation for your obstinacy—but of course there is—

DOCTOR STOCKMANN: What do you mean by that?

MAYOR STOCKMANN: You know perfectly well. But as your brother, and as someone who understands these things, let me advise you not to proceed too confidently on assumptions which could easily go wrong.

DOCTOR STOCKMANN: What on earth are you driving at?

MAYOR STOCKMANN: Do you really expect me to believe that you're ignorant of Morten Kiil's will?

DOCTOR STOCKMANN: I know that what little he has is going to a home for unemployed workers. But how does that affect me?

MAYOR STOCKMANN: To begin with, it's not such a small sum we're talking about. Morten Kiil is a very wealthy man.

DOCTOR STOCKMANN: I had no idea—!

MAYOR STOCKMANN: Oh—Really? And I suppose you also had no idea that a not inconsiderable part of his fortune will come to your children—and that you and your wife will receive the interest during your lifetimes. He hasn't told you about this?

DOCTOR STOCKMANN: No, on my soul, he hasn't. On the contrary—he runs around complaining day in and day out about the outrageous taxes he has to pay. Are you sure of all this, Peter?

MAYOR STOCKMANN: I have it from a completely reliable source.

DOCTOR STOCKMANN: But, my God, then Katherine's provided for—and the children! I've got to tell them right away. (*Shouts.*) Katherine, Katherine!

MAYOR STOCKMANN: (*Holding him back.*) Shh. Not yet.

MRS. STOCKMANN: (*Opening the door.*) What's the matter?

DOCTOR STOCKMANN: Nothing, my love. Just go back in again. (*Mrs. Stockmann closes the door.*) This is a wonderful feeling. Imagine—all of them provided for—for life!

MAYOR STOCKMANN: Yes, but that's precisely what they're not. Morten Kiil can revoke the will any time he wants.

DOCTOR STOCKMANN: But he won't. The Badger is positively jubilant about the way I've gone after you and your infallible friends.

MAYOR STOCKMANN: (*Starts, looking intently at him.*) Well—this puts a new light on things.

DOCTOR STOCKMANN: What things?

MAYOR STOCKMANN: This whole affair has been a plot. These violent, unprincipled attacks that you've launched at our leading citizens—in the name of truth—

DOCTOR STOCKMANN: What? What's that?

MAYOR STOCKMANN:—they were nothing more than a prearranged downpayment for that vindictive old man's will!

DOCTOR STOCKMANN: (*Almost speechless.*) Peter—you are the most worthless creature I've ever known.

MAYOR STOCKMANN: Everything's finished between us. Your dismissal is irrevocable: now we have a weapon against you. (*He goes.*)

DOCTOR STOCKMANN: Uch, uch, uch! (*Calls.*) Katherine! Scrub the floor wherever he's been! Get her in here with a bucket—her—her— what the hell—the girl who's always got a smudgy nose—

MRS. STOCKMANN: (*In the living room.*) Shh, shh, Thomas.

PETRA: Father, Grandfather's here. He's asking if he can speak with you alone.

DOCTOR STOCKMANN: Yes, of course he can. (*By the door.*) Come in! (*Morten Kiil enters. Doctor Stockmann closes the door after him.*) What can I do for you? Please take a seat.

MORTEN KIIL: Won't sit. (*Looks around.*) Things look pretty cozy in here today, Stockmann.

DOCTOR STOCKMANN: Yes, don't you think so?

MORTEN KIIL: Very cozy—and you've got plenty of fresh air, too. You've got enough of that oxygen stuff you were talking about yesterday. Your conscience must be feeling pretty good today, I'd think.

DOCTOR STOCKMANN: Yes—so it is.

MORTEN KIIL: I can imagine. (*Taps his breast pocket.*) But do you know what I've got here?

DOCTOR STOCKMANN: Also a good conscience, I hope.

MORTEN KIIL: Pah! No, it's something much better than that. (*He brings out a thick wallet, opens it, and shows a bundle of papers.*)

DOCTOR STOCKMANN: (*Looks at him, amazed.*) Stock in the baths?

MORTEN KIIL: Not hard to get today.

DOCTOR STOCKMANN: And you went out and bought—

MORTEN KIIL: As much as I could afford.

DOCTOR STOCKMANN: But with the baths in such a precarious position right now—

MORTEN KIIL: If you behave yourself like a reasonable man, you'll soon get them on their feet again.

DOCTOR STOCKMANN: Well, you see for yourself I'm doing all I can— but the people in town are completely crazy.

MORTEN KIIL: You said last night that the worst pollution came from my tannery. If that's true, it means that my grandfather and my father before me, and I myself have been poisoning the town all these years—like three murdering angels. Do you believe I can live with that disgrace?

DOCTOR STOCKMANN: I'm sorry, but you'll have to.

MORTEN KIIL: No thanks. I want my good name and reputation. I've heard that people call me the Badger—that's some kind of pig, isn't it?—but they're not going to be right about that. I'm going to live and die like a clean human being.

DOCTOR STOCKMANN: And how are you going to take care of that?

MORTEN KIIL: You're going to clear me, Stockmann.

DOCTOR STOCKMANN: I—!

MORTEN KIIL: Do you know how I paid for these shares? No, how could you?—but now I'll tell you. It's the money that Katherine and Petra and the boys will get when I'm gone. You know I managed to put away a nice little sum.

DOCTOR STOCKMANN: (*Flaring up.*) You've taken Katherine's money for this?

MORTEN KIIL: Yes, every last bit of it is tied up in the baths now. And now I'll see if you're really so completely—suicidally—insane. If you go on talking about how little animals and other horrors are coming down from my tannery, it will be just the same as flaying great strips from Katherine's skin, and Petra's, and the boys' too. But no decent father would do that—unless he was a madman.

DOCTOR STOCKMANN: (*Pacing up and down.*) But I *am* a madman, I am a madman!

MORTEN KIIL: You won't be so crazy when it comes to your wife and children.

DOCTOR STOCKMANN: (*Stopping in front of him.*) Why couldn't you have talked to me before you went out and bought all that garbage?

MORTEN KIIL: What's done is done.

DOCTOR STOCKMANN: (*Pacing uneasily.*) If only I wasn't so certain about this—! But I'm right! I know I'm right!

MORTEN KIIL: (*Weighing the wallet in his hand.*) If you go on being stupid, this here won't be worth very much. (*He puts the wallet in his pocket.*)

DOCTOR STOCKMANN: But, God damn it, science should be able to find some sort of counter-agent, some preventive treatment—

MORTEN KIIL: You mean something to kill the animals with?

DOCTOR STOCKMANN: Yes, or make them harmless.

MORTEN KIIL: Why don't you try rat poison?

DOCTOR STOCKMANN: Stop talking nonsense! Everyone here says it's just my imagination—so let it be nothing but imagination! Let them have what they want! Didn't these ignorant mongrels brand me an enemy of the people? Weren't they ready to rip the clothes from my back?

MORTEN KIIL: And then they smashed your windows for you too!

DOCTOR STOCKMANN: Yes. And there's my family to think about. I've got to talk to Katherine—she's so practical about these things.

MORTEN KIIL: That's right. Listen to a sensible woman's advice.

DOCTOR STOCKMANN: (*Turning on him.*) How could you have behaved so stupidly! Putting Katherine's money at risk—and me in this horrible dilemma! I look at you now and I see the devil himself!

MORTEN KIIL: Time for me to go. But by two o'clock I want an answer from you. Yes or no. If it's no, the shares go to charity before the day's out.

DOCTOR STOCKMANN: And what will Katherine get?

MORTEN KIIL: Not a scrap.

(*The hall door opens. Hovstad and Aslaksen can be seen outside.*) Well, look who's here.

DOCTOR STOCKMANN: (*Staring at them.*) What is this? You still dare come to my house?

HOVSTAD: Yes, we dare.

ASLAKSEN: We have something to discuss with you, you see.

MORTEN KIIL: (*Whispers.*) Yes or no—by two o'clock.

ASLAKSEN: (*With a glance at Hovstad.*) Aha.

(*Morten Kiil leaves.*)

DOCTOR STOCKMANN: Now what do you want to say to me. Make it quick.

HOVSTAD: I can easily understand that you might resent the position we took at yesterday's meeting—

DOCTOR STOCKMANN: You call that a position! Oh, yes, what a wonderful position. I call it spinelessness—uch, God damn it—

HOVSTAD: Call it what you like: we couldn't have done anything else.

DOCTOR STOCKMANN: You didn't dare do anything else—isn't that so?

HOVSTAD: If you like.

ASLAKSEN: You might have leaked something to us beforehand. All that was required was a hint to Hovstad or me.

DOCTOR STOCKMANN: A hint? What about?

HOVSTAD: About what was behind it all.

DOCTOR STOCKMANN: I'm not understanding you.

ASLAKSEN: (*Nodding confidentially.*) Oh yes you are, Dr. Stockmann.

HOVSTAD: There's no point in keeping it secret any longer.

DOCTOR STOCKMANN: (*Looking from one to the other.*) What in the name of Hell—

ASLAKSEN: May I ask—hasn't your father-in-law been going around buying up all the stock in the baths?

DOCTOR STOCKMANN: Yes, he's been buying stock today, but—?

ASLAKSEN: It would have been smarter to get someone else to do it—someone not so close to you—

HOVSTAD: And you shouldn't have done it in your own name. No one needed to know that you were launching an attack on the baths. You should have taken me into your confidence, Dr. Stockmann.

DOCTOR STOCKMANN: (*Staring ahead; a light seems to dawn on him and he says, as though thunderstruck.*) Are such things conceivable? Are they possible?

ASLAKSEN: (*Smiling.*) It seems they are. But they're best done with finesse, if you take my meaning.

HOVSTAD: And it's best when a few more people are involved—the risk is less to the individual when he has some others along with him.

DOCTOR STOCKMANN: (*Composedly.*) Briefly, gentlemen—what do you want?

ASLAKSEN: Mr. Hovstad can best—

HOVSTAD: No, you explain it.

ASLAKSEN: Well, it's this: now that we know how everything fits together, we think we might venture to put *The People's Herald* at your disposal.

DOCTOR STOCKMANN: Now you dare to do it. But what about public opinion? Aren't you afraid they'll whip up a storm against us?

HOVSTAD: We'll ride it out.

ASLAKSEN: And you'll have to be ready to change your tack quickly, Doctor. As soon as your campaign has taken effect—

DOCTOR STOCKMANN: You mean as soon as my father-in-law has got his hands on the shares for a cheap price—

HOVSTAD: Of course, it was mainly scientific considerations that made you want to take control of the baths.

DOCTOR STOCKMANN: That's right. And those same scientific considerations made me get the old Badger to come in on the deal with me. And so we'll tinker a bit with the water pipes and dig up the beach a little without costing the town half a kroner. That should do it, don't you think? Well?

HOVSTAD: I think so—if you have *The People's Herald* with you.

ASLAKSEN: The press has great power in a free society, Doctor.

DOCTOR STOCKMANN: Ah, yes. And then there's always public opinion. And you, Mr. Aslaksen, you'll take responsibility for the Homeowners' Association?

ASLAKSEN: And the Temperance Union too—you can depend on it.

DOCTOR STOCKMANN: Now, gentlemen—I'm embarrassed to mention this, but—what about compensation—?

HOVSTAD: Ideally, we'd like to help you for absolutely nothing, you understand. But *The People's Herald* isn't really on a firm footing—it's not doing so well right now in fact—and to close it down just when there's so much to fight for in the larger political arena would be extremely unfortunate.

DOCTOR STOCKMANN: Of course—that would be a severe blow to a friend of the people like yourself. (*An outburst.*) But I am an enemy of the people, you see. (*Rushing around the room.*) Where did I put my stick? Where the hell is that stick?

HOVSTAD: What does this mean?

ASLAKSEN: You're not going to—

DOCTOR STOCKMANN: (*Stopping.*) And what if I didn't give you a single share of stock? Don't forget we rich folk are not so free with our assets.

HOVSTAD: And don't you forget that this business with the shares can be presented from two angles.

DOCTOR STOCKMANN: Yes, and you're just the man for the job. If I don't help *The Herald* you'll smear this matter and me all over the paper—I guess you'll hunt me down, grab me, choke me like a dog chokes a rabbit!

HOVSTAD: That's the law of nature. Every animal wants to survive.

ASLAKSEN: You have to take your food where you find it, you know.

DOCTOR STOCKMANN: Then see if you can find any in the gutter! (*Runs around the room.*) Because now, by the fires of Hell, we'll see who is the strongest animal. (*Finds his umbrella and waves it around.*) Look out!

HOVSTAD: You're not going to attack us!

ASLAKSEN: Watch out with that umbrella!

DOCTOR STOCKMANN: Out the window with you, Mr. Hovstad!

HOVSTAD: Are you completely mad?

DOCTOR STOCKMANN: Out the window, Mr. Aslaksen! Jump, I tell you! First or last, I don't care.

ASLAKSEN: (*Running around the table.*) Moderation, Doctor—my condition—I'm not up to this—(*Shrieks*) Help! Help!

(*Mrs. Stockmann, Petra, and Captain Horster enter from the living room.*)

MRS. STOCKMANN: Lord have mercy on us, Thomas, what's going on here?

DOCTOR STOCKMANN: (*Waving the umbrella.*) Jump, I tell you. Down into the gutter!

HOVSTAD: Attacking a defenseless man! You're a witness, Captain Horster.

(*Hovstad scurries out through the hall door.*)

ASLAKSEN: (*Confused.*) If I only knew the floorplan here—(*Sneaks through the living room door.*)

MRS. STOCKMANN: (*Holding on to the Doctor.*) Now get a hold of yourself, Thomas.

DOCTOR STOCKMANN: Damn it, they got away after all.

MRS. STOCKMANN: What did they want with you?

DOCTOR STOCKMANN: I'll tell you all about it later; right now I've got other things to think about. (*Goes to the desk and writes on a visiting card.*) Look, Katherine: what does it say.

MRS. STOCKMANN: "No," three times in big letters. What's that for?

DOCTOR STOCKMANN: You'll hear about that later too. (*Holds out the card.*) Here, Petra, tell smudge-nose to run over to the Badger with this, as fast as she can. Hurry!

(*Petra takes the card and leaves by the hall door.*)

DOCTOR STOCKMANN: Well, if I haven't been visited by the devil's emissaries, I don't know what. But now I'll sharpen my pen against them like a knife. I'll dip it in vinegar and gall. I'll sling my inkstand at their skulls!

MRS. STOCKMANN: But we're leaving here, Thomas.

(*Petra returns.*)

DOCTOR STOCKMANN: Well?

PETRA: Taken care of.

DOCTOR STOCKMANN: Good. Leaving, did you say? No, I'll be damned if we are. We're staying here, Katherine!

PETRA: We're staying?

MRS. STOCKMANN: Here in town?

DOCTOR STOCKMANN: Yes, right here and nowhere else. This is the battlefield: here the fight will be fought, and here I'll win the war. As soon as I've had my trousers stitched, I'll go through town and look for a house. We'll need a roof over our heads by winter.

CAPTAIN HORSTER: You can share mine.

DOCTOR STOCKMANN: Can I?

CAPTAIN HORSTER: Yes, you're more than welcome. I have plenty of room, and I'm hardly ever home.

MRS. STOCKMANN: That's very kind of you, Captain Horster.

PETRA: Thanks!

DOCTOR STOCKMANN: (*Shaking his hand.*) Thanks, thanks! So that's taken care of. And now I'll really get to work. There are so many things that need to be gone into right down to the roots, Katherine. And it's great that I'll have so much time at my disposal—that's right, you should know that I've been fired from the baths—

MRS. STOCKMANN: (*Sighing.*) Yes, I was expecting that.

DOCTOR STOCKMANN: And they want to take my practice away from me too. All right, let them! I'll keep the poor people, at least—the ones who can never pay anything. And, God knows, they're the ones who need me the most. But, God damn it, they're going to have to listen to what I've got to say. I'll preach to them both in season and out of season—as it is written someplace.

MRS. STOCKMANN: But Thomas—I think you've seen how much good preaching does.

DOCTOR STOCKMANN: You're really ridiculous, Katherine. Maybe I should let myself be driven from the field by public opinion and the solid majority and all the other devils? No thank you! What I'm asking for is so simple and straightforward and clear. I only want to knock a few ideas into the heads of these mongrels: that the so-called liberals are free men's most dangerous enemies; that party platforms wring the necks of every young and promising truth; and that party-political-opportunism turns morality and justice upside down, so that living here's becoming a horror. Captain Horster—don't you think I can get people to see that?

CAPTAIN HORSTER: It could well be. I don't understand these things very well.

DOCTOR STOCKMANN: Yes, you see, let me tell you how! We have to get rid of the party bosses—a party boss is just like a wolf—a ravenous wolf who needs this many sheep and this many goats for its existence. Just look at Hovstad and Aslaksen! How many sheep and goats have they sacrificed! Or else they maul and maim them so badly that they can never be anything else but homeowners and subscribers to *The People's Herald.* (*Sitting on the edge of the table.*) Come here, Katherine! See how beautifully the sun streams in today. And there's a blessedly fresh breeze blowing all around me.

MRS. STOCKMANN: Yes, if only we could live off sunshine and fresh air, Thomas.

DOCTOR STOCKMANN: Well, you'll have to scrimp and scrape a bit, but we'll be all right. That's the least of my worries. No, the worst thing is that I don't know any man whose mind is free enough to take up my mission after me.

PETRA: Oh, don't think about that, father. You've got plenty of time for that. Look, the boys are back—

(*Eilif and Morten enter from the living room.*)

MRS. STOCKMANN: Did they let you out early?

MORTEN: No, we got into a fight at recess—

EILIF: That's not true—the others picked a fight with us—

MORTEN: Yes, and so Mr. Rørlund said it was best if we stayed home a few days.

DOCTOR STOCKMANN: (*Snaps his fingers and jumps down from the table.*) I've got it! I've got it, by God! You'll never set foot in that school again.

THE BOYS: No more school!

MRS. STOCKMANN: Thomas, no—

DOCTOR STOCKMANN: Never, I said. I'll teach you myself. Yes, just wait and see—you won't learn a single blessed thing—

MORTEN: Yay!

DOCTOR STOCKMANN: But I'll make you into free, accomplished men. Listen, Petra, you'll have to help me.

PETRA: You can count on me, Father.

DOCTOR STOCKMANN: As for school—that'll be held in the same room where they called me an enemy of the people. But there should be more of us. I need at least twelve to begin with.

MRS. STOCKMANN: You won't get that many in this town.

DOCTOR STOCKMANN: We'll see about that. (*To the boys.*) Do you know any poor kids—kids from the street?

MORTEN: Sure, Father, I know lots of them.

DOCTOR STOCKMANN: That's great. Bring me a few specimens. I want to experiment with mongrels for a change—there could be some remarkable minds among them.

MORTEN: What will we do when we're free and accomplished men?

DOCTOR STOCKMANN: You'll hunt all the wolves into the far West, my boys!

(*Eilif looks somewhat dubious; Morten jumps around cheering.*)

MRS. STOCKMANN: Just be careful that the wolves don't hunt you down, Thomas.

DOCTOR STOCKMANN: Are you completely crazy, Katherine? Hunt me! Now, when I'm the strongest man in town?

MRS. STOCKMANN: The strongest—now?

DOCTOR STOCKMANN: Yes, I'd say that now I am one of the strongest men in the whole world.

MORTEN: You really mean it?

DOCTOR STOCKMANN: (*Lowering his voice.*) Shh. Don't say anything about it yet. But I've made a great discovery.

MRS. STOCKMANN: Again?

DOCTOR STOCKMANN: It's true, it's true! (*Gathers them around him and speaks confidentially.*) The fact is, you see, that the strongest man in the world is the one who stands most alone.

MRS. STOCKMANN: (*Smiles and shakes her head.*) Oh, Thomas, Thomas . . .

PETRA: (*Confidently, grasping his hands.*) Father!

END OF PLAY

Hedda Gabler

HEDDA GABLER was originally produced at the Harris Theater October 8-10, 1993 and October 14-16, 1993 under the direction of Rick Davis. The cast was as follows:

MRS. ELVSTED . . . . Tina Anderson
BERTA . . . . Abigail Gullo
HEDDA GABLER . . . . Antionette de Franca
JUDGE BRACK . . . . Dave Wright
ELBERT LOVBORG . . . . Orlando Pabotoy
ANUT JULIE. . . . . Christa Killelea
GEORGE TESMON . . . . Scott Rinker

Hedda Gabler

ACT ONE

A large, pleasantly and tastefully furnished drawing room, decorated in somber tones. In the rear wall is a wide doorway with the curtains pulled back. This doorway leads into a smaller room decorated in the same style. In the right wall of the drawing room is a folding door leading into the hall. In the opposite wall, a glass door, also with its curtains pulled back. Outside, through the windows, part of a covered veranda can be seen, along with trees in their autumn colors. In the foreground, an oval table surrounded by chairs. Downstage, near the right wall, is a broad, dark porcelain stove, a high-backed armchair, a footstool with cushions and two stools. Up in the right hand corner, a corner-sofa and a small round table. Downstage, on the left side, a little distance from the wall, a sofa. Beyond the glass door, a piano. On both sides of the upstage doorway stand shelves displaying terra cotta and majolica objects. By the back wall of the inner room, a sofa, a table and a couple of chairs can be seen. Above the sofa hangs the portrait of a handsome elderly man in a general's uniform. Above the table, a hanging lamp with an opalescent glass shade. There are many flowers arranged in vases and glasses all around the drawing room. More flowers lie on the tables. The floors of both rooms are covered with thick rugs.

Morning light. The sun shines in through the glass door.

(Miss Julie Tesman, with hat and parasol, comes in from the hall, followed by Berta, who carries a bouquet wrapped in paper. Miss Tesman is a kindly, seemingly good-natured lady of about sixty-five, neatly but simply dressed in a grey visiting outfit. Berta is a housemaid, getting on in years, with a homely and somewhat rustic appearance.)

MISS TESMAN: (*Stops just inside the doorway, listens, and speaks softly.*) Well—I believe they're just now getting up!

BERTA: (*Also softly.*) That's what I said, Miss. Just think—the steamer got in so late last night, and then—Lord, the young mistress wanted so much unpacked before she could settle down.

MISS TESMAN: Well, well. Let them have a good night's sleep at least. But—they'll have some fresh morning air when they come down. (*She crosses to the glass door and throws it wide open.*)

BERTA: (*By the table, perplexed, holding the bouquet.*) Hmm. Bless me if I can find a spot for these. I think I'd better put them down here, Miss. (*Puts the bouquet down on the front of the piano.*)

MISS TESMAN: So, Berta dear, now you have a new mistress. As God's my witness, giving you up was a heavy blow.

BERTA: And me, Miss—what can I say? I've been in yours and Miss Rina's service for so many blessed years—

MISS TESMAN: We must bear it patiently, Berta. Truly, there's no other way. You know George has to have you in the house with him—he simply has to. You've looked after him since he was a little boy.

BERTA: Yes, but Miss—I keep worrying about her, lying there at home—so completely helpless, poor thing. And that new girl! She'll never learn how to take care of sick people.

MISS TESMAN: Oh, I'll teach her how soon enough. And I'll be doing most of the work myself, you know. Don't you worry about my sister, Berta dear.

BERTA: Yes, but there's something else, Miss. I'm so afraid I won't satisfy the new mistress—

MISS TESMAN: Ffft—Good Lord—there might be a thing or two at first—

BERTA: Because she's so particular about things—

MISS TESMAN: Well, what do you expect? General Gabler's daughter—the way she lived in the general's day! Do you remember how she would go out riding with her father? In that long black outfit, with the feather in her hat?

BERTA: Oh, yes—I remember that all right. But I never thought she'd make a match with our Mr. Tesman.

MISS TESMAN: Neither did I. But—while I'm thinking about it, don't call George "Mister Tesman" any more. Now it's "Doctor Tesman."

BERTA: Yes—that's what the young mistress said as soon as they came in last night. So it's true?

MISS TESMAN: Yes, it's really true. Think of it, Berta—they've made him a doctor. While he was away, you understand. I didn't know a thing about it, until he told me himself, down at the pier.

BERTA: Well, he's so smart he could be anything he wanted to be. But I never thought he'd take up curing people too!

MISS TESMAN: No, no, no. He's not that kind of doctor. (*Nods significantly.*) As far as that goes, you might have to start calling him something even grander soon.

BERTA: Oh no! What could that be?

MISS TESMAN: (*Smiling.*) Hmm—wouldn't you like to know? (*Emotionally.*) Oh, dear God . . . if our sainted Joseph could look up from his grave and see what's become of his little boy. (*She looks around.*) But, Berta—what's this now? Why have you taken all the slipcovers off the furniture?

BERTA: The mistress told me to. She said she can't stand covers on chairs.

MISS TESMAN: But are they going to use this for their everyday living room?

BERTA: Yes, they will. At least she will. He—the doctor—he didn't say anything.

(*George Tesman enters, humming, from the right of the inner room, carrying an open, empty suitcase. He is a youthful looking man of 33, of medium height, with an open, round, and cheerful face, blond hair and beard. He wears glasses and is dressed in comfortable, somewhat disheveled clothes.*)

MISS TESMAN: Good morning, good morning, George!

TESMAN: Aunt Julie! Dear Aunt Julie! (*Goes over and shakes her hand.*) All the way here—so early in the day! Hm!

MISS TESMAN: Yes, you know me—I just had to peek in on you a little.

TESMAN: And after a short night's sleep at that!

MISS TESMAN: Oh, that's nothing at all to me.

TESMAN: So—you got home all right from the pier, hm?

MISS TESMAN: Yes, as it turned out, thanks be to God. The Judge was kind enough to see me right to the door.

TESMAN: We felt so bad that we couldn't take you in the carriage—but you saw how many trunks and boxes Hedda had to bring.

MISS TESMAN: Yes, it was amazing.

BERTA: (*To Tesman.*) Perhaps I should go in and ask the mistress if there's anything I can help her with.

TESMAN: No, thank you, Berta. You don't have to do that. If she needs you, she'll ring—that's what she said.

BERTA: (*Going out to right.*) Very well.

TESMAN: Ah—but—Berta—take this suitcase with you.

BERTA: (*Takes the case.*) I'll put it in the attic.

TESMAN: Just imagine, Auntie. I'd stuffed that whole suitcase with notes—just notes! The things I managed to collect in those archives—really incredible! Ancient, remarkable things that no one had any inkling of.

MISS TESMAN: Ah yes—you certainly haven't wasted any time on your honeymoon.

TESMAN: Yes—I can really say that's true. But, Auntie, take off your hat—Here, let's see. Let me undo that ribbon, hm?

MISS TESMAN: (*While he does so.*) Ah, dear God—this is just what it was like when you were home with us.

TESMAN: (*Examining the hat as he holds it.*) My, my—isn't this a fine, elegant hat you've got for yourself.

MISS TESMAN: I bought it for Hedda's sake.

TESMAN: For Hedda's—hm?

MISS TESMAN: Yes, so Hedda won't feel ashamed of me if we go out for a walk together.

TESMAN: (*Patting her cheek.*) You think of everything, Auntie Julie, don't you? (*Putting her hat on a chair by the table.*) And now—let's just settle down here on the sofa until Hedda comes. (*They sit. She puts her parasol down near the sofa.*)

MISS TESMAN: (*Takes both his hands and gazes at him.*) What a blessing to have you here, bright as day, right before my eyes again, George. Sainted Joseph's own boy!

TESMAN: For me too. To see you again, Aunt Julie—who've been both father and mother to me.

MISS TESMAN: Yes, I know you'll always have a soft spot for your old aunts.

TESMAN: But no improvement at all with Rina, hm?

MISS TESMAN: Oh dear no—and none to be expected, poor thing. She lies there just as she has all these years. But I pray that Our Lord lets me keep her just a little longer. Otherwise I don't know what I'd do with my life, George. Especially now, you know—when I don't have you to take care of any more.

TESMAN: (*Patting her on the back.*) There. There. There.

MISS TESMAN: Oh—just to think that you've become a married man, George. And that you're the one who carried off Hedda Gabler! Beautiful Hedda Gabler. Imagine—with all her suitors.

TESMAN: (*Hums a little and smiles complacently.*) Yes, I believe I have quite a few friends in town who envy me, hm?

MISS TESMAN: And then—you got to take such a long honeymoon—more than five—almost six months . . .

TESMAN: Yes, but it was also part of my research, you know. All those archives I had to wade through—and all the books I had to read!

MISS TESMAN: I suppose you're right. (*Confidentially and more quietly.*) But listen, George—isn't there something—something extra you want to tell me?

TESMAN: About the trip?

MISS TESMAN: Yes.

TESMAN: No—I can't think of anything I didn't mention in my letters. I was given my doctorate—but I told you that yesterday.

MISS TESMAN: So you did. But I mean—whether you might have any—any kind of—prospects—?

TESMAN: Prospects?

MISS TESMAN: Good Lord, George—I'm your old aunt.

TESMAN: Well of course I have prospects.

MISS TESMAN: Aha!

TESMAN: I have excellent prospects of becoming a professor one of these days. But Aunt Julie dear, you already know that.

MISS TESMAN: (*With a little laugh.*) You're right, I do. (*Changing the subject.*) But about your trip. It must have cost a lot.

TESMAN: Well, thank God, that huge fellowship paid for a good part of it.

MISS TESMAN: But how did you make it last for the both of you?

TESMAN: That's the tricky part, isn't it?

MISS TESMAN: And on top of that, when you're travelling with a lady! That's always going to cost you more, or so I've heard.

TESMAN: You're right—it was a bit more costly. But Hedda just had to have that trip, Auntie. She really had to. There was no choice.

MISS TESMAN: Well, I suppose not. These days a honeymoon trip is essential, it seems. But now tell me—have you had a good look around the house?

TESMAN: Absolutely! I've been up since dawn.

MISS TESMAN: And what do you think about all of it?

TESMAN: It's splendid! Only I can't think of what we'll do with those two empty rooms between the back parlor and Hedda's bedroom.

MISS TESMAN: (*Lightly laughing.*) My dear George—when the time comes, you'll think of what to do with them.

TESMAN: Oh, of course—as I add to my library, hm?

MISS TESMAN: That's right, my boy—of course I was thinking about your library.

TESMAN: Most of all I'm just so happy for Hedda. Before we got engaged she'd always say how she couldn't imagine living anywhere but here—in Prime Minister Falk's house.

MISS TESMAN: Yes—imagine. And then it came up for sale just after you left for your trip.

TESMAN: Aunt Julie, we really had luck on our side, hm?

MISS TESMAN: But the expense, George. This will all be costly for you.

TESMAN: (*Looks at her disconcertedly.*) Yes. It might be. It might be, Auntie.

MISS TESMAN: Ah, God only knows.

TESMAN: How much, do you think? Approximately. Hm?

MISS TESMAN: I can't possibly tell before all the bills are in.

TESMAN: Luckily Judge Brack lined up favorable terms for me—he wrote as much to Hedda.

MISS TESMAN: That's right—don't you ever worry about that, my boy. All this furniture, and the carpets? I put up the security for it.

TESMAN: Security? You? Dear Auntie Julie, what kind of security could you give?

MISS TESMAN: I took out a mortgage on our annuity.

TESMAN: What? On your—and Aunt Rina's annuity!

MISS TESMAN: I couldn't think of any other way.

TESMAN: (*Standing in front of her.*) Have you gone completely out of your mind, Auntie? That annuity is all you and Aunt Rina have to live on.

MISS TESMAN: Now, now, take it easy. It's just a formality, you understand. Judge Brack said so. He was good enough to arrange it all for me. Just a formality, he said.

TESMAN: That could very well be, but all the same . . .

MISS TESMAN: You'll be earning your own living now, after all. And, good Lord, so what if we do have to open the purse a little, spend a little bit at first? That would only make us happy.

TESMAN: Auntie . . . you never get tired of sacrificing yourself for me.

MISS TESMAN: (*Rises and lays her hands on his shoulders.*) What joy do I have in the world, my dearest boy, other than smoothing out the path for you? You, without a father or mother to take care of you . . . but we've reached our destination, my dear. Maybe things looked black from time to time. But, praise God, George, you've come out on top!

TESMAN: Yes, it's really amazing how everything has gone according to plan.

MISS TESMAN: And those who were against you—those who would have blocked your way—they're at the bottom of the pit. They've fallen, George. And the most dangerous one, he fell the farthest. Now he just lies there where he fell, the poor sinner.

TESMAN: Have you heard anything about Eilert—since I went away, I mean?

MISS TESMAN: Nothing, except they say he published a new book.

TESMAN: What? Eilert Løvborg? Just recently, hm?

MISS TESMAN: That's what they say. God only knows how there could be anything to it. But when *your* book comes out—now that will be something else again, won't it, George? What's it going to be about?

TESMAN: It will deal with the Domestic Craftsmanship Practices of Medieval Brabant.

MISS TESMAN: Just think—you can write about that kind of thing too.

TESMAN: However, it might be quite awhile before that book is ready. I've got all these incredible collections that have to be put in order first.

MISS TESMAN: Ordering and collecting—you're certainly good at that. You're not the son of sainted Joseph for nothing.

TESMAN: And I'm so eager to get going. Especially now that I've got my own snug house and home to work in.

MISS TESMAN: And most of all, now that you've got her—your heart's desire, dear, dear George!

TESMAN: (*Embracing her.*) Yes, Auntie Julie! Hedda . . . that's the most beautiful thing of all! (*Looking towards the doorway.*) I think that's her, hm?

(*Hedda comes in from the left side of the inner room. She is a lady of twenty-nine. Her face and figure are aristocratic and elegant. Her complexion is pale. Her eyes are steel grey, cold and clear. Her hair is an attractive medium brown but not particularly full. She is wearing a tasteful, somewhat loose-fitting morning gown.*)

MISS TESMAN: (*Going to meet Hedda.*) Good morning, Hedda, my dear. Good morning.

HEDDA: (*Extending her hand.*) Good morning, Miss Tesman, my dear. You're here so early. How nice of you.

MISS TESMAN: (*Looking somewhat embarrassed.*) Well now, how did the young mistress sleep in her new home?

HEDDA: Fine thanks. Well enough.

TESMAN: (*Laughing.*) Well enough! That's a good one, Hedda. You were sleeping like a log when I got up.

HEDDA: Yes, lucky for me. But of course, you have to get used to anything new, Miss Tesman. A little at a time. (*Looks toward the window.*) Uch! Look at that. The maid opened the door. I'm drowning in all this sunlight.

MISS TESMAN: (*Going to the door.*) Well then, let's close it.

HEDDA: No, no, don't do that. Tesman my dear, just close the curtains. That gives a gentler light.

TESMAN: (*By the door.*) All right, all right. Now then, Hedda. You've got both fresh air and sunlight.

HEDDA: Yes, fresh air. That's what I need with all these flowers all over the place. But Miss Tesman, won't you sit down?

MISS TESMAN: No, but thank you. Now that I know everything's all right here I've got to see about getting home again. Home to that poor dear who's lying there in pain.

TESMAN: Be sure to give her my respects, won't you? And tell her I'll stop by and look in on her later today.

MISS TESMAN: Yes, yes I'll certainly do that. But would you believe it George? (*She rustles around in the pocket of her skirt.*) I almost forgot. Here, I brought something for you.

TESMAN: And what might that be Auntie, hm?

MISS TESMAN: (*Brings out a flat package wrapped in newspaper and hands it to him.*) Here you are, my dear boy.

TESMAN: (*Opening it.*) Oh my Lord. You kept them for me, Aunt Julie. Hedda, isn't this touching, hm?

HEDDA: Well, what is it?

TESMAN: My old house slippers. My slippers.

HEDDA: Oh yes, I remember how often you talked about them on our trip.

TESMAN: Yes, well I really missed them. (*Goes over to her.*) Now you can see them for yourself, Hedda.

HEDDA: (*Moves over to the stove.*) Oh no thanks, I don't really care to.

TESMAN: (*Following after her.*) Just think, Aunt Rina lying there embroidering for me sick as she was. Oh, you couldn't possibly believe how many memories are tangled up in these slippers.

HEDDA: (*By the table.*) Not for me.

MISS TESMAN: Hedda's quite right about that, George.

TESMAN: Yes, but now that she's in the family I thought—

HEDDA: That maid won't last, Tesman.

MISS TESMAN: Berta—?

TESMAN: What makes you say that, hm?

HEDDA: (*Pointing.*) Look, she's left her old hat lying there on that chair.

TESMAN: (*Terrified, dropping the slippers on the floor.*) Hedda—!

HEDDA: What if someone came in and saw that.

TESMAN: But Hedda—that's Aunt Julie's hat.

HEDDA: Really?

MISS TESMAN: (*Taking the hat.*) Yes, it really is. And for that matter it's not so old either, my dear little Hedda.

HEDDA: Oh I really didn't get a good look at it, Miss Tesman.

MISS TESMAN: (*Tying the hat on her head.*) Actually I've never worn it before today—and the good Lord knows that's true.

TESMAN: And an elegant hat it is too. Really magnificent.

MISS TESMAN: (*She looks around.*) Oh that's as may be, George. My parasol? Ah, here it is. (*She takes it.*) That's mine too. (*She mutters.*) Not Berta's.

TESMAN: A new hat and a new parasol. Just think, Hedda.

HEDDA: Very charming, very attractive.

TESMAN: That's true, hm? But Auntie, take a good look at Hedda before you go. Look at how charming and attractive she is.

MISS TESMAN: Oh my dear, that's nothing new. Hedda's been lovely all her life. (*She nods and goes across to the right.*)

TESMAN: (*Following her.*) Yes but have you noticed how she's blossomed, how well she's filled out on our trip?

HEDDA: Oh leave it alone!

MISS TESMAN: (*Stops and turns.*) Filled out?

TESMAN: Yes, Aunt Julie. You can't see it so well right now in that gown—but I, who have a little better opportunity to—

HEDDA: (*By the glass door impatiently.*) Oh you don't have the opportunity for anything.

TESMAN: It was that mountain air down in the Tyrol.

HEDDA: (*Curtly interrupting.*) I'm the same as when I left.

TESMAN: You keep saying that. But it's true isn't it Auntie?

MISS TESMAN: (*Folding her hands and gazing at Hedda.*) Lovely . . . lovely . . . lovely. That's Hedda. (*She goes over to her and with both her hands takes her head, bends it down, kisses her hair.*) God bless and keep Hedda Tesman for George's sake.

HEDDA: (*Gently freeing herself.*) Ah—! Let me out!

MISS TESMAN: (*With quiet emotion.*) I'll come look in on you two every single day.

TESMAN: Yes, Auntie, do that won't you, hm?

MISS TESMAN: Good-bye, good-bye.

(*She goes out through the hall door. Tesman follows her out. The door remains half open. Tesman is heard repeating his greetings to Aunt Rina and his thanks for the slippers. While this is happening, Hedda walks around the room raising her arms and clenching her fists as if in a rage. Then she draws the curtains back from the door, stands there and looks out. After a short time, Tesman comes in and closes the door behind him.*)

TESMAN: (*Picking up the slippers from the floor.*) What are you looking at, Hedda?

HEDDA: (*Calm and controlled again.*) Just the leaves. So yellow and so withered.

TESMAN: (*Wrapping up the slippers and placing them on the table.*) Yes, well—we're into September now.

HEDDA: (*Once more uneasy.*) Yes,—It's already—Already September.

TESMAN: Didn't you think Aunt Julie was acting strange just now, almost formal? What do you suppose got into her?

HEDDA: I really don't know her. Isn't that the way she usually is?

TESMAN: No, not like today.

HEDDA: (*Leaving the glass door.*) Do you think she was upset by the hat business?

TESMAN: Not really. Maybe a little, for just a moment—

HEDDA: But where did she get her manners, flinging her hat around any way she likes here in the drawing room. People don't act that way.

TESMAN: Well I'm sure she won't do it again.

HEDDA: Anyway, I'll smooth everything over with her soon enough.

TESMAN: Yes, Hedda, if you would do that.

HEDDA: When you visit them later today, invite her here for the evening.

TESMAN: Yes, that's just what I'll do. And there's one more thing you can do that would really make her happy.

HEDDA: Well?

TESMAN: If you just bring yourself to call her Aunt Julie, for my sake, Hedda, hm?

HEDDA: Tesman, for God's sake, don't ask me to do that. I've told you that before. I'll try to call her Aunt once in a while and that's enough.

TESMAN: Oh well, I just thought that now that you're part of the family . . .

HEDDA: Hmm. I don't know— (*She crosses upstage to the doorway.*)

TESMAN: (*After a pause.*) Is something the matter, Hedda?

HEDDA: I was just looking at my old piano. It really doesn't go with these other things.

TESMAN: As soon as my salary starts coming in, we'll see about trading it in for a new one.

HEDDA: Oh, no, don't trade it in. I could never let it go. We'll leave it in the back room instead. And then we'll get a new one to put in here. I mean, as soon as we get the chance.

TESMAN: (*A little dejectedly.*) Yes, I suppose we could do that.

HEDDA: (*Taking the bouquet from the piano.*) These flowers weren't here when we got in last night.

TESMAN: I suppose Aunt Julie brought them.

HEDDA: (*Looks into the bouquet.*) Here's a card. (*Takes it out and reads.*) "Will call again later today." Guess who it's from?

TESMAN: Who is it, hm?

HEDDA: It says Mrs. Elvsted.

TESMAN: Really. Mrs. Elvsted. She used to be Miss Rysing.

HEDDA: Yes, that's the one. She had all that irritating hair she'd always be fussing with. An old flame of yours, I've heard.

TESMAN: (*Laughs.*) Oh, not for long and before I knew you, Hedda. And she's here in town. How about that.

HEDDA: Strange that she should come visiting us. I hardly know her except from school.

TESMAN: Yes and of course I haven't seen her since—well God knows how long. How could she stand it holed up out there so far from everything, hm?

HEDDA: (*Reflects a moment and then suddenly speaks.*) Just a minute, Tesman. Doesn't he live out that way, Eilert Løvborg, I mean?

TESMAN: Yes, right up in that area.

(*Berta comes in from the hallway.*)

BERTA: Ma'am, she's back again. The lady who came by with the flowers an hour ago. (*Pointing.*) Those you've got in your hand, Ma'am.

HEDDA: Is she then? Please ask her to come in.

(*Berta opens the door for Mrs. Elvsted and then leaves. Mrs. Elvsted is slender with soft, pretty features. Her eyes are light blue, large, round and slightly protruding. Her expression is one of alarm and question. Her hair is remarkably light, almost a white gold and exceptionally rich and full. She is a couple of years younger than Hedda. Her costume is a dark, visiting dress, tasteful but not of the latest fashion.)*

HEDDA: (*Goes to meet her in a friendly manner.*) Hello my dear Mrs. Elvsted. So delightful to see you again.

MRS. ELVSTED: (*Nervous, trying to control herself.*) Yes, it's been so long since we've seen each other.

TESMAN: (*Shakes her hand.*) And we could say the same, hm?

HEDDA: Thank you for the lovely flowers.

MRS. ELVSTED: I would have come yesterday right away but I heard you were on a trip—

TESMAN: So you've just come into town, hm?

MRS. ELVSTED: Yesterday around noon. I was absolutely desperate when I heard you weren't home.

HEDDA: Desperate, why?

TESMAN: My dear Miss Rysing—I mean Mrs. Elvsted.

HEDDA: There isn't some sort of trouble—?

MRS. ELVSTED: Yes there is—and I don't know another living soul to turn to here in town.

HEDDA: (*Sets the flowers down on the table.*) All right then, let's sit down here on the sofa.

MRS. ELVSTED: Oh no, I'm too upset to sit down.

HEDDA: No you're not. Come over here. (*She draws Mrs. Elvsted to the sofa and sits beside her.*)

TESMAN: Well, and now Mrs.—

HEDDA: Did something happen up at your place?

MRS. ELVSTED: Yes—That's it—well, not exactly—Oh, I don't want you to misunderstand me—

HEDDA: Well then the best thing is just to tell it straight out, Mrs. Elvsted—

TESMAN: That's why you came here, hm?

MRS. ELVSTED: Yes, of course. So I'd better tell you, if you don't already know, that Eilert Løvborg is in town.

HEDDA: Løvborg?

TESMAN: Eilert Løvborg's back again? Just think, Hedda.

HEDDA: Good Lord, Tesman, I can hear.

MRS. ELVSTED: He's been back now for about a week. The whole week alone here where he can fall in with all kinds of bad company. This town's a dangerous place for him.

HEDDA: But my dear Mrs. Elvsted, how does this involve you?

MRS. ELVSTED: (*With a scared expression, speaking quickly.*) He was the children's tutor.

HEDDA: Your children?

MRS. ELVSTED: My husband's. I don't have any.

HEDDA: The stepchildren then?

MRS. ELVSTED: Yes.

TESMAN: (*Somewhat awkwardly.*) But was he sufficiently I don't know how to say this—sufficiently regular in his habits to be trusted with that kind of job, hm?

MRS. ELVSTED: For the past two years no one could say anything against him.

TESMAN: Really, nothing. Just think, Hedda.

HEDDA: I hear.

MRS. ELVSTED: Nothing at all I assure you. Not in any way. But even so, now that I know he's here in the city alone and with money in his pocket I'm deathly afraid for him.

TESMAN: But why isn't he up there with you and your husband, hm?

MRS. ELVSTED: When the book came out he was too excited to stay up there with us.

TESMAN: Yes, that's right. Aunt Julie said he'd come out with a new book.

MRS. ELVSTED: Yes, a major new book on the progress of civilization— in its entirety I mean. That was two weeks ago. And it's been selling wonderfully. Everyone's reading it. It's created a huge sensation—

TESMAN: All that, really? Must be something he had lying around from his better days.

MRS. ELVSTED: From before you mean?

TESMAN: Yes.

MRS. ELVSTED: No, he wrote the whole thing while he was up there living with us. Just in the last year.

TESMAN: That's wonderful to hear, Hedda. Just think!

MRS. ELVSTED: Yes, if only it continues.

HEDDA: Have you met him here in town?

MRS. ELVSTED: No, not yet. I had a terrible time hunting down his address but this morning I finally found it.

HEDDA: (*Looks searchingly.*) I can't help thinking this is a little odd on your husband's part.

MRS. ELVSTED: (*Starts nervously.*) My husband—What?

HEDDA: That he'd send you to town on this errand. That he didn't come himself to look for his friend.

MRS. ELVSTED: Oh no, no, no. My husband doesn't have time for that. And anyway I had to do some shopping too.

HEDDA: (*Smiling slightly.*) Oh well, that's different then.

MRS. ELVSTED: (*Gets up quickly, ill at ease.*) And now I beg you, Mr. Tesman, please be kind to Eilert Løvborg if he comes here—and I'm sure he will. You were such good friends in the old days. You have interests in common. The same area of research as far as I can tell.

TESMAN: Yes, that used to be the case anyway.

MRS. ELVSTED: Yes, that's why I'm asking you—from the bottom of my heart to be sure to—that you'll—that you'll keep a watchful eye on him. Oh, Mr. Tesman, will you do that—will you promise me that?

TESMAN: Yes, with all my heart, Mrs. Rysing.

HEDDA: Elvsted.

TESMAN: I'll do anything in my power for Eilert. You can be sure of it.

MRS. ELVSTED: Oh that is so kind of you. (*She presses his hands.*) Many, many thanks. (*Frightened.*) Because my husband thinks so highly of him.

HEDDA: (*Rising.*) You should write to him, Tesman. He might not come to you on his own.

TESMAN: Yes, that's the way to do it, Hedda, hm?

HEDDA: And the sooner the better. Right now I think.

MRS. ELVSTED: (*Beseechingly.*) Yes, if you only could.

TESMAN: I'll write to him this moment. Do you have his address, Mrs. Elvsted?

MRS. ELVSTED: Yes. (*She takes a small slip of paper from her pocket and hands it to him.*) Here it is.

TESMAN: Good, good. I'll go write him—(*Looks around just a minute.*) —Where are my slippers? Ah, here they are. (*Takes the packet and is about to leave.*)

HEDDA: Make sure your note is very friendly—nice and long too.

TESMAN: Yes, you can count on me.

MRS. ELVSTED: But please don't say a word about my asking you to do it.

TESMAN: Oh, that goes without saying.

(*Tesman leaves to the right through the rear room.*)

HEDDA: (*Goes over to Mrs. Elvsted, smiles and speaks softly.*) There, now we've killed two birds with one stone.

MRS. ELVSTED: What do you mean?

HEDDA: Didn't you see that I wanted him out of the way?

MRS. ELVSTED: Yes, to write the letter—

HEDDA: So I could talk to you alone.

MRS. ELVSTED: (*Confused.*) About this thing?

HEDDA: Yes, exactly, about this thing.

MRS. ELVSTED: (*Apprehensively.*) But there's nothing more to it, Mrs. Tesman, really there isn't.

HEDDA: Ah, but there is indeed. There's a great deal more. I can see that much. Come here, let's sit down together. Have a real heart-to-heart talk. (*She forces Mrs. Elvsted into the armchair by the stove and sits down herself on one of the small stools.*)

MRS. ELVSTED: (*Nervously looking at her watch.*) Mrs. Tesman, I was just thinking of leaving.

HEDDA: Now you can't be in such a hurry, can you? Talk to me a little bit about how things are at home.

MRS. ELVSTED: Oh, that's the last thing I want to talk about.

HEDDA: But to me? Good Lord, we went to the same school.

MRS. ELVSTED: Yes but you were one class ahead of me. Oh, I was so afraid of you then.

HEDDA: Afraid of me?

MRS. ELVSTED: Horribly afraid. Whenever we'd meet on the stairs you always used to pull my hair.

HEDDA: No, did I do that?

MRS. ELVSTED: Yes you did—and once you said you'd burn it off.

HEDDA: Oh, just silly talk, you know.

MRS. ELVSTED: Yes but I was so stupid in those days, and anyway since then we've gotten to be so distant from each other. Our circles have just been totally different.

HEDDA: Well let's see if we can get closer again. Listen now, I know we were good friends in school. We used to call each other by our first names.

MRS. ELVSTED: No, no I think you're mistaken.

HEDDA: I certainly am not. I remember it perfectly and so we have to be perfectly open with each other just like in the old days. (*Moves the stool closer.*) There now. (*Kisses her cheek.*) Now you must call me Hedda.

MRS. ELVSTED: (*Pressing and patting her hands.*) Oh, you're being so friendly to me. I'm just not used to that.

HEDDA: There, there, there. I'll stop being so formal with you and I'll call you my dear Thora.

MRS. ELVSTED: My name is Thea.

HEDDA: That's right, of course, I meant Thea. (*Looks at her compassionately.*) So you're not used to friendship, Thea, in your own home?

MRS. ELVSTED: If I only had a home, but I don't. I've never had one.

HEDDA: (*Glances at her.*) I suspected it might be something like that.

MRS. ELVSTED: (*Staring helplessly before her.*) Yes, yes, yes.

HEDDA: I can't exactly remember now, but didn't you go up to Sheriff Elvsted's as a housekeeper?

MRS. ELVSTED: Actually I was supposed to be a governess but his wife—at that time—she was an invalid, mostly bedridden, so I had to take care of the house too.

HEDDA: So in the end you became mistress of your own house.

MRS. ELVSTED: (*Heavily.*) Yes, that's what I became.

HEDDA: Let me see. How long has that been?

MRS. ELVSTED: Since I was married?

HEDDA: Yes.

MRS. ELVSTED: Five years now.

HEDDA: That's right, it must be about that.

MRS. ELVSTED: Oh these five years—! Or the last two or three anyway—! Ah, Mrs. Tesman, if you could just imagine.

HEDDA: (*Slaps her lightly on the hand.*) Mrs. Tesman; really Thea.

MRS. ELVSTED: No, no, of course, I'll try to remember. Any way, Hedda, if you could only imagine.

HEDDA: (*Casually.*) It seems to me that Eilert Løvborg's been living up there for about three years hasn't he?

MRS. ELVSTED: (*Looks uncertainly at her.*) Eilert Løvborg? Yes, that's about right.

HEDDA: Did you know him from before—from here in town?

MRS. ELVSTED: Hardly at all. I mean his name of course.

HEDDA: But up there he'd come to visit you at the house?

MRS. ELVSTED: Yes, every day. He'd read to the children. I couldn't manage everything myself, you see.

HEDDA: No, of course not. And what about your husband? His work must take him out of the house quite a bit.

MRS. ELVSTED: Yes, as you might imagine. He's the sheriff so he has to go traveling around the whole district.

HEDDA: (*Leaning against the arm of the chair.*) Thea, my poor sweet Thea—You've got to tell me everything just the way it is.

MRS. ELVSTED: All right but you've got to ask the questions.

HEDDA: So, Thea, what's your husband really like? I mean, you know, to be with? Is he good to you?

MRS. ELVSTED: (*Evasively.*) He thinks he does everything for the best.

HEDDA: I just think he's a little too old for you. He's twenty years older isn't he?

MRS. ELVSTED: (*Irritatedly.*) There's that too. There's a lot of things. I just can't stand being with him. We don't have a single thought in common, not a single thing in the world, he and I.

HEDDA: But doesn't he care for you at all in his own way?

MRS. ELVSTED: I can't tell what he feels. I think I'm just useful to him, and it doesn't cost very much to keep me. I'm very inexpensive.

HEDDA: That's a mistake.

MRS. ELVSTED: (*Shaking her head.*) Can't be any other way, not with him. He only cares about himself and maybe about the children a little.

HEDDA: And also for Eilert Løvborg, Thea.

MRS. ELVSTED: (*Stares at her.*) For Eilert Løvborg? Why do you think that?

HEDDA: Well, my dear, he sent you all the way into town to look for him. (*Smiling almost imperceptibly.*) And besides you said so yourself, to Tesman.

MRS. ELVSTED: (*With a nervous shudder.*) Oh yes, I suppose I did. No, I'd better just tell you the whole thing. It's bound to come to light sooner or later anyway.

HEDDA: But my dear Thea.

MRS. ELVSTED: All right, short and sweet. My husband doesn't know that I'm gone.

HEDDA: What, your husband doesn't know?

MRS. ELVSTED: Of course not. Anyway he's not at home. He was out traveling. I just couldn't stand it any longer, Hedda, it was impossible. I would have been so completely alone up there.

HEDDA: Well then what?

MRS. ELVSTED: Then I packed some of my things, just the necessities, all in secret, and I left the house.

HEDDA: Just like that?

MRS. ELVSTED: Yes, and I took the train to town.

HEDDA: Oh my good, dear Thea. You dared to do that!

MRS. ELVSTED: (*Gets up and walks across the floor.*) Well, what else could I do?

HEDDA: What do you think your husband will say when you go home again?

MRS. ELVSTED: (*By the table looking at her.*) Up there, to him?

HEDDA: Of course, of course.

MRS. ELVSTED: I'm never going back up there.

HEDDA: (*Gets up and goes closer to her.*) So you've really done it? You've really run away from everything.

MRS. ELVSTED: Yes, I couldn't think of anything else to do.

HEDDA: But you did it—so openly.

MRS. ELVSTED: Oh you can't keep something like that a secret anyway.

HEDDA: Well, what do you think people will say about you, Thea?

MRS. ELVSTED: They'll say whatever they want, God knows. (*She sits tired and depressed on the sofa.*) But I only did what I had to do.

HEDDA: (*After a brief pause.*) So what will you do with yourself now?

MRS. ELVSTED: I don't know yet. All I know is that I've got to live here where Eilert Løvborg lives if I'm going to live at all.

HEDDA: (*Moves a chair closer from the table, sits beside her and strokes her hands.*) Thea, my dear, how did it come about, this—bond between you and Eilert Løvborg?

MRS. ELVSTED: Oh, it just happened, little by little. I started to have a kind of power over him.

HEDDA: Really?

MRS. ELVSTED: He gave up his old ways—and not because I begged him to. I never dared to do that. But he started to notice that those kind of things upset me, so he gave them up.

HEDDA: (*Concealing an involuntary, derisive smile.*) So you rehabilitated him as they say. You, little Thea.

MRS. ELVSTED: That's what he said anyway. And for his part he's made a real human being out of me. Taught me to think, to understand all sorts of things.

HEDDA: So he read to you too did he?

MRS. ELVSTED: No, not exactly, but he talked to me. Talked without stopping about all sorts of great things. And then there was that wonderful time when I shared in his work, when I helped him.

HEDDA: You got to do that?

MRS. ELVSTED: Yes. Whenever he wrote anything, we had to agree on it first.

HEDDA: Like two good comrades.

MRS. ELVSTED: (*Eagerly.*) Yes, comrades. Imagine, Hedda, that's what he called it too. I should feel so happy, but I can't yet because I don't know how long it will last.

HEDDA: Are you that unsure of him?

MRS. ELVSTED: (*Dejectedly.*) There's the shadow of a woman between Eilert Løvborg and me.

HEDDA: (*Stares intently at her.*) Who could that be?

MRS. ELVSTED: I don't know. Someone from his past. Someone he's never really been able to forget.

HEDDA: What has he told you about all this?

MRS. ELVSTED: He's only talked about it once and very vaguely.

HEDDA: Yes, what did he say?

MRS. ELVSTED: He said that when they broke up she was going to shoot him with a pistol.

HEDDA: (*Calm and controlled.*) That's nonsense, people just don't act that way here.

MRS. ELVSTED: No they don't—so I think it's got to be that red haired singer that he once—

HEDDA: Yes, that could well be.

MRS. ELVSTED: Because I remember they used to say about her that she went around with loaded pistols.

HEDDA: Well then it's her of course.

MRS. ELVSTED: (*Wringing her hands.*) Yes, but Hedda just think, I hear this singer is in town again. Oh, I'm so afraid.

HEDDA: (*Glancing toward the back room.*) Shh, here comes Tesman. (*She gets up and whispers.*) Now, Thea, all of this is strictly between you and me.

MRS. ELVSTED: (*Jumping up.*) Oh yes, yes for God's sake!

(*George Tesman, a letter in his hand, comes in from the right side of the inner room.*)

TESMAN: There now, the epistle is prepared.

HEDDA: Well done—but Mrs. Elvsted's got to leave now, I think. Just a minute, I'll follow you as far as the garden gate.

TESMAN: Hedda dear, do you think Berta could see to this?

HEDDA: (*Takes the letter.*) I'll instruct her.

(*Berta comes in from the hall.*)

BERTA: Judge Brack is here. Says he'd like to pay his respects.

HEDDA: Yes, ask the Judge to be so good as to come in, and then— listen here now—Put this letter in the mailbox.

BERTA: (*Takes the letter.*) Yes Ma'am.

(*She opens the door for Judge Brack and then goes out. Judge Brack is forty-five years old, short, well built and moves easily. He has a round face and an aristocratic profile. His short hair is still almost black. His eyes are lively and ironic. He has thick eyebrows*)

*and a thick moustache, trimmed square at the ends. He is wearing
outdoor clothing, elegant, but a little too young in style. He has a
monocle in one eye. Now and then he lets it drop.)*

BRACK: (*Bows with his hat in his hand.*) Does one dare to call so
early?

HEDDA: One does dare.

TESMAN: (*Shakes his hand.*) You're welcome any time. Judge Brack,
Mrs. Rysing. (*Hedda sighs.*)

BRACK: (*Bows.*) Aha, delighted.

HEDDA: (*Looks at him laughing.*) Nice to see you by daylight, for a
change, Judge.

BRACK: Do I look different?

HEDDA: Yes, younger.

BRACK: You're too kind.

TESMAN: Well, how about Hedda, hm? Doesn't she look fine? Hasn't
she filled out?

HEDDA: Stop it now. You should be thanking Judge Brack for all of
his hard work—

BRACK: Nonsense. It was my pleasure.

HEDDA: There's a loyal soul. But here's my friend burning to get away.
Excuse me Judge, I'll be right back.

(*Mutual good-byes. Mrs. Elvsted and Hedda leave by the hall
door.*)

BRACK: Well now, your wife's satisfied, more or less?

TESMAN: Oh yes, we can't thank you enough. I gather there might be a
little more rearrangement here and there and one or two things
still missing. A couple of small things yet to be procured.

BRACK: Is that so?

TESMAN: But nothing for you to worry about. Hedda said that she'd
look for everything herself. Let's sit down.

BRACK: Thanks. Just for a minute. (*Sits by the table.*) Now my dear
Tesman, there's something we need to talk about.

TESMAN: Oh yes, ah, I understand. (*Sits down.*) Time for a new topic.
Time for the serious part of the celebration, hm?

BRACK: Oh, I wouldn't worry too much about the finances just yet—
although I must tell you that it would have been better if we'd
managed things a little more frugally.

TESMAN: But there was no way to do that. You know Hedda, Judge,
you know her well. I couldn't possibly ask her to live in a middle
class house.

BRACK: No, that's precisely the problem.

TESMAN: And luckily it can't be too long before I get my appointment.

BRACK: Well, you know, these things often drag on and on.

TESMAN: Have you heard anything further, hm?

BRACK: Nothing certain. (*Changing the subject.*) But there is one thing. I've got a piece of news for you.

TESMAN: Well?

BRACK: Your old friend Eilert Løvborg's back in town.

TESMAN: I already know.

BRACK: Oh, how did you find out?

TESMAN: She told me, that lady who just left with Hedda.

BRACK: Oh, I see. I didn't quite get her name.

TESMAN: Mrs. Elvsted.

BRACK: Ah yes, the Sheriff's wife. Yes, he's been staying up there with them.

TESMAN: And I'm so glad to hear that he's become a responsible person again.

BRACK: Yes, one is given to understand that.

TESMAN: And he's come out with a new book, hm?

BRACK: He has indeed.

TESMAN: And it's caused quite a sensation.

BRACK: It's caused an extraordinary sensation.

TESMAN: Just think, isn't that wonderful to hear. With all his remarkable talents I was absolutely certain he was down for good.

BRACK: That was certainly the general opinion.

TESMAN: But I can't imagine what he'll do with himself now. What will he live on, hm?

(*During these last words, Hedda has entered from the hallway.*)

HEDDA: (*To Brack, laughing a little scornfully.*) Tesman is constantly going around worrying about what to live on.

TESMAN: My Lord, we're talking about Eilert Løvborg, dear.

HEDDA: (*Looking quickly at him.*) Oh yes? (*Sits down in the armchair by the stove and asks casually.*) What's the matter with him?

TESMAN: Well he must have spent his inheritance a long time ago, and he can't really write a new book every year, hm? So I was just asking what was going to become of him.

BRACK: Perhaps I can enlighten you on that score.

TESMAN: Oh?

BRACK: You might remember that he has some relatives with more than a little influence.

TESMAN: Unfortunately they've pretty much washed their hands of him.

BRACK: In the old days they thought of him as the family's great shining hope.

TESMAN: Yes, in the old days, possibly, but he took care of that himself.

HEDDA: Who knows? (*Smiles slightly.*) Up at the Elvsteds' he's been the target of a reclamation project.

BRACK: And there's this new book.

TESMAN: Well, God willing, they'll help him out some way or another. I've just written to him, Hedda, asking him to come over this evening.

BRACK: But my dear Tesman, you're coming to my stag party this evening. You promised me on the pier last night.

HEDDA: Had you forgotten, Tesman?

TESMAN: Yes, to be perfectly honest, I had.

BRACK: For that matter, you can be sure he won't come.

TESMAN: Why do you say that, hm?

BRACK: (*Somewhat hesitantly getting up and leaning his hands on the back of his chair.*) My dear Tesman, you too, Mrs. Tesman, in good conscience I can't let you go on living in ignorance of something like this.

TESMAN: Something about Eilert, hm?

BRACK: About both of you.

TESMAN: My dear Judge, tell me what it is.

BRACK: You ought to prepare yourself for the fact that your appointment might not come through as quickly as you expect.

TESMAN: (*Jumps up in alarm.*) Has something held it up?

BRACK: The appointment might just possibly be subject to a competition.

TESMAN: A competition! Just think of that, Hedda!

HEDDA: (*Leans further back in her chair.*) Ah yes—yes.

TESMAN: But who on earth would it—surely not with—?

BRACK: Yes, precisely, with Eilert Løvborg.

TESMAN: (*Clasping his hands together.*) No, no, this is absolutely unthinkable, absolutely unthinkable, hm?

BRACK: Hmm—well we might just have to learn to get used to it.

TESMAN: No, but Judge Brack, that would be incredibly inconsiderate. (*Waving his arms.*) Because—well—just look, I'm a married man. We went and got married on this very prospect, Hedda and I. Went and got ourselves heavily into debt. Borrowed money from

Aunt Julie too. I mean, good Lord, I was as much as promised the position, hm?

BRACK: Now, now, you'll almost certainly get it but first there'll have to be a contest.

HEDDA: (*Motionless in the armchair.*) Just think, Tesman, it will be a sort of match.

TESMAN: But Hedda my dear, how can you be so calm about this?

HEDDA: Oh I'm not, not at all. I can't wait for the final score.

BRACK: In any case, Mrs. Tesman, it's a good thing that you know how matters stand. I mean, before you embark on any more of these little purchases I hear you're threatening to make.

HEDDA: What's that got to do with this?

BRACK: Well, well that's another matter. Good-bye. (*To Tesman.*) I'll come by for you when I take my afternoon walk.

TESMAN: Oh yes, yes, forgive me—I don't know if I'm coming or going.

HEDDA: (*Reclining, stretching out her hand.*) Good-bye, Judge, and do come again.

BRACK: Many thanks. Good-bye, good-bye.

TESMAN: (*Following him to the door.*) Good-bye Judge. You'll have to excuse me.

(*Judge Brack goes out through the hallway door.*)

TESMAN: (*Pacing about the floor.*) We should never let ourselves get lost in a wonderland, Hedda, hm?

HEDDA: (*Looking at him and smiling.*) Do you do that?

TESMAN: Yes, well, it can't be denied. It was like living in wonderland to go and get married and set up housekeeping on nothing more than prospects.

HEDDA: You may be right about that.

TESMAN: Well, at least we have our home, Hedda, our wonderful home. The home both of us dreamt about, that both of us craved, I could almost say, hm?

HEDDA: (*Rises slowly and wearily.*) The agreement was that we would live in society, that we would entertain.

TESMAN: Yes, good Lord, I was so looking forward to that. Just think, to see you as a hostess in our own circle. Hm. Well, well, well, for the time being at least we'll just have to make do with each other, Hedda. We'll have Aunt Julie here now and then. Oh you, you should have such a completely different—

HEDDA: To begin with, I suppose I can't have the liveried footmen.

TESMAN: Ah no, unfortunately not. No footmen. We can't even think about that right now.

HEDDA: And the horse!

TESMAN: (*Horrified.*) The horse.

HEDDA: I suppose I mustn't think about that any more.

TESMAN: No, God help us, you can see that for yourself.

HEDDA: (*Walking across the floor.*) Well, at least I've got one thing to amuse myself with.

TESMAN: (*Beaming with pleasure.*) Ah, thank God for that, and what is that, Hedda?

HEDDA: (*In the center doorway looking at him with veiled scorn.*) My pistols, George.

TESMAN: (*Alarmed.*) Pistols?

HEDDA: (*With cold eyes.*) General Gabler's pistols.

(*She goes through the inner room and out to the left.*)

TESMAN: (*Running to the center doorway and shouting after her.*) No, for the love of God, Hedda, dearest, don't touch those dangerous things. For my sake, Hedda, hm?

END OF ACT ONE

ACT TWO

The Tesmans' rooms as in the first act except that the piano has been moved out and an elegant little writing table with a bookshelf has been put in its place. Next to the sofa a smaller table has been placed. Most of the bouquets have been removed. Mrs. Elvsted's bouquet stands on the larger table in the foreground. It is afternoon.

(Hedda, dressed to receive visitors, is alone in the room. She stands by the open glass door loading a pistol. The matching pistol lies in an open pistol case on the writing table.)

HEDDA: (*Looking down into the garden and calling.*) Hello again, Judge.

BRACK: (*Is heard some distance below.*) Likewise, Mrs. Tesman.

HEDDA: (*Raises the pistol and aims.*) Now, Judge Brack, I am going to shoot you.

BRACK: (*Shouting from below.*) No, no, no. Don't stand there aiming at me like that.

HEDDA: That's what you get for coming up the back way. (*She shoots.*)

BRACK: Are you out of your mind?

HEDDA: Oh, good Lord, did I hit you?

BRACK: (*Still outside.*) Stop this nonsense.

HEDDA: Then come on in Judge.

(Judge Brack, dressed for a bachelor party, comes in through the glass doors. He carries a light overcoat over his arm.)

BRACK: In the devil's name, are you still playing this game? What were you shooting at?

HEDDA: Oh, I just stand here and shoot at the sky.

BRACK: (*Gently taking the pistol out of her hands.*) With your permission, Ma'am? (*Looks at it.*) Ah, this one. I know it well. (*Looks around.*) And where do we keep the case? I see, here it is. (*Puts the pistol inside and shuts the case.*) All right, we're through with these little games for today.

HEDDA: Then what in God's name am I to do with myself?

BRACK: No visitors?

HEDDA: (*Closes the glass door.*) Not a single one. Our circle is still in the country.

BRACK: Tesman's not home either I suppose.

HEDDA: (*At the writing table, locks the pistol case in the drawer.*) No, as soon as he finished eating he was off to the aunts. He wasn't expecting you so early.

BRACK: Hmm, I never thought of that. Stupid of me.

HEDDA: (*Turns her head, looks at him.*) Why stupid?

BRACK: Then I would have come a little earlier.

HEDDA: (*Going across the floor.*) Then you wouldn't have found anyone here at all. I've been in my dressing room since lunch.

BRACK: Isn't there even one little crack in the door wide enough for a negotiation?

HEDDA: Now that's something you forgot to provide for.

BRACK: That was also stupid of me.

HEDDA: So we'll just have to flop down here and wait. Tesman won't be home any time soon.

BRACK: Well, well, Lord knows I can be patient.

(*Hedda sits in the corner of the sofa. Brack lays his overcoat over the back of the nearest chair and sits down, keeps his hat in his hand. Short silence. They look at each other.*)

HEDDA: So?

BRACK: (*In the same tone.*) So?

HEDDA: I asked first.

BRACK: (*Leaning a little forward.*) Yes, why don't we allow ourselves a cozy little chat, Mrs. Hedda.

HEDDA: (*Leaning further back in the sofa.*) Doesn't it feel like an eternity since we last talked together? A few words last night and this morning but I don't count them.

BRACK: Like this, between ourselves, just the two of us?

HEDDA: Well, yes, more or less.

BRACK: I wished you were back home every single day.

HEDDA: The whole time I was wishing the same thing.

BRACK: You, really, Mrs. Hedda? Here I thought you were having a wonderful time on your trip.

HEDDA: Oh yes, you can just imagine.

BRACK: But that's what Tesman always wrote.

HEDDA: Yes, him! He thinks it's the greatest thing in the world to go scratching around in libraries. He loves sitting and copying out old parchments or whatever they are.

BRACK: (*Somewhat maliciously.*) Well, that's his calling in the world, at least in part.

HEDDA: Yes, so it is, and no doubt it's—but for me, oh dear Judge, I've been so desperately bored.

BRACK: (*Sympathetically.*) Do you really mean that? You're serious?

HEDDA: Yes, you can imagine it for yourself. Six whole months never meeting with a soul who knew the slightest thing about our circle. No one we could talk with about our kind of things.

BRACK: Ah no, I'd agree with you there. That would be a loss.

HEDDA: Then what was most unbearable of all.

BRACK: Yes?

HEDDA: To be together forever and always with one and the same person.

BRACK: (*Nodding agreement.*) Early and late, yes, night and day, every waking and sleeping hour.

HEDDA: That's it, forever and always.

BRACK: Yes, all right, but with our excellent Tesman I would have imagined that you might—

HEDDA: Tesman is—a specialist, dear Judge.

BRACK: Undeniably.

HEDDA: And specialists aren't so much fun to travel with. Not for the long run anyway.

BRACK: Not even the specialist that one loves?

HEDDA: Uch, don't use that syrupy word.

BRACK: (*Startled.*) Mrs. Hedda.

HEDDA: (*Half laughing, half bitterly.*) Well, give it a try for yourself. Hearing about the history of civilization every hour of the day.

BRACK: Forever and always.

HEDDA: Yes, yes, yes. And then his particular interest, domestic crafts in the middle ages. Uch, the most revolting thing of all.

BRACK: (*Looks at her curiously.*) But, tell me now, I don't quite understand how—hmmm.

HEDDA: That we're together? George Tesman and I, you mean?

BRACK: Well, yes. That's a good way of putting it.

HEDDA: Good Lord, do you think it's so remarkable?

BRACK: I think—yes and no, Mrs. Hedda.

HEDDA: I'd danced myself out dear Judge. My time was up. (*Shudders slightly.*) Uch, no, I'm not going to say that or even think it.

BRACK: You certainly have no reason to think it.

HEDDA: Ah, reasons—(*Looks watchfully at him.*) And George Tesman? Well, he'd certainly be called a most acceptable man in every way.

BRACK: Acceptable and solid, God knows.

HEDDA: And I can't find anything about him that's actually ridiculous, can you?

BRACK: Ridiculous? No—I wouldn't quite say that.

HEDDA: Hmm. Well he's a very diligent archivist anyway. Some day he might do something interesting with all of it. Who knows.

BRACK: (*Looking at her uncertainly.*) I thought you believed, like everyone else, that he'd turn out to be a great man.

HEDDA: (*With a weary expression.*) Yes, I did. And then when he went around constantly begging with all his strength, begging for permission to let him take care of me, well, I didn't see why I shouldn't take him up on it.

BRACK: Ah well, from that point of view . . .

HEDDA: It was a great deal more than any of my other admirers were offering.

BRACK: (*Laughing.*) Well, of course I can't answer for all the others, but as far as I'm concerned you know very well that I've always maintained a certain respect for the marriage bond, that is in an abstract kind of way, Mrs. Hedda.

HEDDA: (*Playfully.*) Oh, I never had any hopes for you.

BRACK: All I ask is an intimate circle of good friends, friends I can be of service to in any way necessary. Places where I am allowed to come and go as a trusted friend.

HEDDA: Of the man of the house you mean.

BRACK: (*Bowing.*) No, to be honest, of the lady. Of the man as well, you understand, because you know that kind of,—how should I put this—that kind of triangular arrangement is really a magnificent convenience for everyone concerned.

HEDDA: Yes, you can't imagine how many times I longed for a third person on that trip. Ach, huddled together alone in a railway compartment.

BRACK: Fortunately the wedding trip is over now.

HEDDA: (*Shaking her head.*) Oh no, it's a very long trip. It's nowhere near over. I've only come to a little stopover on the line.

BRACK: Then you should jump out, stretch your legs a little, Mrs. Hedda.

HEDDA: I'd never jump out.

BRACK: Really?

HEDDA: No, because there's always someone at the stop who—

BRACK: (*Laughing.*) Who's looking at your legs you mean?

HEDDA: Yes, exactly.

BRACK: Yes, but for heavens sake.

HEDDA: (*With a disdainful gesture.*) I don't hold with that sort of thing. I'd rather remain sitting, just like I am now, a couple alone. On a train.

BRACK: But what if a third man climbed into the compartment with the couple?

HEDDA: Ah yes. Now that's quite different.

BRACK: An understanding friend, a proven friend—

HEDDA: Who can be entertaining on all kinds of topics—

BRACK: And not a specialist in any way!

HEDDA: (*With an audible sigh.*) Yes, that would be a relief.

BRACK: (*Hears the front door open and glances toward it.*) The triangle is complete.

HEDDA: (*Half audibly.*) And there goes the train.

(*George Tesman in a gray walking suit and with a soft felt hat comes in from the hallway. He is carrying a large stack of unbound books under his arm and in his pockets.*)

TESMAN: (*Goes to the table by the corner sofa.*) Phew—hot work lugging all these here. (*Puts the books down.*) Would you believe I'm actually sweating, Hedda? And you're already here, Judge, hm. Berta didn't mention anything about that.

BRACK: (*Getting up.*) I came up through the garden.

HEDDA: What are all those books you've got there?

TESMAN: (*Stands leafing through them.*) All the new works by my fellow specialists. I've absolutely got to have them.

HEDDA: By your fellow specialists.

BRACK: Ah, the specialists, Mrs. Tesman. (*Brack and Hedda exchange a knowing smile.*)

HEDDA: You need even more of these specialized works?

TESMAN: Oh yes, my dear Hedda, you can never have too many of these. You have to keep up with what's being written and published.

HEDDA: Yes, you certainly must do that.

TESMAN: (*Searches among the books.*) And look here, I've got Eilert Løvborg's new book too. (*Holds it out.*) Maybe you'd like to look at it, Hedda, hm?

HEDDA: No thanks—or maybe later.

TESMAN: I skimmed it a little on the way.

HEDDA: And what's your opinion as a specialist?

TESMAN: I think the argument's remarkably thorough. He never wrote like this before. (*Collects the books together.*) Now I've got to get all these inside. Oh, it's going to be such fun to cut the pages. Then I'll go and change. (*To Brack.*) We don't have to leave right away, hm?

BRACK: No, not at all. No hurry at all.

TESMAN: Good, I'll take my time then. (*Leaves with the books but stands in the doorway and turns.*) Oh, Hedda, by the way, Aunt Julie won't be coming over this evening.

HEDDA: Really? Because of that hat business?

TESMAN: Not at all. How could you think that of Aunt Julie? No, it's just that Aunt Rina is very ill.

HEDDA: She always is.

TESMAN: Yes, but today she's gotten quite a bit worse.

HEDDA: Well then it's only right that the other one should stay at home with her. I'll just have to make the best of it.

TESMAN: My dear, you just can't believe how glad Aunt Julie was, in spite of everything, at how healthy and rounded out you looked after the trip.

HEDDA: (*Half audibly getting up.*) Oh, these eternal aunts.

TESMAN: Hm?

HEDDA: (*Goes over to the glass door.*) Nothing.

TESMAN: Oh, all right. (*He goes out through the rear room and to the right.*)

BRACK: What were you saying about a hat?

HEDDA: Oh, just a little run-in with Miss Tesman this morning. She'd put her hat down there on that chair (*Looks at him smiling.*) and I pretended I thought it was the maid's.

BRACK: (*Shaking his head.*) My dear Mrs. Hedda, how could you do such a thing to that harmless old lady.

HEDDA: (*Nervously walking across the floor.*) Oh, you know—these things just come over me like that and I can't resist them. (*Flings herself into the armchair by the stove.*) I can't explain it, even to myself.

BRACK: (*Behind the armchair.*) You're not really happy—that's the heart of it.

HEDDA: (*Staring in front of her.*) And why should I be happy? Maybe you can tell me.

BRACK: Yes. Among other things, be happy you've got the home that you've always longed for.

HEDDA: (*Looks up at him and laughs.*) You also believe that myth?

BRACK: There's nothing to it?

HEDDA: Yes, heavens, there's something to it.

BRACK: So?

HEDDA: And here's what it is. I used George Tesman to walk me home from parties last summer.

BRACK: Yes, regrettably I had to go another way.

HEDDA: Oh yes, you certainly were going a different way last summer.

BRACK: (*Laughs.*) Shame on you, Mrs. Hedda. So you and Tesman . . .

HEDDA: So we walked past here one evening and Tesman, the poor thing, was twisting and turning in his agony because he didn't have the slightest idea what to talk about and I felt sorry that such a learned man—

BRACK: (*Smiling skeptically.*) You did . . .

HEDDA: Yes, if you will, I did, and so just to help him out of his torment I said, without really thinking about it, that this was the house I would love to live in.

BRACK: That was all?

HEDDA: For that evening.

BRACK: But afterwards?

HEDDA: Yes, dear Judge, my thoughtlessness has had its consequences.

BRACK: Unfortunately our thoughtlessness often does, Mrs. Hedda.

HEDDA: Thanks I'm sure. But it so happens that George Tesman and I found our common ground in this passion for Prime Minister Falk's villa. And after that it all followed. The engagement, the marriage, the honeymoon and everything else. Yes, yes, Judge, I almost said: you make your bed, you have to lie in it.

BRACK: That's priceless. Essentially what you're telling me is you didn't care about any of this here.

HEDDA: God knows I didn't.

BRACK: What about now, now that we've made it into a lovely home for you?

HEDDA: Ach, I feel an air of lavender and dried roses in every room— or maybe Aunt Julie brought that in with her.

BRACK: (*Laughing.*) No, I think that's probably a relic of the eminent prime minister's late wife.

HEDDA: Yes, that's it, there's something deathly about it. It reminds me of a corsage the day after the ball. (*Folds her hands at the back of her neck, leans back in her chair and gazes at him.*) Oh my dear Judge, you can't imagine how I'm going to bore myself out here.

BRACK: What if life suddenly should offer you some purpose or other, something to live for? What about that, Mrs. Hedda?

HEDDA: A purpose? Something really tempting for me?

BRACK: Preferably something like that, of course.

HEDDA: God knows what sort of purpose that would be. I often wonder if—(*Breaks off.*) No, that wouldn't work out either.

BRACK: Who knows, let me hear.

HEDDA: If I could get Tesman to go into politics, I mean.

BRACK: (*Laughing.*) Tesman? No, you have to see that politics, anything like that, is not for him. Not in his line at all.

HEDDA: No, I can see that. But what if I could get him to try just the same?

BRACK: Yes, but why should he do that if he's not up to it? Why would you want him to?

HEDDA: Because I'm bored, do you hear me? (*After a pause.*) So you don't think there's any way that Tesman could become a cabinet minister?

BRACK: Hmm, you see my dear Mrs. Hedda, that requires a certain amount of wealth in the first place.

HEDDA: (*Rises impatiently.*) Yes, that's it, this shabby little world I've ended up in. (*Crosses the floor.*) That's what makes life so contemptible, so completely ridiculous. That's just what it is.

BRACK: I think the problem's somewhere else.

HEDDA: Where's that?

BRACK: You've never had to live through anything that really shakes you up.

HEDDA: Anything serious you mean.

BRACK: Yes, you could call it that. Perhaps now though it's on its way.

HEDDA: (*Tosses her head.*) You mean that competition for that stupid professorship? That's Tesman's business. I'm not going to waste a single thought on it.

BRACK: No, forget about that. But when you find yourself facing what one calls in elegant language a profound and solemn calling— (*Smiling.*) a new calling, my dear little Mrs. Hedda.

HEDDA: (*Angry.*) Quiet. You'll never see anything like that.

BRACK: (*Gently.*) We'll talk about it again in a year's time, at the very latest.

HEDDA: (*Curtly.*) I don't have any talent for that, Judge. I don't want anything to do with that kind of calling.

BRACK: Why shouldn't you, like most other women, have an innate talent for a vocation that—

HEDDA: (*Over by the glass door.*) Oh, please be quiet. I often think I only have one talent, one talent in the world.

BRACK: (*Approaching.*) And what is that may I ask?

HEDDA: (*Standing, staring out.*) Boring the life right out of me. Now you know. (*Turns, glances toward the inner room and laughs.*) Perfect timing, here comes the professor.

BRACK: (*Warning softly.*) Now, now, now, Mrs. Hedda.

(*George Tesman in evening dress carrying his gloves and hat comes in from the right of the rear room.*)

TESMAN: Hedda, no message from Eilert Løvborg?

HEDDA: No.

BRACK: Do you really think he'll come?

TESMAN: Yes, I'm almost certain he will. What you told us this morning was just idle gossip.

BRACK: Oh?

TESMAN: Yes, at least Aunt Julie said she couldn't possibly believe that he would stand in my way any more. Just think.

BRACK: So, then everything's all right.

TESMAN: (*Puts his hat with his gloves inside on a chair to the right.*) Yes, but I'd like to wait for him as long as I can.

BRACK: We have plenty of time. No one's coming to my place until seven or even half past.

TESMAN: Meanwhile we can keep Hedda company and see what happens, hm?

HEDDA: (*Sets Brack's overcoat and hat on the corner sofa.*) At the very worst, Mr. Løvborg can stay here with me.

BRACK: (*Offering to take his things.*) At the worst, Mrs. Tesman, what do you mean?

HEDDA: If he won't go out with you and Tesman.

TESMAN: (*Looking at her uncertainly.*) But, Hedda dear, do you think that would be quite right, him staying here with you? Remember, Aunt Julie can't come.

HEDDA: No, but Mrs. Elvsted will be coming and the three of us can have a cup of tea together.

TESMAN: Yes, that's all right then.

BRACK: (*Smiling.*) And I might add, that would be the best plan for him.

HEDDA: Why so?

BRACK: Good Lord, Mrs. Tesman, you've had enough to say about my little bachelor parties in the past. Don't you agree they should be open only to men of the highest principle?

HEDDA: That's just what Mr. Løvborg is now, a reclaimed sinner.

(*Berta comes in from the hall doorway.*)

BERTA: Madam, there's a gentleman who wishes to—

HEDDA: Yes, please, show him in.

TESMAN: (*Softly.*) It's got to be him. Just think.

(*Eilert Løvborg enters from the hallway. He is slim and lean, the same age as Tesman but he looks older and somewhat haggard.*

His hair and beard are dark brown. His face is longish, pale, with patches of red over the cheekbones. He is dressed in an elegant suit, black, quite new, dark gloves and top hat. He stops just inside the doorway and bows hastily. He seems somewhat embarrassed.)

TESMAN: (*Goes to him and shakes his hands.*) Oh my dear Eilert, we meet again at long last.

LØVBORG: (*Speaks in a low voice.*) Thanks for the letter, George. (*Approaches Hedda.*) May I shake your hand also, Mrs. Tesman?

HEDDA: (*Takes his hand.*) Welcome, Mr. Løvborg. (*With a gesture.*) I don't know if you two gentlemen—

LØVBORG: (*Bowing.*) Judge Brack, I believe.

BRACK: (*Similarly.*) Indeed. It's been quite a few years—

TESMAN: (*To Løvborg, his hands on his shoulders.*) And now Eilert, make yourself completely at home. Right, Hedda? I hear you're going to settle down here in town, hm?

LØVBORG: Yes I will.

TESMAN: Well, that's only sensible. Listen, I got your new book. I haven't really had time to read it yet.

LØVBORG: You can save yourself the trouble.

TESMAN: What do you mean?

LØVBORG: There's not much to it.

TESMAN: How can you say that?

BRACK: But everyone's been praising it so highly.

LØVBORG: Exactly as I intended—so I wrote the sort of book that everyone can agree with.

BRACK: Very clever.

TESMAN: Yes but my dear Eilert.

LØVBORG: Because I want to reestablish my position, begin again.

TESMAN: (*A little downcast.*) Yes, I suppose you'd want to, hm.

LØVBORG: (*Smiling, putting down his hat and pulling a package wrapped in paper from his coat pocket.*) But when this comes out, George Tesman—this is what you should read. It's the real thing. I've put my whole self into it.

TESMAN: Oh yes? What's it about?

LØVBORG: It's the sequel.

TESMAN: Sequel to what?

LØVBORG: To my book.

TESMAN: The new one?

LØVBORG: Of course.

TESMAN: But my dear Eilert, that one takes us right to the present day.

LØVBORG: So it does—and this one takes us into the future.

TESMAN: The future. Good Lord! We don't know anything about that.

LØVBORG: No, we don't—but there are still one or two things to say about it, just the same. (*Opens the package.*) Here, you'll see.

TESMAN: That's not your handwriting is it?

LØVBORG: I dictated it. (*Turns the pages.*) It's written in two sections. The first is about the cultural forces which will shape the future and this other section (*Turning the pages.*) is about the future course of civilization.

TESMAN: Extraordinary. It would never occur to me to write about something like that.

HEDDA: (*By the glass door, drumming on the pane.*) Hmm, no, no.

LØVBORG: (*Puts the papers back in the packet and sets it on the table.*) I brought it along because I thought I might read some of it to you tonight.

TESMAN: Ah, that was very kind of you, Eilert, but this evening (*Looks at Brack.*) I'm not sure it can be arranged—

LØVBORG: Some other time then, there's no hurry.

BRACK: I should tell you, Mr. Løvborg, we're having a little party at my place this evening, mostly for Tesman you understand—

LØVBORG: (*Looking for his hat.*) Aha, well then I'll—

BRACK: No, listen, why don't you join us?

LØVBORG: (*Briefly but firmly.*) No, that I can't do but many thanks just the same.

BRACK: Oh come now, you certainly can do that. We'll be a small, select circle and I guarantee we'll be "lively" as Mrs. Hed—Mrs. Tesman would say.

LØVBORG: No doubt, but even so—

BRACK: And then you could bring your manuscript along and read it to Tesman at my place. I've got plenty of rooms.

TESMAN: Think about that, Eilert. You could do that, hm?

HEDDA: (*Intervening.*) Now, my dear, Mr. Løvborg simply doesn't want to. I'm quite sure Mr. Løvborg would rather settle down here and have supper with me.

LØVBORG: (*Staring at her.*) With you, Mrs. Tesman?

HEDDA: And with Mrs. Elvsted.

LØVBORG: Ah—(*Casually.*) I saw her this morning very briefly.

HEDDA: Oh did you? Well, she's coming here; so you might almost say it's essential that you stay here, Mr. Løvborg. Otherwise she'll have no one to see her home.

LØVBORG: That's true. Yes, Mrs. Tesman, many thanks. I'll stay.

HEDDA: I'll go and have a word with the maid.

(*She goes over to the hall door and rings. Berta enters. Hedda speaks quietly to her and points toward the rear room. Berta nods and goes out again.*)

TESMAN: (*At the same time to Løvborg.*) Listen, Eilert, your lecture—Is it about this new subject? About the future?

LØVBORG: Yes.

TESMAN: Because I heard down at the bookstore that you'd be giving a lecture series here this fall.

LØVBORG: I plan to. Please don't hold it against me.

TESMAN: No, God forbid, but—?

LØVBORG: I can easily see how this might make things awkward.

TESMAN: (*Dejectedly.*) Oh, for my part, I can't expect you to—

LØVBORG: But I'll wait until you get your appointment.

TESMAN: You will? Yes but—yes but—you won't be competing then?

LØVBORG: No. I only want to conquer you in the marketplace of ideas.

TESMAN: But, good Lord, Aunt Julie was right after all. Oh yes, yes, I was quite sure of it. Hedda, imagine, my dear—Eilert Løvborg won't stand in our way.

HEDDA: (*Curtly.*) Our way? Leave me out of it.

(*She goes up toward the rear room where Berta is placing a tray with decanters and glasses on the table. Hedda nods approvingly, comes forward again. Berta goes out.*)

TESMAN: (*Meanwhile.*) So, Judge Brack, what do you say about all this?

BRACK: Well now, I say that honor and victory, hmm—they have a powerful appeal—

TESMAN: Yes, yes I suppose they do but all the same—

HEDDA: (*Looking at Tesman with a cold smile.*) You look like you've been struck by lightning.

TESMAN: Yes, that's about it—or something like that I think—

BRACK: That was quite a thunderstorm that passed over us, Mrs. Tesman.

HEDDA: (*Pointing toward the rear room.*) Won't you gentlemen go in there and have a glass of punch.

BRACK: (*Looking at his watch.*) For the road? Yes, not a bad idea.

TESMAN: Wonderful, Hedda, wonderful! And I'm in such a fantastic mood now.

HEDDA: You too, Mr. Løvborg, if you please.

LØVBORG: (*Dismissively.*) No thank you, not for me.

BRACK: Good Lord, cold punch isn't exactly poison, you know.

LØVBORG: Maybe not for everybody.

HEDDA: Then I'll keep Mr. Løvborg company in the meantime.

TESMAN: Yes, yes, Hedda dear, you do that.

(*Tesman and Brack go into the rear room, sit down and drink punch, smoking cigarettes and talking animatedly during the following. Eilert Løvborg remains standing by the stove and Hedda goes to the writing table.*)

HEDDA: (*In a slightly raised voice.*) Now, if you like, I'll show you some photographs. Tesman and I—we took a trip to the Tyrol on the way home.

(*She comes over with an album and lays it on the table by the sofa seating herself in the farthest corner. Eilert Løvborg comes closer, stooping and looking at her. Then he takes a chair and sits on her left side with his back to the rear room.*)

HEDDA: (*Opening the album.*) Do you see these mountains, Mr. Løvborg? That's the Ortler group. Tesman's written a little caption. Here. "The Ortler group near Meran."

LØVBORG: (*Who has not taken his eyes off her from the beginning, says softly and slowly.*) Hedda Gabler.

HEDDA: (*Glances quickly at him.*) Shh, now.

LØVBORG: (*Repeating softly.*) Hedda Gabler.

HEDDA: (*Staring at the album.*) Yes, so I was once, when we knew each other.

LØVBORG: And from now—for the rest of my life—do I have to teach myself never to say Hedda Gabler?

HEDDA: (*Turning the pages.*) Yes, you have to. And I think you'd better start practicing now. The sooner the better I'd say.

LØVBORG. (*In a resentful voice.*) Hedda Gabler married—and then—with George Tesman.

HEDDA: That's how it goes.

LØVBORG: Ah, Hedda, Hedda—how could you have thrown yourself away like that?

HEDDA: (*Looks sharply at him.*) What? Now stop that.

LØVBORG: Stop what, what do you mean?

HEDDA: Calling me Hedda and—*

(*Tesman comes in and goes toward the sofa.*)

HEDDA: (*Hears him approaching and says casually.*) And this one here, Mr. Løvborg, this was taken from the Ampezzo Valley.

Would you just look at these mountain peaks. (*Looks warmly up at Tesman.*) George, dear, what were these extraordinary mountains called?

TESMAN: Let me see. Ah, yes, those are the Dolomites.

HEDDA: Of course. Those, Mr. Løvborg, are the Dolomites.

TESMAN: Hedda, dear, I just wanted to ask you if we should bring some punch in here, for you at least.

HEDDA: Yes, thank you my dear. And a few pastries perhaps.

TESMAN: Any cigarettes?

HEDDA: No.

TESMAN: Good.

(*He goes off into the rear room and off to the right. Brack remains sitting, from time to time keeping his eye on Hedda and Løvborg.*)

LØVBORG: (*Quietly, as before.*) Then answer me, Hedda—how could you go and do such a thing?

HEDDA: (*Apparently absorbed in the album.*) If you keep talking to me that way I just won't speak to you.

LØVBORG: Not even when we're alone together?

HEDDA: No. You can think whatever you want but you can't talk about it.

LØVBORG: Ah, I see. It offends your love for George Tesman.

HEDDA: (*Glances at him and smiles.*) Love? Don't be absurd.

LØVBORG: Not love then either?

HEDDA: But even so—nothing unfaithful. I will not allow it.

LØVBORG: Answer me just one thing—

HEDDA: Shh.

(*Tesman, with a tray, enters from the rear room.*)

TESMAN: Here we are, here come the treats. (*He places the tray on the table.*)

*HEDDA: Why are you serving us yourself?

TESMAN: (*Filling the glasses.*) I have such a good time waiting on you, Hedda.

HEDDA: But now you've gone and poured two drinks and Mr. Løvborg definitely does not want—

* *TRANSLATOR'S NOTE: This line is interpolated in an attempt to suggest the difference between the informal du (thee or thy) and the formal de (you) in the Norwegian text. Løvborg has just addressed Hedda in the informal manner and she is warning him not to.]*

TESMAN: No, but Mrs. Elvsted's coming soon.

HEDDA: Yes, that's right, Mrs. Elvsted.

TESMAN: Did you forget about her?

HEDDA: We were just sitting here so completely wrapped up in these. (*Shows him a picture.*) Do you remember this little village?

TESMAN: Yes, that's the one below the Brenner Pass. We spent the night there—

HEDDA: —and ran into all those lively summer visitors.

TESMAN: Ah yes, that was it. Imagine—if you could have been with us, Eilert, just think. (*He goes in again and sits with Brack.*)

LØVBORG: Just answer me one thing—

HEDDA: Yes?

LØVBORG: In our relationship—wasn't there any love there either? No trace? Not a glimmer of love in any of it?

HEDDA: I wonder if there really was. For me it was like we were two good comrades, two really good, faithful friends. (*Smiling.*) I remember you were particularly frank and open.

LØVBORG: That's how you wanted it.

HEDDA: When I look back on it, there was something really beautiful—something fascinating, something brave about this secret comradeship, this secret intimacy that no living soul had any idea about.

LØVBORG: Yes, Hedda, that's true isn't it? That was it. When I'd come to your father's in the afternoon—and the General would sit in the window reading his newspaper with his back toward the room—

HEDDA: And us on the corner sofa.

LØVBORG: Always with the same illustrated magazine in front of us.

HEDDA: Instead of an album, yes.

LØVBORG: Yes, Hedda and when I made all those confessions to you—telling you things about myself that no one else knew in those days. Sat there and told you how I'd lost whole days and nights in drunken frenzy, frenzy that would last for days on end. Ah, Hedda—what kind of power was in you that drew these confessions out of me?

HEDDA: You think it was a power in me?

LØVBORG: Yes. I can't account for it in any other way. And you'd ask me all those ambiguous leading questions—

HEDDA: Which you understood implicitly—

LØVBORG: How did you sit there and question me so fearlessly?

HEDDA: Ambiguously?

LØVBORG: Yes, but fearlessly all the same. Questioning me about— About things like that.

HEDDA: And how could you answer them, Mr. Løvborg?

LØVBORG: Yes, yes. That's just what I don't understand any more. But now tell me, Hedda, wasn't it love underneath it all? Wasn't that part of it? You wanted to purify me, to cleanse me—when I'd seek you out to make my confessions. Wasn't that it?

HEDDA: No, no not exactly.

LØVBORG: Then what drove you?

HEDDA: Do you find it so hard to explain that a young girl—when it becomes possible—in secret—

LØVBORG: Yes?

HEDDA: That she wants a glimpse of a world that—

LØVBORG: That—

HEDDA: That is not permitted to her.

LØVBORG: So that was it.

HEDDA: That too, that too—I almost believe it.

LØVBORG: Comrades in a quest for life. So why couldn't it go on?

HEDDA: That was your own fault.

LØVBORG: You broke it off.

HEDDA: Yes, when it looked like reality threatened to spoil the situation. Shame on you, Eilert Løvborg, how could you do violence to your comrade in arms?

LØVBORG: (*Clenching his hands together.*) Well why didn't you do it for real? Why didn't you shoot me dead right then and there like you threatened to?

HEDDA: Oh, I'm much too afraid of scandal.

LØVBORG: Yes, Hedda, underneath it all, you're a coward.

HEDDA: A terrible coward. (*Changes her tone.*) Lucky for you. And now you've got plenty of consolation up there at the Elvsteds'.

LØVBORG: I know what Thea's confided to you.

HEDDA: And no doubt you've confided to her about us.

LØVBORG: Not one word. She's too stupid to understand things like this.

HEDDA: Stupid?

LØVBORG: In things like this she's stupid.

HEDDA: And I'm a coward. (*Leans closer to him without looking him in the eyes and says softly.*) Now I'll confide something to you.

LØVBORG: (*In suspense.*) What?

HEDDA: My not daring to shoot you—

LØVBORG: Yes?!

HEDDA: —that wasn't my worst cowardice that evening.

LØVBORG: (*Stares at her a moment, understands and whispers passionately.*) Ah, Hedda Gabler, now I see the hidden reason why we're such comrades. This craving for life in you—

HEDDA: (*Quietly with a sharp glance at him.*) Watch out, don't believe anything of the sort.

(*It starts to get dark. The hall door is opened by Berta.*)

HEDDA: (*Clapping the album shut and crying out with a smile.*) Ah, finally. Thea, darling, do come in.

(*Mrs. Elvsted enters from the hall. She is in evening dress. The door is closed after her.*)

HEDDA: (*On the sofa, stretching out her arms.*) Thea, my sweet, you can't imagine how I've been expecting you.

(*Mrs. Elvsted, in passing, exchanges a greeting with the gentlemen in the inner room, crosses to the table, shakes Hedda's hand. Eilert Løvborg has risen. He and Mrs. Elvsted greet each other with a single nod.*)

MRS. ELVSTED: Perhaps I should go in and have a word with your husband.

HEDDA: Not at all. Let them sit there. They'll be on their way soon.

MRS. ELVSTED: They're leaving?

HEDDA: Yes, they're going out on a little binge.

MRS. ELVSTED: (*Quickly to Løvborg.*) You're not?

LØVBORG.: No.

HEDDA: Mr. Løvborg . . . he'll stay here with us.

MRS. ELVSTED: (*Takes a chair and sits down beside him.*) It's so nice to be here.

HEDDA: No you don't, little Thea, not there. Come right over here next to me. I want to be in the middle between you.

MRS. ELVSTED: All right, whatever you like. (*She goes around the table and sits on the sofa to the right of Hedda. Løvborg takes his chair again.*)

LØVBORG: (*After a brief pause, to Hedda.*) Isn't she lovely to look at?

HEDDA: (*Gently stroking her hair.*) Only to look at?

LØVBORG: Yes. We're true comrades, the two of us. We trust each other completely and that's why we can sit here and talk so openly and boldly together.

HEDDA: With no ambiguity, Mr. Løvborg.

LØVBORG: Well—

MRS. ELVSTED: (*Softly, clinging to Hedda.*) Oh, Hedda, I'm so lucky. Just think, he says I've inspired him too.

HEDDA: (*Regards her with a smile.*) No dear, does he say that?

LØVBORG: And she has the courage to take action, Mrs. Tesman.

MRS. ELVSTED: Oh God, me, courage?

LØVBORG: Tremendous courage when it comes to comradeship.

HEDDA: Yes, courage—yes! That's the crucial thing.

LØVBORG: Why that do you suppose?

HEDDA: Because then—maybe—life has a chance to be lived. (*Suddenly changing her tone.*) But now my dearest Thea. Why don't you treat yourself to a nice cold glass of punch?

MRS. ELVSTED: No thank you, I never drink anything like that.

HEDDA: Then for you, Mr. Løvborg.

LØVBORG: No thank you, not for me either.

MRS. ELVSTED: No, not for him either.

HEDDA: (*Looking steadily at him.*) But if I insisted.

LØVBORG: Doesn't matter.

HEDDA: (*Laughing.*) Then I have absolutely no power over you? Ah, poor me.

LØVBORG: Not in that area.

HEDDA: But seriously now, I really think you should, for your own sake.

MRS. ELVSTED: No, Hedda—

LØVBORG: Why is that?

HEDDA: Or to be more precise, for others' sakes.

LØVBORG: Oh?

HEDDA: Because otherwise people might get the idea that you don't, deep down inside, feel really bold, really sure of yourself.

LØVBORG: Oh, from now on people can think whatever they like.

MRS. ELVSTED: Yes, that's right, isn't it.

HEDDA: I saw it so clearly with Judge Brack a few minutes ago.

LØVBORG: What did you see?

HEDDA: That condescending little smile when you didn't dare join them at the table.

LØVBORG: Didn't dare? I'd just rather stay here and talk with you, of course.

MRS. ELVSTED: That's only reasonable, Hedda.

HEDDA: How was the Judge supposed to know that? I saw how he smiled and shot a glance at Tesman when you didn't dare join them in their silly little party.

LØVBORG: Didn't dare. You're saying I don't dare.

HEDDA: Oh, I'm not. But that's how Judge Brack sees it.

LØVBORG: Well let him.

HEDDA: So you won't join them?

LØVBORG: I'm staying here with you and Thea.

MRS. ELVSTED: Yes, Hedda, you can be sure he is.

HEDDA: (*Smiling and nodding approvingly to Løvborg.*) What a strong foundation you've got. Principles to last a lifetime. That's what a man ought to have. (*Turns to Mrs. Elvsted.*) See now, wasn't that what I told you when you came here this morning in such a panic—

LØVBORG: (*Startled.*) Panic?

MRS. ELVSTED: (*Terrified.*) Hedda, Hedda, no.

HEDDA: Just see for yourself. No reason at all to come running here in mortal terror. (*Changing her tone.*) There, now all three of us can be quite jolly.

LØVBORG: (*Shocked.*) What does this mean, Mrs. Tesman?

MRS. ELVSTED: Oh God, oh God, Hedda. What are you doing? What are you saying?

HEDDA: Keep calm now. That disgusting Judge is sitting there watching you.

LØVBORG: In mortal terror on my account?

MRS. ELVSTED: (*Quietly wailing.*) Oh, Hedda—

LØVBORG: (*Looks at her steadily for a moment, his face is drawn.*) So that, then, was how my brave, bold comrade trusted me.

MRS. ELVSTED: (*Pleading.*) Oh, my dearest friend, listen to me—

LØVBORG: (*Takes one of the glasses of punch, raises it and says in a low, hoarse voice.*) Your health, Thea. (*Empties the glass, takes another.*)

MRS. ELVSTED: (*Softly.*) Oh Hedda, Hedda how could you want this to happen?

HEDDA: Want it? I want this? Are you mad?

LØVBORG: And your health too, Mrs. Tesman. Thanks for the truth. Long may it live. (*He drinks and goes to refill the glass.*)

HEDDA: (*Placing her hand on his arm.*) That's enough for now. Remember, you're going to the party.

MRS. ELVSTED: No, no, no.

HEDDA: Shh. They're watching us.

LØVBORG: (*Putting down the glass.*) Thea, be honest with me now.

MRS. ELVSTED: Yes.

LØVBORG: Was your husband told that you came here to look for me?

MRS. ELVSTED: (*Wringing her hands.*) Oh, Hedda, listen to what he's asking me!

LØVBORG: Did he arrange for you to come to town to spy on me? Maybe he put you up to it himself. Aha, that's it. He needed me back in the office again. Or did he just miss me at the card table?

MRS. ELVSTED: (*Softly moaning.*) Oh, Løvborg, Løvborg—

LØVBORG: (*Grabs a glass intending to fill it.*) Skøal to the old Sheriff too.

HEDDA: (*Preventing him.*) No more now. Remember, you're going out to read to Tesman.

LØVBORG: (*Calmly putting down his glass.*) Thea, that was stupid of me. What I did just now. Taking it like that I mean. Don't be angry with me my dear, dear comrade. You'll see. Both of you, and everyone else will see that even though I once was fallen— now I've raised myself up again, with your help, Thea.

MRS. ELVSTED: (*Radiant with joy.*) Oh God be praised.
    (*Meanwhile Brack has been looking at his watch. He and Tesman get up and come into the drawing room.*)

BRACK: (*Taking his hat and overcoat.*) Well, Mrs. Tesman, our time is up.

HEDDA: Yes, it must be.

LØVBORG: (*Rising.*) Mine too.

MRS. ELVSTED: (*Quietly pleading.*) Løvborg, don't do it.

HEDDA: (*Pinching her arm.*) They can hear you.

MRS. ELVSTED: (*Crying out faintly.*) Ow.

LØVBORG: (*To Brack.*) You were kind enough to ask me along.

BRACK: So you're coming after all.

LØVBORG: Yes, thanks.

BRACK: I'm delighted.

LØVBORG: (*Putting the manuscript packet in his pocket and saying to Tesman.*) I'd really like you to look at one or two things before I send it off.

TESMAN: Just think, that will be splendid. But, Hedda dear, how will you get Mrs. Elvsted home?

HEDDA: Oh, there's always a way out.

LØVBORG: (*Looking at the ladies.*) Mrs. Elvsted? Well, of course, I'll come back for her. (*Coming closer.*) Around ten o'clock, Mrs. Tesman, will that do?

HEDDA: Yes, that will be fine.

TESMAN: Well, everything's all right then; but don't expect me that early, Hedda.

HEDDA: No dear, you stay just as long—as long as you like.

MRS. ELVSTED: (*With suppressed anxiety.*) Mr. Løvborg—I'll stay here until you come.

LØVBORG: (*His hat in his hand.*) That's understood.

BRACK: All aboard then, the party train's pulling out. Gentlemen, I trust it will be a lively trip, as a certain lovely lady suggested.

HEDDA: Ah yes, if only that lovely lady could be there—invisible, of course.

BRACK: Why invisible?

HEDDA: To hear a little of your liveliness, Judge, uncensored.

BRACK: (*Laughing.*) Not recommended for the lovely lady.

TESMAN: (*Also laughing.*) You really are the limit, Hedda. Think of it.

BRACK: Well, well my ladies. Good night. Good night.

LØVBORG: (*Bowing as he leaves.*) Until ten o'clock then.

(*Brack, Løvborg and Tesman leave through the hall door. At the same time Berta comes in from the rear room with a lighted lamp which she places on the drawing room table, going out the way she came in.*)

MRS. ELVSTED: (*Has gotten up and wanders uneasily about the room.*) Oh, Hedda, where is all this going?

HEDDA: Ten o'clock—then he'll appear. I see him before me with vine leaves in his hair, burning bright and bold.

MRS. ELVSTED: Yes, if only it could be like that.

HEDDA: And then you'll see—then he'll have power over himself again. Then he'll be a free man for the rest of his days.

MRS. ELVSTED: Oh God yes—if only he'd come back just the way you see him.

HEDDA: He'll come back just that way and no other. (*Gets up and comes closer.*) You can doubt him as much as you like. I believe in him. And so we'll see—

MRS. ELVSTED: There's something behind this, something else you're trying to do.

HEDDA: Yes, there is. Just once in my life I want to help shape someone's destiny.

MRS. ELVSTED: Don't you do that already?

HEDDA: I don't and I never have.

MRS. ELVSTED: Not even your husband?

HEDDA: Oh yes, that was a real bargain. Oh, if you could only understand how destitute I am while you get to be so rich. (*She passionately throws her arms around her.*) I think I'll burn your hair off after all.

MRS. ELVSTED: Let me go, let me go. I'm afraid of you.

BERTA: (*In the doorway.*) Tea is ready in the dining room, Madam.

HEDDA: Good. We're on our way.

MRS. ELVSTED: No, no, no! I'd rather go home alone! Right now!

HEDDA: Nonsense! First you're going to have some tea, you little bubble-head, and then—at ten o'clock—Eilert Løvborg—with vine leaves in his hair! (*She pulls Mrs. Elvsted toward the doorway almost by force.*)

END OF ACT TWO

ACT THREE

*The room at the Tesmans'. The curtains are drawn across the
center doorway and also across the glass door. The lamp covered
with a shade burns low on the table. In the stove, with its door
standing open, there has been a fire that is almost burned out.*

*(Mrs. Elvsted, wrapped in a large shawl and with her feet on a foot
stool, sits sunk back in an armchair. Hedda, fully dressed, lies
sleeping on the sofa with a rug over her.)*

MRS. ELVSTED: *(After a pause suddenly straightens herself in the chair
and listens intently. Then she sinks back wearily and moans
softly.)* Still not back . . . Oh God, oh God . . . Still not back.
*(Berta enters tiptoeing carefully through the hall doorway; she has
a letter in her hand.)*

MRS. ELVSTED: Ah—did someone come?

BERTA: Yes, a girl came by just now with this letter.

MRS. ELVSTED: *(Quickly stretching out her hand.)* A letter? Let me have it.

BERTA: No ma'am, it's for the doctor.

MRS. ELVSTED: Oh.

BERTA: It was Miss Tesman's maid who brought it. I'll put it on the
table here.

MRS. ELVSTED: Yes, do that.

BERTA: *(Puts down the letter.)* I'd better put out the lamp, it's starting
to smoke.

MRS. ELVSTED: Yes, put it out. It'll be light soon anyway.

BERTA: *(Putting out the light.)* Oh, Ma'am, it's already light.

MRS. ELVSTED: So, morning and still not back—!

BERTA: Oh, dear Lord—I knew all along it would go like this.

MRS. ELVSTED: You knew?

BERTA: Yes, when I saw a certain person was back in town. And then
when he went off with them—oh we'd heard plenty about that
gentleman.

MRS. ELVSTED: Don't speak so loud, you'll wake your mistress.

BERTA: *(Looks over to the sofa and sighs.)* No, dear Lord—let her sleep
poor thing. Shouldn't I build the stove up a little more?

MRS. ELVSTED: Not for me, thanks.

BERTA: Well, well then. *(She goes out quietly through the hall
doorway.)*

HEDDA: *(Awakened by the closing door, looks up.)* What's that?

MRS. ELVSTED: Only the maid.

HEDDA: (*Looking around.*) In here—! Oh, now I remember. (*Straightens up, stretches sitting on the sofa and rubs her eyes.*) What time is it, Thea?

MRS. ELVSTED: (*Looks at her watch.*) It's after seven.

HEDDA: What time did Tesman get in?

MRS. ELVSTED: He hasn't.

HEDDA: Still?

MRS. ELVSTED: (*Getting up.*) No one's come back.

HEDDA: And we sat here waiting and watching until almost four.

MRS. ELVSTED: (*Wringing her hands.*) Waiting for him!

HEDDA: (*Yawning and speaking with her hand over her mouth.*) Oh yes—we could have saved ourselves the trouble.

MRS. ELVSTED: Did you finally manage to sleep?

HEDDA: Yes, I think I slept quite well. Did you?

MRS. ELVSTED: Not a wink. I couldn't, Hedda. It was just impossible for me.

HEDDA: (*Gets up and goes over to her.*) Now, now, now. There's nothing to worry about. I know perfectly well how it all turned out.

MRS. ELVSTED: Yes, what do you think? Can you tell me?

HEDDA: Well, of course they dragged it out dreadfully up at Judge Brack's.

MRS. ELVSTED: Oh God yes—that must be true. But all the same—

HEDDA: And then you see, Tesman didn't want to come home and create a fuss by ringing the bell in the middle of the night. (*Laughing.*) He probably didn't want to show himself either right after a wild party like that.

MRS. ELVSTED: For goodness sake—where would he have gone?

HEDDA: Well, naturally, he went over to his aunt's and laid himself down to sleep there. They still have his old room standing ready for him.

MRS. ELVSTED: No, he's not with them. A letter just came for him from Miss Tesman. It's over there.

HEDDA: Oh? (*Looks at the inscription.*) Yes, that's Aunt Julie's hand all right. So then, he's still over at Judge Brack's and Eilert Løvborg— he's sitting—reading aloud with vine leaves in his hair.

MRS. ELVSTED: Oh, Hedda, you don't even believe what you're saying.

HEDDA: You are such a little noodle head, Thea.

MRS. ELVSTED: Yes, unfortunately I probably am.

HEDDA: And you look like you're dead on your feet.

MRS. ELVSTED: Yes, I am. Dead on my feet.

HEDDA: And so now you're going to do what I tell you. You'll go into my room and lie down on my bed.

MRS. ELVSTED: Oh no, no—I couldn't get to sleep anyway.

HEDDA: Yes, you certainly will.

MRS. ELVSTED: But your husband's bound to be home any time now and I've got to find out right away—

HEDDA: I'll tell you as soon as he comes.

MRS. ELVSTED: Promise me that, Hedda?

HEDDA: Yes, that you can count on. Now just go in and sleep for awhile.

MRS. ELVSTED: Thanks. At least I'll give it a try. (*She goes in through the back room.*)

(*Hedda goes over to the glass door and draws back the curtains. Full daylight floods the room. She then takes a small hand mirror from the writing table, looks in it and arranges her hair. Then she goes to the hall door and presses the bell. Soon after Berta enters the doorway.*)

BERTA: Did Madam want something?

HEDDA: Yes, build up the stove a little bit. I'm freezing in here.

BERTA: Lord, in no time at all it'll be warm in here. (*She rakes the embers and puts a log inside. She stands and listens.*) There's the front doorbell Madam.

HEDDA: So, go answer it. I'll take care of the stove myself.

BERTA: It'll be burning soon enough. (*She goes out through the hall door.*)

(*Hedda kneels on the footstool and puts more logs into the stove. After a brief moment, George Tesman comes in from the hall. He looks weary and rather serious. He creeps on tiptoes toward the doorway and is about to slip through the curtains.*)

HEDDA: (*By the stove, without looking up.*) Good morning.

TESMAN: (*Turning around.*) Hedda. (*Comes nearer.*) What in the world—Up so early, hm?

HEDDA: Yes, up quite early today.

TESMAN: And here I was so sure you'd still be in bed. Just think, Hedda.

HEDDA: Not so loud. Mrs. Elvsted's lying down in my room.

TESMAN: Has Mrs. Elvsted been here all night?

HEDDA: Yes. No one came to pick her up.

TESMAN: No, no, they couldn't have.

HEDDA: (*Shuts the door of the stove and gets up.*) So, did you have a jolly time at the Judge's?

TESMAN: Were you worried about me?

HEDDA: No, that would never occur to me. I asked if you had a good time.

TESMAN: Yes, I really did, for once, in a manner of speaking—Mostly in the beginning I'd say. We'd arrived an hour early. How about that? And Brack had so much to get ready. But then Eilert read to me.

HEDDA: (*Sits at the right of the table.*) So, tell me.

TESMAN: Hedda, you can't imagine what this new work will be like. It's one of the most brilliant things ever written, no doubt about it. Think of that.

HEDDA: Yes, yes, but that's not what I'm interested in.

TESMAN: But, I have to confess something, Hedda. After he read— something horrible came over me.

HEDDA: Something horrible?

TESMAN: I sat there envying Eilert for being able to write like that. Think of it, Hedda.

HEDDA: Yes, yes, I'm thinking.

TESMAN: And then, that whole time, knowing that he—Even with all the incredible powers at his command—is still beyond redemption.

HEDDA: You mean he's got more of life's courage in him than the others?

TESMAN: No, for heaven sakes—he just has no control over his pleasures.

HEDDA: And what happened then—at the end?

TESMAN: Well, Hedda, I guess you'd have to say it was a bacchanal.

HEDDA: Did he have vine leaves in his hair?

TESMAN: Vine leaves? No, I didn't see anything like that. But he did make a long wild speech for the woman who had inspired him in his work. Yes—that's how he put it.

HEDDA: Did he name her?

TESMAN: No, he didn't but I can only guess that it must be Mrs. Elvsted. Wouldn't you say?

HEDDA: Hmm—where did you leave him?

TESMAN: On the way back. Most of our group broke up at the same time and Brack came along with us to get a little fresh air. And you see, we agreed to follow Eilert home because—well—he was so far gone.

HEDDA: He must have been.

TESMAN: But here's the strangest part, Hedda! Or maybe I should say the saddest. I'm almost ashamed for Eilert's sake—to tell you—

HEDDA: So?

TESMAN: There we were walking along, you see, and I happened to drop back a bit, just for a couple of minutes, you understand.

HEDDA: Yes, yes, good Lord but—

TESMAN: And then when I was hurrying to catch up—can you guess what I found in the gutter, hm?

HEDDA: How can I possibly guess?

TESMAN: Don't ever tell a soul, Hedda. Do you hear? Promise me that for Eilert's sake. (*Pulls a package out of his coat pocket.*) Just think—this is what I found.

HEDDA: That's the package he had with him here yesterday, isn't it?

TESMAN: That's it. His precious, irreplaceable manuscript—all of it. And he's lost it—without even noticing it. Oh just think, Hedda— the pity of it—

HEDDA: Well, why didn't you give it back to him right away?

TESMAN: Oh, I didn't dare do that—The condition he was in—

HEDDA: You didn't tell any of the others that you found it either?

TESMAN: Absolutely not. I couldn't, you see, for Eilert's sake.

HEDDA: So nobody knows you have Eilert's manuscript? Nobody at all?

TESMAN: No. And they mustn't find out either.

HEDDA: What did you talk to him about later?

TESMAN: I didn't get a chance to talk to him any more. We got to the city limits, and he and a couple of the others went a different direction. Just think—

HEDDA: Aha, they must have followed him home then.

TESMAN: Yes, I suppose so. Brack also went his way.

HEDDA: And, in the meantime, what became of the bacchanal?

TESMAN: Well, I and some of the others followed one of the revelers up to his place and had morning coffee with him—or maybe we should call it morning after coffee, hm? Now, I'll rest a bit—and as soon as I think Eilert has managed to sleep it off, poor man, then I've got to go over to him with this.

HEDDA: (*Reaching out for the envelope.*) No, don't give it back. Not yet, I mean. Let me read it first.

TESMAN: Oh no.

HEDDA: Oh, for God's sake.

TESMAN: I don't dare do that.

HEDDA: You don't dare?

TESMAN: No, you can imagine how completely desperate he'll be when he wakes up and realizes he can't find the manuscript. He's got no copy of it. He said so himself.

HEDDA: (*Looks searchingly at him.*) Couldn't it be written again?

TESMAN: No, I don't believe that could ever be done because the inspiration—you see—

HEDDA: Yes, yes—That's the thing, isn't it? (*Casually.*) But, oh yes— there's a letter here for you.

TESMAN: No, think of that.

HEDDA: (*Hands it to him.*) It came early this morning.

TESMAN: From Aunt Julie, Hedda. What can it be? (*Puts the manuscript on the other stool, opens the letter and jumps up.*) Oh Hedda— poor Aunt Rina's almost breathing her last.

HEDDA: It's only what's expected.

TESMAN: And if I want to see her one more time, I've got to hurry. I'll charge over there right away.

HEDDA: (*Suppressing a smile.*) You'll charge?

TESMAN: Oh, Hedda dearest—if you could just bring yourself to follow me. Just think.

HEDDA: (*Rises and says wearily and dismissively.*) No, no. Don't ask me to do anything like that. I won't look at sickness and death. Let me stay free from everything ugly.

TESMAN: Oh, good Lord then—(*Darting around.*) My hat—? My overcoat—? Ah, in the hall— Oh, I hope I'm not too late, Hedda, hm?

HEDDA: Then charge right over—

(*Berta appears in the hallway.*)

BERTA: Judge Brack is outside.

HEDDA: Ask him to come in.

TESMAN: At a time like this! No, I can't possibly deal with him now.

HEDDA: But I can. (*To Berta.*) Ask the Judge in.

(*Berta goes out.*)

HEDDA: (*In a whisper.*) The package, Tesman. (*She snatches it off the stool.*)

TESMAN: Yes, give it to me.

HEDDA: No, I'll hide it until you get back.

(*She goes over to the writing table and sticks the package in the bookcase. Tesman stands flustered, and can't get his gloves on. Brack enters through the hall doorway.*)

HEDDA: (*Nodding to him.*) Well, you're an early bird.

BRACK: Yes, wouldn't you say. (*To Tesman.*) You're going out?

TESMAN: Yes, I've got to go over to my aunt's. Just think, the poor dear is dying.

BRACK: Good Lord, is she really? Then don't let me hold you up for even a moment, at a time like this—

TESMAN: Yes, I really must run—Good-bye. Good-bye. (*He hurries through the hall doorway.*)

HEDDA: (*Approaches.*) So, things were livelier than usual at your place last night, Judge.

BRACK: Oh yes, so much so that I haven't even been able to change clothes, Mrs. Hedda.

HEDDA: You too.

BRACK: As you see. But, what has Tesman been telling you about last night's adventures?

HEDDA: Oh, just some boring things. He went someplace to drink coffee.

BRACK: I've already looked into the coffee party. Eilert Løvborg wasn't part of that group, I presume.

HEDDA: No, they followed him home before that.

BRACK: Tesman too?

HEDDA: No, but a couple of others he said.

BRACK: (*Smiles.*) George Tesman is a very naïve soul, Mrs. Hedda.

HEDDA: God knows, he is. But is there something more behind this?

BRACK: I'd have to say so.

HEDDA: Well then, Judge, let's be seated. Then you can speak freely. (*She sits to the left side of the table, Brack at the long side near her.*) Well, then—

BRACK: I had certain reasons for keeping track of my guests—or, more precisely, some of my guests' movements last night.

HEDDA: For example, Eilert Løvborg?

BRACK: Yes, indeed.

HEDDA: Now I'm hungry for more.

BRACK: Do you know where he and a couple of the others spent the rest of the night, Mrs. Hedda?

HEDDA: Why don't you tell me, if it can be told.

BRACK: Oh, it's certainly worth the telling. It appears that they found their way into a particularly animated soirée.

HEDDA: A lively one?

BRACK: The liveliest.

HEDDA: Tell me more, Judge.

BRACK: Løvborg had received an invitation earlier—I knew all about that. But he declined because, as you know, he's made himself into a new man.

HEDDA: Up at the Elvsteds', yes. But he went just the same?

BRACK: Well, you see, Mrs. Hedda—unfortunately, the spirit really seized him at my place last evening.

HEDDA: Yes, I hear he was quite inspired.

BRACK: Inspired to a rather powerful degree. And so, he started to reconsider, I assume, because we men, alas, are not always so true to our principles as we ought to be.

HEDDA: Present company excepted, Judge Brack. So, Løvborg—?

BRACK: Short and sweet—He ended up at the salon of a certain Miss Diana.

HEDDA: Miss Diana?

BRACK: Yes, it was Miss Diana's soirée for a select circle of ladies and their admirers.

HEDDA: Is she a red head?

BRACK: Exactly.

HEDDA: A sort of a—singer?

BRACK: Oh, yes—She's also that. And a mighty huntress—of men, Mrs. Hedda. You must have heard of her. Eilert Løvborg was one of her most strenuous admirers—in his better days.

HEDDA: And how did all this end?

BRACK: Apparently less amicably than it began. Miss Diana, after giving him the warmest of welcomes, soon turned to assault and battery.

HEDDA: Against Løvborg?

BRACK: Oh, yes. He accused her, or one of her ladies, of robbing him. He insisted that his pocketbook was missing, along with some other things. In short, he seems to have created a dreadful spectacle.

HEDDA: And what did that lead to?

BRACK: A regular brawl between both the men and the women. Luckily the police finally got there.

HEDDA: The police too?

BRACK: Yes. It's going to be quite a costly little romp for Eilert Løvborg. What a madman.

HEDDA: Well!

BRACK: Apparently, he resisted arrest. It seems he struck one of the officers on the ear, and ripped his uniform to shreds, so he had to go to the police station.

HEDDA: How do you know all this?

BRACK: From the police themselves.

HEDDA: (*Gazing before her.*) So, that's how it ended? He had no vine leaves in his hair.

BRACK: Vine leaves, Mrs. Hedda?

HEDDA: (*Changing her tone.*) Tell me now, Judge, why do you go around snooping and spying on Eilert Løvborg?

BRACK: For starters, I'm not a completely disinterested party— especially if the hearing uncovers the fact that he came straight from my place.

HEDDA: There's going to be a hearing?

BRACK: You can count on it. Be that as it may, however—My real concern was my duty as a friend of the house to inform you and Tesman of Løvborg's nocturnal adventures.

HEDDA: Why, Judge Brack?

BRACK: Well, I have an active suspicion that he'll try to use you as a kind of screen.

HEDDA: Oh! What makes you think that?

BRACK: Good God—we're not that blind, Mrs. Hedda. Wait and see. This Mrs. Elvsted—she won't be in such a hurry to leave town again.

HEDDA: If there's anything going on between those two, there's plenty of places they can meet.

BRACK: Not one single home. Every respectable house will be closed to Eilert Løvborg from now on.

HEDDA: And mine should be too—Is that what you're saying?

BRACK: Yes. I have to admit it would be more than painful for me if this man secured a foothold here. If this—utterly superfluous— and intrusive individual—were to force himself into—

HEDDA: Into the triangle?

BRACK: Precisely! It would leave me without a home.

HEDDA: (*Looks smilingly at him.*) I see—The one cock of the walk— That's your goal.

BRACK: (*Slowly nodding and dropping his voice.*) Yes, that's my goal. And it's a goal that I'll fight for—with every means at my disposal.

HEDDA: (*Her smile fading.*) You're really a dangerous man, aren't you—when push comes to shove.

BRACK: You think so?

HEDDA: Yes, I'm starting to. And that's all right—just as long as you don't have any kind of hold on me.

BRACK: (*Laughing ambiguously.*) Yes, Mrs. Hedda—you might be right about that. Of course, then, who knows whether I might not find some way or other—

HEDDA: Now listen, Judge Brack! That sounds like you're threatening me.

BRACK: (*Gets up.*) Oh, far from it. A triangle, you see—is best fortified by free defenders.

HEDDA: I think so too.

BRACK: Well, I've had my say so I should be getting back. Good-bye, Mrs. Hedda. (*He goes toward the glass doors.*)

HEDDA: Out through the garden?

BRACK: Yes, it's shorter for me.

HEDDA: And then, it's also the back way.

BRACK: That's true. I have nothing against back ways. Sometimes they can be very piquant.

HEDDA: When there's sharp shooting.

BRACK: (*In the doorway, laughing at her.*) Oh, no—you never shoot your tame cocks.

HEDDA: (*Also laughing.*) Oh, no, especially when there's only one—

(*Laughing and nodding they take their farewells. He leaves. She closes the door after him. Hedda stands for awhile, serious, looking out. Then she goes and peers through the curtains in the back wall. She goes to the writing table, takes Løvborg's package from the bookcase, and is about to leaf through it. Berta's voice, raised in indignation, is heard out in the hall. Hedda turns and listens. She quickly locks the package in the drawer, and sets the key on the writing table. Eilert Løvborg, wearing his overcoat and carrying his hat, bursts through the hall doorway. He looks somewhat confused and excited.*)

LØVBORG: (*Turned toward the hallway.*) And I'm telling you, I've got to go in! And that's that! (*He closes the door, sees Hedda, controls himself immediately, and bows.*)

HEDDA: (*By the writing table.*) Well, Mr. Løvborg, it's pretty late to be calling for Thea.

LØVBORG: Or a little early to be calling on you. I apologize.

HEDDA: How do you know that she's still here?

LØVBORG: I went to where she was staying. They told me she'd been out all night.

HEDDA: (*Goes to the table.*) Did you notice anything special when they told you that?

LØVBORG: (*Looks inquiringly at her.*) Notice anything?

HEDDA: I mean—did they seem to have any thought on the subject— one way or the other?

LØVBORG: (*Suddenly understanding.*) Oh, of course, it's true. I'm dragging her down with me. Still, I didn't notice anything. Tesman isn't up yet, I suppose?

HEDDA: No, I don't think so.

LØVBORG: When did he get home?

HEDDA: Very late.

LØVBORG: Did he tell you anything?

HEDDA: Yes. I heard Judge Brack's was very lively.

LØVBORG: Nothing else?

HEDDA: No, I don't think so. I was terribly tired, though—

(*Mrs. Elvsted comes in through the curtains at the back.*)

MRS. ELVSTED: (*Runs toward him.*) Oh, Løvborg—at last!

LØVBORG: Yes, at last, and too late.

MRS. ELVSTED: (*Looking anxiously at him.*) What's too late?

LØVBORG: Everything's too late. I'm finished.

MRS. ELVSTED: Oh no, no—Don't say that!

LØVBORG: You'll say it too, when you've heard—

MRS. ELVSTED: I won't listen—

HEDDA: Shall I leave you two alone?

LØVBORG: No stay—You too, I beg you.

MRS. ELVSTED: But I won't listen to anything you tell me.

LØVBORG: I don't want to talk about last night.

MRS. ELVSTED: What is it then?

LØVBORG: We've got to go our separate ways.

MRS. ELVSTED: Separate!

HEDDA: (*Involuntarily.*) I knew it!

LØVBORG: Because I have no more use for you, Thea.

MRS. ELVSTED: You can stand there and say that! No more use for me! Can't I help you now, like I did before? Won't we go on working together?

LØVBORG: I don't plan to work any more.

MRS. ELVSTED: (*Desperately.*) Then what do I have to live for?

LØVBORG: Just try to live your life as if you'd never known me.

MRS. ELVSTED: I can't do that.

LØVBORG: Try, Thea. Try, if you can. Go back home.

MRS. ELVSTED: (*Defiantly.*) Where you are, that's where I want to be. I won't let myself be just driven off like this. I want to stay at your side—Be with you when the book comes out.

HEDDA: (*Half aloud, tensely.*) Ah, the book—Yes.

LØVBORG: (*Looking at her.*) Mine and Thea's, because that's what it is.

MRS. ELVSTED: Yes, that's what I feel it is. That's why I have a right to be with you when it comes out. I want to see you covered in honor and glory again, and the joy. I want to share that with you too.

LØVBORG: Thea—our book's never coming out.

HEDDA: Ah!

MRS. ELVSTED: Never coming out?

LØVBORG: It can't ever come out.

MRS. ELVSTED: (*In anxious foreboding.*) Løvborg, what have you done with the manuscript?

HEDDA: (*Looking intently at him.*) Yes, the manuscript—?

MRS. ELVSTED: What have you—?

LØVBORG: Oh, Thea, don't ask me that.

MRS. ELVSTED: Yes, yes, I've got to know. I have the right to know.

LØVBORG: The manuscript—all right then, the manuscript—I've ripped it up into a thousand pieces.

MRS. ELVSTED: (*Screams.*) Oh no, no!

HEDDA: (*Involuntarily.*) But that's just not—!

LØVBORG: (*Looking at her.*) Not true, you think?

HEDDA: (*Controls herself.*) All right then. Of course it is, if you say so. It sounds so ridiculous.

LØVBORG: But, it's true, just the same.

MRS. ELVSTED: (*Wringing her hands.*) Oh God—oh God, Hedda. Torn his own work to pieces.

LØVBORG: I've torn my own life to pieces. I might as well tear up my life's work too—

MRS. ELVSTED: And you did that last night!

LØVBORG: Yes. Do you hear me? A thousand pieces. Scattered them all over the fjord. Way out where there's pure salt water. Let them drift in it. Drift with the current in the wind. Then, after awhile, they'll sink. Deeper and deeper. Like me, Thea.

MRS. ELVSTED: You know, Løvborg, all this with the book—? For the rest of my life, it will be just like you'd killed a little child.

LØVBORG: You're right. Like murdering a child.

MRS. ELVSTED: But then, how could you—! That child was partly mine, too.

HEDDA: (*Almost inaudibly.*) Ah, the child—

MRS. ELVSTED: (*Sighs heavily.*) So, it's finished? All right, Hedda, now I'm going.

HEDDA: You're not going back?

MRS. ELVSTED: Oh, I don't know what I'm going to do. I can't see anything out in front of me. (*She goes out through the hall doorway.*)

HEDDA: (*Standing awhile, waiting.*) Don't you want to see her home, Mr. Løvborg?

LØVBORG: Through the streets? So that people can get a good look at us together?

HEDDA: I don't know what else happened to you last night but if it's so completely beyond redemption—

LØVBORG: It won't stop there. I know that much. And I can't bring myself to live that kind of life again either. Not again. Once I had the courage to live life to the fullest, to break every rule. But she's taken that out of me.

HEDDA: (*Staring straight ahead.*) That sweet little fool has gotten hold of a human destiny. (*Looks at him.*) And you're so heartless to her.

LØVBORG: Don't call it heartless.

HEDDA: To go and destroy the thing that has filled her soul for this whole long, long time. You don't call that heartless?

LØVBORG: I can tell you the truth, Hedda.

HEDDA: The truth?

LØVBORG: First, promise me—Give me your word that Thea will never find out what I'm about to confide to you.

HEDDA: You have my word.

LØVBORG: Good. Then I'll tell you—What I stood here and described—It wasn't true.

HEDDA: About the manuscript?

LØVBORG: Yes. I haven't ripped it up. I didn't throw it in the fjord, either.

HEDDA: No, well—so—Where is it?

LØVBORG: I've destroyed it just the same. Utterly and completely, Hedda!

HEDDA: I don't understand any of this.

LØVBORG: Thea said that what I'd done seemed to her like murdering a child.

HEDDA: Yes, she did.

LØVBORG: But killing his child—that's not the worst thing a father can do to it.

HEDDA: Not the worst?

LØVBORG: No. And the worst—that is what I wanted to spare Thea from hearing.

HEDDA: And what is the worst?

LØVBORG: Imagine, Hedda, a man—in the very early hours of the morning—after a wild night of debauchery, came home to the mother of his child and said, "Listen—I've been here and there to this place and that place, and I had our child with me in this place and that place. And the child got away from me. Just got away. The devil knows whose hands it's fallen into, who's got a hold of it."

HEDDA: Well—when you get right down to it—it's only a book—

LØVBORG: All of Thea's soul was in that book.

HEDDA: Yes, I can see that.

LØVBORG: And so, you must also see that there's no future for her and me.

HEDDA: So, what will your road be now?

LØVBORG: None. Only to see to it that I put an end to it all. The sooner the better.

HEDDA: (*Comes a step closer.*) Eilert Løvborg—Listen to me now—Can you see to it that—that when you do it, you bathe it in beauty.

LØVBORG: In beauty? (*Smiles.*) With vine leaves in my hair as you used to imagine?

HEDDA: Ah, no. No vine leaves—I don't believe in them any longer. But in beauty, yes! For once! Good-bye. You've got to go now. And don't come here any more.

LØVBORG: Good-bye, Mrs. Tesman. And give my regards to George Tesman. (*He is about to leave.*)

HEDDA: No, wait! Take a souvenir to remember me by.
(*She goes over to the writing table, opens the drawer and the pistol case. She returns to Løvborg with one of the pistols.*)

LØVBORG: (*Looks at her.*) That's the souvenir?

HEDDA: (*Nodding slowly.*) Do you recognize it? It was aimed at you once.

LØVBORG: You should have used it then.

HEDDA: Here, you use it now.

LØVBORG: (*Puts the pistol in his breast pocket.*) Thanks.

HEDDA: In beauty, Eilert Løvborg. Promise me that.

LØVBORG: Good-bye, Hedda Gabler. (*He goes out the hall doorway.*)

(*Hedda listens a moment at the door. Afterwards, she goes to the writing table and takes out the package with the manuscript, looks inside the wrapper, pulls some of the pages half out and looks at them. She then takes it all over to the armchair by the stove and sits down. She has the package in her lap. Soon after she opens the stove door and then opens the package.*)

HEDDA: (*Throws one of the sheets into the fire and whispers to herself.*) Now, I'm burning your child, Thea—You with your curly hair. (*Throws a few more sheets into the fire.*) Your child and Eilert Løvborg's. (*Throws in the rest.*) Now I'm burning—burning the child.

END OF ACT THREE

ACT FOUR

The same room at the Tesmans'. It is evening. The drawing room is in darkness. The rear room is lit with a hanging lamp over the table. The curtains are drawn across the glass door.

(Hedda, dressed in black, wanders up and down in the darkened room. Then she goes into the rear room, and over to the left side. Some chords are heard from the piano. Then she emerges again, and goes into the drawing room. Berta comes in from the right of the rear room, with a lighted lamp, which she places on the table in front of the sofa, in the salon. Her eyes show signs of crying, and she has black ribbons on her cap. She goes quietly and carefully to the right. Hedda goes over to the glass door, draws the curtains aside a little, and stares out into the darkness. Soon after, Miss Tesman enters from the hallway dressed in black with a hat and a veil. Hedda goes over to her, and shakes her hand.)

MISS TESMAN: Yes, here I am, Hedda—in mourning black. My poor sister's struggle is over at last.

HEDDA: As you can see, I've already heard. Tesman sent me a note.

MISS TESMAN: Yes, he promised he would but I thought I should bring the news myself. This news of death into this house of life.

HEDDA: That was very kind of you.

MISS TESMAN: Ah, Rina shouldn't have left us right now. Hedda's house is no place for sorrow at a time like this.

HEDDA: (*Changing the subject.*) She died peacefully, Miss Tesman?

MISS TESMAN: Yes, so gently—Such a peaceful release. And she was happy beyond words that she got to see George once more, and could say a proper good bye to him. Is it possible he's not home yet?

HEDDA: No. He wrote saying I shouldn't expect him too early. But, please sit down.

MISS TESMAN: No, thank you, my dear—blessed Hedda. I'd like to, but I have so little time. She'll be dressed and arranged the best that I can. She'll look really splendid when she goes to her grave.

HEDDA: Can I help you with anything?

MISS TESMAN: Oh, don't even think about it. These kinds of things aren't for Hedda Tesman's hands or her thoughts either. Not at this time. No, no.

HEDDA: Ah—thoughts—Now they're not so easy to master—

MISS TESMAN: (*Continuing.*) Yes, dear God, that's how this world goes.

Over at my house we'll be sewing a linen shroud for Aunt Rina, and here there will be sewing too, but of a whole different kind, praise God.

(*George Tesman enters through a hall door.*)

HEDDA: Well, it's good you're finally here.

TESMAN: You here, Aunt Julie, with Hedda. Just think.

MISS TESMAN: I was just about to go, my dear boy. Well. Did you manage to finish everything you promised to?

TESMAN: No, I'm afraid I've forgotten half of it. I have to run over there tomorrow again. Today my brain is just so confused. I can't keep hold of two thoughts in a row.

MISS TESMAN: George, my dear, you mustn't take it like that.

TESMAN: Oh? How should I take it do you think?

MISS TESMAN: You must be joyful in your sorrow. You must be glad for what has happened, just as I am.

TESMAN: Ah, yes. You're thinking of Aunt Rina.

HEDDA: You'll be lonely now, Miss Tesman.

MISS TESMAN: For the first few days, yes. But that won't last long I hope. Our sainted Rina's little room won't stand empty. That much I know.

TESMAN: Really? Who'll be moving in there, hm?

MISS TESMAN: Oh, there's always some poor invalid or other who needs care and attention, unfortunately.

HEDDA: You'd really take on a cross like that again?

MISS TESMAN: Cross? God forgive you child. It's not a cross for me.

HEDDA: But a complete stranger—

MISS TESMAN: It's easy to make friends with sick people. And I so badly need someone to live for. Well, God be praised and thanked—there'll be a thing or two to keep an old aunt busy here in this house soon enough.

HEDDA: Oh, please don't think about us.

TESMAN: Yes. The three of us could be quite cozy here if only—

HEDDA: If only—?

TESMAN: (*Uneasily.*) Oh, it's nothing. Everything'll be fine. Let's hope, hm?

MISS TESMAN: Well, well, you two have plenty to talk about, I'm sure. (*Smiling.*) And Hedda may have something to tell you, George. Now it's home to Rina. (*Turning in the doorway.*) Dear, Lord, isn't it strange to think about. Now Rina's both with me and our sainted Joseph.

TESMAN: Yes, just think, Aunt Julie, hm?

(*Miss Tesman leaves through the hall door.*)

HEDDA: (*Follows Tesman with cold, searching eyes.*) I think all this has hit you harder than your aunt.

TESMAN: Oh, it's not just this death. It's Eilert I'm worried about.

HEDDA: (*Quickly.*) Any news?

TESMAN: I wanted to run to him this afternoon and tell him that his manuscript was safe—in good hands.

HEDDA: Oh? Did you find him?

TESMAN: No, he wasn't home. But later I met Mrs. Elvsted, and she told me he'd been here early this morning.

HEDDA: Yes, just after you left.

TESMAN: And apparently he said that he'd ripped the manuscript up into a thousand pieces, hm?

HEDDA: That's what he said.

TESMAN: But, good God, he must have been absolutely crazy. So you didn't dare give it back to him, Hedda?

HEDDA: No, he didn't get it back.

TESMAN: But, you told him we had it?

HEDDA: No. (*Quickly.*) Did you tell Mrs. Elvsted?

TESMAN: No, I didn't want to. But you should have told him. What would happen if in his desperation he went and did something to himself? Let me have the manuscript, Hedda. I'll run it over to him right away. Where did you put it?

HEDDA: (*Cold and impassively leaning on the armchair.*) I don't have it any more.

TESMAN: Don't have it! What in the world do you mean?

HEDDA: I burned it up—every page.

TESMAN: (*Leaps up in terror.*) Burned? Burned? Eilert's manuscript!

HEDDA: Don't shout like that. The maid will hear you.

TESMAN: Burned! But good God—! No, no, no—That's absolutely impossible.

HEDDA: Yes, but all the same it's true.

TESMAN: Do you have any idea what you've done, Hedda? That's— that's criminal appropriation of lost property. Think about that. Yes, just ask Judge Brack, then you'll see.

HEDDA: Then it's probably wise for you not to talk about it, isn't it? To the Judge or anyone else.

TESMAN: How could you have gone and done something so appalling? What came over you? Answer me that, Hedda, hm?

HEDDA: (*Suppressing an almost imperceptible smile.*) I did it for your sake, George.

TESMAN: My sake?

HEDDA: Remember you came home this morning and talked about how he had read to you?

TESMAN: Yes, yes.

HEDDA: You confessed that you envied him.

TESMAN: Good God, I didn't mean it literally.

HEDDA: Nevertheless, I couldn't stand the idea that someone would overshadow you.

TESMAN: (*Exclaiming between doubt and joy.*) Hedda—oh, is this true? —What you're saying? —Yes, but. Yes, but. I never noticed that you loved me this way before. Think of that!

HEDDA: Well, you need to know—that at a time like this— (*Violently breaking off.*) No, no—go and ask your Aunt Julie. She'll provide all the details.

TESMAN: Oh, I almost think I understand you, Hedda. (*Clasps his hands together.*) No, good God—Can it be, hm?

HEDDA: Don't shout like that. The maid can hear you.

TESMAN: (*Laughing in extraordinary joy.*) The maid! Oh, Hedda, you are priceless. The maid—why it's—why it's Berta. I'll go tell Berta myself.

HEDDA: (*Clenching her hands as if frantic.*) Oh, I'm dying—Dying of all this.

TESMAN: All what, Hedda, what?

HEDDA: (*Coldly controlled again.*) All this—absurdity—George.

TESMAN: Absurdity? I'm so incredibly happy. Even so, maybe I shouldn't say anything to Berta.

HEDDA: Oh yes, go ahead. Why not?

TESMAN: No, no. Not right now. But Aunt Julie, yes, absolutely. And then, you're calling me George. Just think. Oh, Aunt Julie will be so happy—so happy.

HEDDA: When she hears I've burned Eilert Løvborg's manuscript for your sake?

TESMAN: No, no, you're right. All this with the manuscript. No. Of course, nobody can find out about that. But, Hedda—you're burning for me—Aunt Julie really must share in that. But I wonder—all this—I wonder if it's typical with young wives, hm?

HEDDA: You'd better ask Aunt Julie about that too.

TESMAN: Oh yes, I certainly will when I get the chance. (*Looking *uneasy and thoughtful again.*) No, but, oh no, the manuscript. Good Lord, it's awful to think about poor Eilert, just the same. (*Mrs. Elvsted, dressed as for her first visit with hat and coat, enters through the hall door.*)

MRS. ELVSTED: (*Greets them hurriedly and speaks in agitation.*) Oh, Hedda, don't be offended that I've come back again.

HEDDA: What happened to you, Thea?

TESMAN: Something about Eilert Løvborg?

MRS. ELVSTED: Oh yes, I'm terrified that he's had an accident.

HEDDA: (*Grips her arm.*) Ah, do you think so?

TESMAN: Good Lord, where did you get that idea, Mrs. Elvsted?

MRS. ELVSTED: I heard them talking at the boarding house—just as I came in. There are the most incredible rumors about him going around town today.

TESMAN: Oh yes, imagine, I heard them too. And still I can swear he went straight home to sleep. Just think.

HEDDA: So—What were they saying at the boarding house?

MRS. ELVSTED: Oh, I couldn't get any details, either because they didn't know or—or they saw me and stopped talking. And I didn't dare ask.

TESMAN: (*Uneasily pacing the floor.*) Let's just hope—you misunderstood.

MRS. ELVSTED: No, I'm sure they were talking about him. Then I heard them say something about the hospital—

TESMAN: Hospital?

HEDDA: No—That's impossible.

MRS. ELVSTED: I'm deathly afraid for him, so I went up to his lodgings and asked about him there.

HEDDA: You dared to do that?

MRS. ELVSTED: What else should I have done? I couldn't stand the uncertainty any longer.

TESMAN: You didn't find him there either, hm?

MRS. ELVSTED: No. And the people there didn't know anything at all. They said he hadn't been home since yesterday afternoon.

TESMAN: Yesterday? How could they say that?

MRS. ELVSTED: It could only mean one thing—Something terrible's happened to him.

TESMAN: You know, Hedda—What if I were to go into town and ask around at different places—?

HEDDA: No! You stay out of this.

(*Judge Brack, carrying his hat, enters through the hall door which*

Berta opens and closes after him. He looks serious and bows in silence.)

TESMAN: Oh, here you are, Judge, hm?

BRACK: Yes, it was essential for me to see you this evening.

TESMAN: I see you got the message from Aunt Julie.

BRACK: Yes, that too.

TESMAN: Isn't it sad, hm?

BRACK: Well, my dear Tesman, that depends on how you look at it.

TESMAN: (*Looks at him uneasily.*) Has anything else happened?

BRACK: Yes, it has.

HEDDA: (*Tensely.*) Something sad, Judge Brack?

BRACK: Once again, it depends on how you look at it, Mrs. Tesman.

MRS. ELVSTED: (*In an uncontrollable outburst.*) It's Eilert Løvborg.

BRACK: (*Looks briefly at her.*) How did you guess, Mrs. Elvsted? Do you already know something—?

MRS. ELVSTED: (*Confused.*) No, no, I don't know anything but—

TESMAN: Well, for God's sake, tell us what it is.

BRACK: (*Shrugging his shoulders.*) Well then—I'm sorry to tell you— that Eilert Løvborg has been taken to the hospital. He is dying.

MRS. ELVSTED: (*Crying out.*) Oh God, oh God.

TESMAN: Dying?

HEDDA: (*Involuntarily.*) So quickly—?

MRS. ELVSTED: (*Wailing.*) And we were quarrelling when we parted, Hedda.

HEDDA: (*Whispers.*) Now, Thea—Thea.

MRS. ELVSTED: (*Not noticing her.*) I'm going to him. I've got to see him alive.

BRACK: It would do you no good, Mrs. Elvsted. No visitors are allowed.

MRS. ELVSTED: At least tell me what happened. What—?

TESMAN: Yes, because he certainly wouldn't have tried to—hm?

HEDDA: Yes, I'm sure that's what he did.

TESMAN: Hedda. How can you—

BRACK: (*Who is watching her all the time.*) Unfortunately, Mrs. Tesman, you've guessed right.

MRS. ELVSTED: Oh, how awful.

TESMAN: To himself, too. Think of it.

HEDDA: Shot himself!

BRACK: Right again, Mrs. Tesman.

MRS. ELVSTED: (*Tries to compose herself.*) When did this happen, Mr. Brack?

BRACK: Just this afternoon between three and four.

TESMAN: Oh, my God—Where did he do it, hm?

BRACK: (*Slightly uncertain.*) Where? Oh, I suppose at his lodgings.

MRS. ELVSTED: No, that can't be. I was there between six and seven.

BRACK: Well then, some other place. I don't know precisely. All I know is that he was found—he'd shot himself—in the chest.

MRS. ELVSTED: Oh how awful to think that he should die like that.

HEDDA: (*To Brack.*) In the chest?

BRACK: Yes, like I said.

HEDDA: Not through the temple?

BRACK: The chest, Mrs. Tesman.

HEDDA: Well, well. The chest is also good.

BRACK: What was that, Mrs. Tesman?

HEDDA: (*Evasively.*) Oh, nothing—nothing.

TESMAN: And the wound is fatal, hm?

BRACK: The wound is absolutely fatal. In fact, it's probably already over.

MRS. ELVSTED: Yes, yes, I can feel it. It's over. It's all over. Oh, Hedda—!

TESMAN: Tell me, how did you find out about all this?

BRACK: (*Curtly.*) From a police officer. One I spoke with.

HEDDA: (*Raising her voice.*) Finally—an action.

TESMAN: God help us, Hedda, what are you saying?

HEDDA: I'm saying that here, in this—there is beauty.

BRACK: Uhm, Mrs. Tesman.

TESMAN: Beauty! No, don't even think it.

MRS. ELVSTED: Oh, Hedda. How can you talk about beauty?

HEDDA: Eilert Løvborg has come to terms with himself. He's had the courage to do what had to be done.

MRS. ELVSTED: No, don't ever believe it was anything like that. What he did, he did in a moment of madness.

TESMAN: It was desperation.

MRS. ELVSTED: Yes, madness. Just like when he tore his book in pieces.

BRACK: (*Startled.*) The book. You mean his manuscript? Did he tear it up?

MRS. ELVSTED: Yes, last night.

TESMAN: (*Whispering softly.*) Oh, Hedda, we'll never get out from under all this.

BRACK: Hmm, that's very odd.

TESMAN: (*Pacing the floor.*) To think that Eilert Løvborg should leave the world this way. And then not to leave behind the work that would have made his name immortal.

MRS. ELVSTED: Oh, what if it could be put together again.

TESMAN: Yes—just think—what if it could? I don't know what I wouldn't give—

MRS. ELVSTED: Maybe it can, Mr. Tesman.

TESMAN: What do you mean?

MRS. ELVSTED: (*Searching in the pocket of her skirt.*) See this? I saved all the notes he dictated from.

HEDDA: (*A step closer.*) Ah.

TESMAN: You saved them, Mrs. Elvsted, hm?

MRS. ELVSTED: Yes, they're all here. I brought them with me when I came to town, and here they've been. Tucked away in my pocket—

TESMAN: Oh, let me see them.

MRS. ELVSTED: (*Gives him a bundle of small papers.*) But they're all mixed up, completely out of order.

TESMAN: Just think. What if we could sort them out. Perhaps if the two of us helped each other.

MRS. ELVSTED: Oh yes. Let's at least give it a try—

TESMAN: It will happen. It must happen. I'll give my whole life to this.

HEDDA: You, George, your life?

TESMAN: Yes, or, anyway, all the time I have. Every spare minute. My own research will just have to be put aside. Hedda—you understand, don't you, hm? I owe this to Eilert's memory.

HEDDA: Maybe so.

TESMAN: Now, my dear Mrs. Elvsted, let's pull ourselves together. God knows there's no point brooding about what's happened. We've got to try to find some peace of mind so that—

MRS. ELVSTED: Yes, yes, Mr. Tesman. I'll do my best.

TESMAN: Well. So, come along then. We've got to get started on these notes right away. Where should we sit? Here? No. In the back room. Excuse us, Judge. Come with me, Mrs. Elvsted.

MRS. ELVSTED: Oh God—if only it can be done.

(*Tesman and Mrs. Elvsted go into the rear room. She takes her hat and coat off. Both sit at the table under the hanging lamp and immerse themselves in eager examination of the papers. Hedda goes across to the stove, and sits in the armchair. Soon after, Brack goes over to her.*)

HEDDA: (*Softly.*) Ah, Judge—This act of Eilert Løvborg's—there's a sense of liberation in it.

BRACK: Liberation, Mrs. Hedda? Yes, I guess it's a liberation for him all right.

HEDDA: I mean, for me. It's a liberation for me to know that in this world an act of such courage, done in full, free will is possible. Something bathed in a bright shaft of sudden beauty.

BRACK: (*Smiles.*) Hmm—Dear Mrs. Hedda—

HEDDA: Oh, I know what you're going to say because you're a kind of specialist too, after all, just like—Ah well.

BRACK: (*Looking steadily at her.*) Eilert Løvborg meant more to you than you might admit—even to yourself. Or am I wrong?

HEDDA: I don't answer questions like that. All I know is that Eilert Løvborg had the courage to live life his own way, and now—his last great act—bathed in beauty. He—had the will to break away from the banquet of life—so soon.

BRACK: It pains me, Mrs. Hedda—but I'm forced to shatter this pretty illusion of yours.

HEDDA: Illusion?

BRACK: Which would have been taken away from you soon enough.

HEDDA: And what's that?

BRACK: He didn't shoot himself—so freely.

HEDDA: Not freely?

BRACK: No. This whole Eilert Løvborg business didn't come off exactly the way I described it.

HEDDA: (*In suspense.*) Are you hiding something? What is it?

BRACK: I employed a few euphemisms for poor Mrs. Elvsted's sake.

HEDDA: Such as—?

BRACK: First, of course, he's already dead.

HEDDA: At the hospital?

BRACK: Yes. And without regaining consciousness.

HEDDA: What else?

BRACK: The incident took place somewhere other than his room.

HEDDA: That's insignificant.

BRACK: Not completely. I have to tell you—Eilert Løvborg was found shot in—Miss Diana's boudoir.

HEDDA: (*About to jump up but sinks back again.*) That's impossible, Judge. He can't have gone there again today.

BRACK: He was there this afternoon. He came to demand the return of something that he said they'd taken from him. He talked crazily about a lost child.

HEDDA: Ah, so that's why—

BRACK: I thought maybe he was referring to his manuscript but I hear he'd already destroyed that himself so I guess it was his pocketbook.

HEDDA: Possibly. So—that's where he was found.

BRACK: Right there with a discharged pistol in his coat pocket, and a fatal bullet wound.

HEDDA: In the chest, yes?

BRACK: No—lower down.

HEDDA: (*Looks up at him with an expression of revulsion.*) That too! Oh absurdity—! It hangs like a curse over everything I so much as touch.

BRACK: There's still one more thing, Mrs. Hedda. Also in the ugly category.

HEDDA: And what is that?

BRACK: The pistol he had with him—

HEDDA: (*Breathless.*) Well, what about it?

BRACK: He must have stolen it.

HEDDA: (*Jumping up.*) Stolen? That's not true. He didn't.

BRACK: There's no other explanation possible. He must have stolen it—Shh.

(*Tesman and Mrs. Elvsted have gotten up from the table in the rear room and come into the living room.*)

TESMAN: (*With papers in both hands.*) Hedda, my dear—I can hardly see anything in there under that lamp. Just think—

HEDDA: I'm thinking.

TESMAN: Do you think you might let us sit a while at your desk, hm?

HEDDA: Oh, gladly. (*Quickly.*) No, wait. Let me just clean it up a bit first.

TESMAN: Oh, not necessary, Hedda. There's plenty of room.

HEDDA: No, no, I'll just straighten it up, I'm telling you. I'll just move these things here under the piano for a while.

(*She has pulled an object covered with sheet music out of the bookcase. She adds a few more sheets and carries the whole pile out to the left of the rear room. Tesman puts the papers on the desk and brings over the lamp from the corner table. He and Mrs. Elvsted sit and continue their work.*)

HEDDA: Well, Thea, my sweet. Are things moving along with the memorial?

MRS. ELVSTED: (*Looks up at her dejectedly.*) Oh, God—It's going to be so difficult to find the order in all of this.

TESMAN: But it must be done. There's simply no other choice. And finding the order in other people's papers—that's precisely what I'm meant for.

(*Hedda goes over to the stove and sits on one of the stools. Brack stands over her, leaning over the armchair.*)

HEDDA: (*Whispers.*) What were you saying about the pistol?

BRACK: (*Softly.*) That he must have stolen it.

HEDDA: Why stolen exactly?

BRACK: Because there shouldn't be any other way to explain it, Mrs. Hedda.

HEDDA: I see.

BRACK: (*Looks briefly at her.*) Eilert Løvborg was here this morning, am I correct?

HEDDA: Yes.

BRACK: Were you alone with him?

HEDDA: Yes, for a while.

BRACK: You didn't leave the room at all while he was here?

HEDDA: No.

BRACK: Think again. Weren't you out of the room, even for one moment?

HEDDA: Yes. Perhaps. Just for a moment—out in the hallway.

BRACK: And where was your pistol case at that time?

HEDDA: I put it under the—

BRACK: Well, Mrs. Hedda—

HEDDA: It was over there on the writing table.

BRACK: Have you looked since then to see if both pistols are there?

HEDDA: No.

BRACK: It's not necessary. I saw the pistol Løvborg had, and I recognized it immediately from yesterday, and from before, as well.

HEDDA: Have you got it?

BRACK: No, the police have it.

HEDDA: What will the police do with that pistol?

BRACK: Try to track down its owner.

HEDDA: Do you think they can do that?

BRACK: (*Bends over her and whispers.*) No, Hedda Gabler, not as long as I keep quiet.

HEDDA: (*Looking fearfully at him.*) And what if you don't keep quiet—then what?

BRACK: Then the way out is to claim that the pistol was stolen.

HEDDA: I'd rather die.

BRACK: (*Smiling.*) People make those threats but they don't act on them.

HEDDA: (*Without answering.*) So—let's say the pistol is not stolen and the owner is found out? What happens then?

BRACK: Well, Hedda—then there'll be a scandal.

HEDDA: A scandal?

BRACK: Oh, yes, a scandal. Just what you're so desperately afraid of. You'd have to appear in court, naturally. You and Miss Diana. She'd have to detail how it all occurred. Whether it was an accident or a homicide. Was he trying to draw the pistol to threaten her? Is that when the gun went off? Did she snatch it out of his hands to shoot him, and then put the pistol back in his pocket? That would be thoroughly in character for her. She's a feisty little thing, that Miss Diana.

HEDDA: But all this ugliness has got nothing to do with me.

BRACK: No. But you would have to answer one question. Why did you give the pistol to Eilert Løvborg? And what conclusions would people draw from the fact that you gave it to him?

HEDDA: (*Lowers her head.*) That's true. I didn't think of that.

BRACK: Well. Fortunately you have nothing to worry about as long as I keep quiet.

HEDDA: (*Looking up at him.*) So I'm in your power now, Judge. You have a hold over me from now on.

BRACK: (*Whispering more softly.*) Dearest Hedda—Believe me—I won't abuse my position.

HEDDA: But in your power. Totally subject to your demands—And your will. Not free, Not free at all. (*She gets up silently.*) No, that's one thought I just can't stand. Never!

BRACK: (*Looks mockingly at her.*) One can usually learn to live with the inevitable.

HEDDA: (*Returning his look.*) Maybe so. (*She goes over to the writing table suppressing an involuntary smile and imitating Tesman's intonation.*) Well, George, this is going to work out, hm?

TESMAN: Oh, Lord knows, dear. Anyway, at this rate, it's going to be months of work.

HEDDA: (*As before.*) No, just think. (*Runs her fingers lightly through Mrs. Elvsted's hair.*) Doesn't it seem strange, Thea. Here you are, sitting together with Tesman—just like you used to sit with Eilert Løvborg.

MRS. ELVSTED: Oh, God, if only I could inspire your husband too.

HEDDA: Oh, that will come—in time.

TESMAN: Yes, you know what, Hedda—I really think I'm beginning to feel something like that. But why don't you go over and sit with Judge Brack some more.

HEDDA: Can't you two find any use for me here?

TESMAN: No, nothing in the world. (*Turning his head.*) From now on, my dear Judge, you'll have to be kind enough to keep Hedda company.

BRACK: (*With a glance at Hedda.*) That will be an infinite pleasure for me.

HEDDA: Thanks but I'm tired tonight. I'll go in there and lie down on the sofa for a while.

TESMAN: Yes, do that, Hedda, hm?

(*Hedda goes into the rear room and draws the curtains after her. Short pause. Suddenly she is heard to play a wild dance melody on the piano.*)

MRS. ELVSTED: (*Jumping up from her chair.*) Oh—what's that?

TESMAN: (*Running to the doorway.*) Oh, Hedda, my dear—Don't play dance music tonight. Just think of poor Aunt Rina and of Eilert Løvborg too.

HEDDA: (*Putting her head out from between the curtains.*) And Aunt Julie and all the rest of them too. From now on I shall be quiet. (*She closes the curtains again.*)

TESMAN: (*At the writing table.*) This can't be making her very happy—Seeing us at this melancholy work. You know what, Mrs. Elvsted—You're going to move in with Aunt Julie. Then I can come over in the evening, and we can sit and work there, hm?

MRS. ELVSTED: Yes, maybe that would be the best—

HEDDA: (*From the rear room.*) I can hear you perfectly well, Tesman. So, how am I supposed to get through the evenings out here?

TESMAN: (*Leafing through the papers.*) Oh, I'm sure Judge Brack will be good enough to call on you.

BRACK: (*In the armchair, shouts merrily.*) I'd be delighted, Mrs. Tesman. Every evening. Oh, we're going to have some good times together, the two of us.

HEDDA: (*Loudly and clearly.*) Yes, that's what you're hoping for isn't it, Judge? You, the one and only cock of the walk—

(*A shot is heard within. Tesman, Mrs. Elvsted and Brack all jump to their feet.*)

TESMAN: Oh, she's playing around with those pistols again.

(*He pulls the curtains aside and runs in. Mrs. Elvsted follows. Hedda is stretched out lifeless on the sofa. Confusion and cries. Berta comes running in from the right.*)

(*Shrieking to Brack.*) Shot herself! Shot herself in the temple! Just think!

BRACK: (*Half prostrate in the armchair.*) But God have mercy—People don't act that way.

END OF PLAY